ZION

The Third Pillar of Zion
The Law of Consecration

LARRY BARKDULL

Pillars of Zion Series Titles

Introduction: *Portrait of a Zion Person*

Book 1: *Zion—Our Origin and Our Destiny*

Book 2: *The First Pillar of Zion—The New and Everlasting Covenant*

Book 3: *The Second Pillar of Zion—The Oath and Covenant of the Priesthood*

Book 4: *The Third Pillar of Zion—The Law of Consecration*

Book 5: *The Pure in Heart*

Book 6: *No Poor among Them*

Pillars of Zion Publishing
Orem, Utah

Contact

Contact us at info@pillarsofzion.com
Visit our Website at www.PillarsOfZion.com

Disclaimer

This series is heavily documented with some 5,000 references and 400 works cited. Every effort has been made to achieve accuracy. This work is not an official publication of the Church of Jesus Christ of Latter-day Saints, and the views expressed within this work are the sole responsibility of the author and do not necessarily reflect the position of The Church of Jesus Christ of Latter-day Saints or any other entity.

LICENSE USE

Library of Congress Cataloging Publication Data is on file at the Library of Congress.
ISBN: 978-1-937399-10-8

Dedication

To Elizabeth Barkdull
Ron and Bonnie McMillan
David and Lorelea Anderson
Paul and Sharon Meyers

Acknowledgments

My wife, Elizabeth, and I would like to acknowledge a number of people, who, in one way or another, lent their support for the creation of this project.

Lawrence and Georgia Shaw
Lance and Jozet Richardson
Blaine and Kathy Yorgason
Scot and Maurine Proctor
Clay Gorton
Ted Gibbons
Grover Cardon
Gary and Bonnie Leavitt
Bud and Barbara Poduska
Dee Jay Bawden
Steve Glenn
Gavon and Tanya Barkdull

Production Staff

Thanks to Eschler Editing for editorial and design work.

Editors—Jay A. Parry and Michele Preisendorf
Graphic Artist—Douglass Cole
Typesetter—Sean Graham

Note about The Three Pillars of Zion

The complete Zion series contains seven books. The full bibliography, and index are included in each of the books for ease of referencing and navigation. Each volume includes its own table of contents except for the Introduction book, *Portrait of a Zion Person*, includes the table of contents for each volume in order to introduce the entire series.

Table of Contents

Book 4
The Third Pillar of Zion—The Law of Consecration

Book 4
The Third Pillar of Zion—The Law of Consecration

Introduction

"[Zion] commences in the heart of each person"[1]
—*Brigham Young*

In this fourth book of The Three Pillars of Zion series, we will examine in depth the third pillar of Zion: The Law of Consecration. We recall that the "Law of the Church" (D&C 42) states that three covenants are sufficient to establish us as Zion people: "And ye shall hereafter receive church covenants, such as shall be sufficient to establish you, both here and in the New Jerusalem."[2] These covenants are:

1. The New and Everlasting Covenant. (D&C 132:4–7)
2. The Oath and Covenant of the Priesthood. (D&C 84:33–44)
3. The Law of Consecration. (D&C 82:11–15)

In book 1, we learned that Zion was our origin and will be our destiny. She is our ideal, and the antithesis of Babylon. Moreover, Zion is the standard among celestial and celestial-seeking people.[3] Joseph Smith said, "We ought to have the building up of Zion as our greatest object."[4] The obligation to become Zion people rests upon each of us individually.

That obligation begins with formally accepting the Atonement by receiving the new and everlasting covenant (book 2) by way of baptism. The new and everlasting covenant is the umbrella covenant, consisting of two primary covenants: the covenant of baptism, and the oath and covenant of the priesthood (book 3). The priesthood covenant is magnified by (1) ordination for worthy men; (2) temple covenants and ordinances for worthy men and women; and (3) the temple sealing covenant, which is called the Covenant of Exaltation,[5] for worthy men and women.

---

1 Young, *Discourses of Brigham Young,* 118.
2 D&C 42:67.
3 D&C 105:5.
4 Smith, *Teachings of the Prophet Joseph Smith,* 60.
5 Nelson, *The Power within Us,* 136; Smith, *Doctrines of Salvation,* 2:58. Note: Elder McConkie stated that men make a covenant of exaltation twice: once upon ordination to the Melchizedek Priesthood and again at the time of the marriage sealing: "Ordination to office in the Melchizedek priesthood and entering into that 'order of the priesthood' named 'the new and everlasting covenant of marriage' are both occasions when men make the covenant of exaltation, being promised through their faithfulness all that the Father hath (D&C 131:1–4; 84:39–41; 132; Num. 25:13)." (*Mormon Doctrine,* 167.)

As we learned in book 2, the new and everlasting covenant not only provides a way to be cleansed from sin and separated from the world, it also provides us a way to receive God's authority, power, and knowledge—everything we need to become like him and inherit all that he has. This is the essence of the second pillar of Zion—the oath and covenant of the priesthood.

As we learned in book 3, the principles of the priesthood apply to both worthy men and women. The priesthood covenant is received by men at the time of ordination, but its principles are expansive and eventually lead to the temple. There, faithful men and women are endowed with priesthood covenants and ordinances that culminate at a marriage altar. Elder Bruce R. McConkie said, "This covenant, made when the priesthood is received, is renewed when the recipient enters the order of eternal marriage."[6] Clearly, both men and women are involved in the doctrines of the priesthood.

We discussed the history of the priesthood and the men who were great examples in honoring that priesthood. We discussed priesthood keys and their importance in the restored Church of Jesus Christ. Then we surveyed our covenantal agreements and the Father's oath, instructions, and promises. Later we examined "The Constitution of the Priesthood," found in Doctrine and Covenants 121, and we discussed why many are called to eternal life but few are chosen. We also studied the Lord's instructions and rewards for the chosen few. We came to understand that priesthood is more than an ordination; it is a way of life and the power to pursue that life. Without the priesthood and its guiding principles, neither a man nor a woman can achieve Zion in his or her life and thus attain the ultimate form of salvation, exaltation in the celestial kingdom.

In this fourth book of the Zion series, we will examine the law of the celestial kingdom,[7] which is the foundational law of Zion—The Law of Consecration. Few laws of God are as misunderstood. We will discuss what the law of consecration is and what it is not. We will demonstrate how this law is a template that can be used (and has been used) in any number of situations. We will also discuss how living the law of consecration results in equality and unity, two foundational characteristics that describe the celestial kingdom. We will study the guiding principles of consecration and contrast them with the condition of Babylon. Then we will discuss the ultimate test during mortality: the decision we must make between God and mammon.

Finally, we will learn in book 5 that the law of consecration is an outgrowth of the "Royal Law,"[8] which is this: "Thou shalt love the Lord thy God with all thy heart, and with all thy soul, and with all thy mind. This is the first and great commandment. And the second is like unto it, Thou shalt love thy neighbour as thyself." The royal law is "the first and great commandment," according to Jesus, and upon it "hang all the law and the prophets."[9] When all is said and done, we consecrate ourselves and all that we have and are because we love God and his children. Then we are truly Zion, the pure in heart.

---

6   McConkie, *A New Witness for the Articles of Faith*, 313.
7   D&C 105:5.
8   James 2:8.
9   Matthew 22:36–40.

Section 1
What Is the Law of Consecration?

Note: The first time we refer to a covenant or unique doctrine, we may capitalize it to call special attention to it. Thereafter, we will lowercase the name of the covenant or doctrine, with two exceptions: (1) If the name is capitalized in a quotation from another source, we will leave it as found in that source; and (2) if we are referring to the new and everlasting covenant by the shorthand of "the Covenant," we will capitalize it in that setting.

I magine going into partnership with a benevolent billionaire. You express to him your desire to build a company, and to accommodate your desire he makes you a co-owner in his fortune. Now you have unlimited access to his unlimited resources; you need only ask and report responsibly and the fortune is at your disposal. Your agreement with your benefactor is simple: What is his is yours, and what is yours is his. But there is more. Beyond your having access to your partner's incomprehensible wealth, you also have access to his expertise, his influence, and his name. Now there is no knowledge that you cannot tap, no power beyond your reach, and no door you cannot enter.

Could you not succeed in such a situation?

In a similar way, assuming we are living the laws that govern the celestial kingdom, we may draw upon the resources of God's higher kingdom to build our eternal kingdoms. Because we are in a covenant relationship with our Heavenly Father, we may invoke the terms of the new and everlasting covenant and gain unrestricted, unlimited, and indivisible rights to the resources of his kingdom, including access to his knowledge and power. Additionally, he gives us his full time and attention, and he puts upon us his name, allowing us to act authoritatively as his proxies.

Consecration—the Principle of Exaltation

Heavenly Father lives the law of consecration perfectly. He withholds nothing from us—neither his time, ability, knowledge, power, nor his vast kingdom. He does all of this so that we might become like him—*one* with him—in attributes, honor, glory, power, might, and dominion. This is his stated work and glory.[10] To accomplish this, he lives the eternal laws that elevated him to the status of God and that makes gods of all other worthy beings of his race. The capstone of these laws is called *consecration*.

The law of consecration provides that greater beings partner with lesser beings in a covenant relationship—a *family* relationship—to allow the lesser beings to rise to a progressively higher stature by giving them the ability to draw upon the resources of the higher kingdom. This covenant relationship has no end, thus ensuring that the emerging god can progress eternally and expand his kingdom infinitely. In return for this incomprehensible gift, the lesser being, by covenant, consecrates his kingdom to the greater being, whereupon the higher kingdom expands, resulting in both beings enjoying infinite and eternal increase. This is exaltation.

Joseph Smith explained it this way: "What did Jesus do? Why; I do the things I saw my Father do when worlds came rolling into existence. My Father worked out his kingdom with fear and trembling, and I must do the same; and when I get my kingdom, I shall present it to my Father, so that he may obtain kingdom upon kingdom, and it will exalt him in glory. He will then take a higher exaltation, and I will take his place, and thereby become exalted myself. So that Jesus treads in the tracks of his Father, and inherits what God did before; and God is thus glorified and exalted in the salvation and exaltation of all his children."[11]

Considering the covenant relationship that exists between greater and lesser beings, the law of consecration might be better called the *Covenant* of Consecration. When we agree to live the covenant, the Father affixes his signature to it, so to speak, which sets in motion the process of our exaltation. Upon the condition that both parties agree to consecrate to each other their all, we lesser beings obtain license to access the Father's time, abilities, and all that he has and is to establish and grow our personal kingdoms. Then, as Joseph Smith explained, as we consecrate our kingdom back to the Father, essentially assimilating it into the Father's kingdom, his dominion grows and he is further exalted. As he moves up, we take his place, and we both experience extended and eternal exaltation. In this way, we both obtain "kingdom upon kingdom," which results in eternal upward movement and increase. All of this is made possible by the covenant we enter into with God: the covenant of consecration.

Which brings us to consecration in this life.

If we ever hope to achieve the most profound blessings of the gospel, we must embrace the law of consecration. Because "Zion cannot be built up unless it is by the principles of the law of the celestial kingdom,"[12] we can never expect to achieve that holy place, abide its glory, and progress from one exaltation to another unless we abide this law.[13] We have ample opportunities to learn how to live this law of the celestial kingdom here and now. For example, we are commanded to "remember the poor, and consecrate of [our] properties for their support that which [we have] to impart unto them, with

10   Moses 1:39.
11   Smith, *Teachings of the Prophet Joseph Smith*, 347; emphasis added.
12   D&C 105:5.
13   D&C 88:22.

a covenant and a deed which cannot be broken."[14] That is, we prepare to become like God by learning how to reach down and lift up those of lesser means by consecrating our time, talents, and resources to the Lord's work. Thus, by learning to consecrate now we experience an essential principle of exaltation while in the flesh. Perhaps the act of consecration creates and defines Zion's oneness, equality, and pure-heartedness better than anything else.

The Condition of Babylon

The world hands the law of consecration a huge challenge. This foundational law of Zion is wholly foreign to everything we see around us. Consecration simply makes no sense in Babylon. Where in this world do we hear the idea that giving away money and possessions is a principle of prosperity, safety, happiness, and security? We simply cannot wrap our minds around the concept. *Less becomes more?* How can that be? The philosophies of men (which we often attempt to legitimize with scripture) teach us that we live in a dog-eat-dog world where only the smartest, fittest, strongest, and most beautiful survive. We had better conform to the realities of life, they say, or we will find ourselves on the outside looking in.

And there seems to be plenty of evidence that Babylon is right.

From our youth, we have been taught that if we don't look out for ourselves, who will? All of us know the "self-made man's" formula of success: dedicate yourself completely to the accumulation of wealth; never let up, day after day, year after year; let no one get in your way. We are taught that no goal is as worthy as the pursuit of the good life, and we are bombarded with messages that giving away our time, talents, and assets won't get us there. It all sounds so reasonable. Except for one tiny detail: This philosophy is anti-Zion, and therefore it is anti-celestial.

At the opening of the dispensation of the fulness of times, the Lord told his young prophet, "Behold, the world at this time lieth in sin, and there is none that doeth good, *no not one.* And mine anger is kindling against the inhabitants of the earth to visit them according to this ungodliness."[15] It is sobering to note that the Lord said the same thing of Sodom and Gomorrah.[16] What condition could be so prevalent and depraved that it could envelop the entirety of humanity? The Lord gave the answer: "But it is not given that one man should possess that which is above another, wherefore the world lieth in sin."[17] Like pride, this condition is a universal sin.

Moroni taught the same truth. He ends his record of the Book of Mormon dispensation in the same way our dispensation began, with an ominous view of the future. Foreseeing universal latter-day ungodliness, he said, "And wo be unto the children of men . . . for there shall be none that doeth good among you, *no not one.*" Not one person is exempt from this universal sin! How can we escape this woeful condition? Moroni

14   D&C 42:30.
15   Nibley, *Nibley on the Timely and the Timeless*, 280–81.
16   Genesis 18, 19.
17   D&C 49:20; emphasis added.

gave the answer: "For if there be one among you that doeth good, he shall work by the power and gifts of God."[18] Moroni links true goodness with working by the power and gifts of God. In the end, the power and gifts of God are sufficient to help us break free of this universal sin, reject the philosophies of men, release our grasp on the things of this world, and embrace the law of the celestial kingdom.

The solution for protection from this universal sin and establishing a Zion-like life is consecration. The Lord restored this celestial law, in part, for our safety and ultimate salvation. Hugh Nibley taught, "God has always commanded his people to give up that way of life [Babylon], come out of the world, and follow his special instructions. *The main purpose of the Doctrine and Covenants, you will find, is to implement the law of consecration.*"[19]

The Greatest Desire

What is our greatest desire? Although we might have a variety of answers, we would hope that our greatest desire aligns with the great desire of the prophets, whom we covenant to follow. President Lorenzo Snow expressed his "greatest desire," and offered an eloquent list of promised blessings to those whose wish was similar. "For my greatest desire is to see Zion established according to the revelations of God, to see her inhabitants industrious and self-sustaining, filled with wisdom and the power of God, that around us may be built a wall of defense, a protection against the mighty powers of Babylon; and while the disobedient of our Father's family are contending, and filling up their cup of iniquity, even to the brim, and thus preparing themselves for the burning, we who are the acknowledged children of the kingdom, being filled with the righteousness and knowledge of God, may be like the wise virgins, clothed in our wedding garments, and properly prepared for the coming of our Lord and Savior."[20]

President Snow's desire was no different from the desire of every other prophet from Adam to the present: the establishment of a Zion people whose lives are founded upon the law of consecration.

Definition of Consecration

President Ezra Taft Benson made the following statement about consecration's purpose: "We covenant to live the law of consecration. This law is that we consecrate our time, talents, strength, property, and money for the upbuilding of the kingdom of God on this earth and the establishment of Zion. . . . The law of consecration is a celestial law, not an economic experiment."[21]

The law of consecration was given to the Church in its early days. Because a variety of attempts were either suspended or ultimately failed, many members of the Church

---

18   Moroni 10:25; emphasis added.
19   Nibley, *Approaching Zion*, 174; emphasis added.
20   Snow, *The Teachings of Lorenzo Snow*, 180.
21   Benson, *The Teachings of Ezra Taft Benson*, 121.

believe that the law of consecration is for the future and that it will emerge again some-day as a formal, legally-binding economic order. Therefore, they imagine that either the law of consecration does not apply today, or, if it does, it applies in a watered-down form. This assumption is completely erroneous. The lesson we should learn from former attempts is this: The principles of consecration constitute a *template* that can be applied successfully to any number of situations, and it can be adapted to the needs of the few or the many. This template is at once individual, familial, societal, economical, temporal, and spiritual.

That we limit consecration in our minds to a certain application is a mistake of monumental proportions. The future most certainly holds a formal application—or ap-plications—of the law of consecration; formal application(s) will be administered by the prophets in the Lord's own time. But on no occasion has the Lord repealed the consecra-tion covenant that we make in the temple. This law does not lie in some sort of sus-pended state, waiting for an announcement for us to live it. Consecration is current and in full force today, and it must be lived actively by each of us who makes the covenant; otherwise, we can neither build up the kingdom of God nor establish the principles of Zion in our lives. The future Zion priesthood society, which will depend wholly upon consecration, will certainly be established by people who live the law of consecration now, and who thus have become Zion-like.[22]

To consecrate something is to sanctify, purify, and set it apart for a sacred use, to make it holy, to dedicate it solemnly to a special service, or to give it religious sanction, as with an oath or a vow.[23] Joseph Smith defined consecration this way: "When we con-secrate our property to the Lord it is to administer to the wants of the poor and needy, for this is the law of God. . . . Now for a man to consecrate . . . is nothing more nor less than to feed the hungry, clothe the naked, visit the widow and fatherless, the sick and af-flicted, and do all he can to administer to their relief in their afflictions, and for him and his house to serve the Lord. In order to do this, he and all his house must be virtuous, and must shun the very appearance of evil."[24]

Consecration comes down to one thing: the giving of one's whole self to God. This giving of self, which encompasses sacrifice, according to President Spencer W. Kimball, "is the giving of one's own time, talents, and means to care for those in need—whether spiritually or temporally—and in building the Lord's kingdom."[25] That is, we contribute the totality of who we are, what we are, and all that we have or will have—*everything!*[26] Nothing less than our all will do. Such total sacrifice of self cannot be legislated; it is a freewill offering made from the purity of the heart. Thus, we *choose* to consecrate our all because we value the kingdom of God and Zion more than we value anything.

Could there be any misunderstanding that the law of consecration is a covenant that must be lived today? Hugh Nibley writes, "The law of consecration has no histori-

22   Gardner, "Becoming a Zion Society," 31.
23   *American Heritage Dictionary*, s.v. "consecrate," "sanctify."
24   Smith, *Teachings of the Prophet Joseph Smith*, 127.
25   D&C 38:17; 104:11–14; Kimball, *The Teachings of Spencer W. Kimball*, 366.
26   D&C 64:34; 82:19; 88:67–68; 98:12–14.

cal development; the issues are perennial. We like to think that we are living under special conditions today."[27] But we are not. Consecration is an eternal law that does not depend upon man's current economic or social situation. It works in one life or many lives, in poverty or prosperity, in Africa or America, in the days of Adam or the latter days. Consecration simply waits for a covenant person's decision to live it and propel it into action.

The Law We Must Live to Achieve the Celestial Kingdom

The Church welfare plan describes a consecrated person as one who does not seek for worldly riches; who esteems his brother as himself; who, through tithes and offerings, helps to build up the kingdom of God by making his worldly goods, over and above his family's necessities, available for the Lord's work; and who, with his time, talents, and means, takes care of the temporally and spiritually poor. Referring to the Church welfare plan, Elder Bruce R. McConkie wrote, "The practice of the law of consecration is inextricably intertwined with the development of the attributes of godliness in this life and the attainment of eternal life in the world to come. 'The law pertaining to material aid is so formulated that the carrying of it out necessitates practices calculated to root out human traits not in harmony with requirements for living in the celestial kingdom and replacing those inharmonious traits with the virtues and character essential to life in that abode.'"[28]

Therefore, we are left without excuse. We have made the covenant of consecration in the temple, and the covenant is manifested today as a Church-wide program called the welfare plan. Beyond the global application of the welfare plan, consecration espouses the principle of individual choice in giving time, talents, and resources to sustain the Lord's work and to care for family and the temporally and spiritually poor. If and when consecration takes another form, it will not contradict the divine template, but, in any case, we are not excused for failing to live our covenant here and now.

Consecrating the Good and the Bad

When the Lord demands that we consecrate everything to him, he expects that we consecrate *all* that we are: both the good and the bad. How else could he transform us into what we must become to inherit the celestial kingdom? When we lay everything on the altar, including our weaknesses, troubles, and sins, he gladly agrees to take those things, reconstitute them into something positive, and help us manage the affairs of our lives. Hence his declaration: "[God] shall consecrate thine afflictions for thy gain."[29]

This remarkable promise corresponds with the Lord's injunction: "Search diligently, pray always, and be believing, and all things shall work together for your good, if ye walk

27   Nibley, *Approaching Zion*, 463.
28   McConkie, *Mormon Doctrine*, 157, quoting Albert E. Bowen, *The Church Welfare Plan*, 6.
29   2 Nephi 2:2.

uprightly and remember the covenant wherewith ye have covenanted one with another."[30] Here we notice that having all things working together for our good is linked to our abiding in the covenant wherewith we have covenanted with each other. That covenant is consecration.[31] Nephi learned the same principle of consecration: "But behold, I say unto you that ye must pray always, and not faint; that ye must not perform any thing unto the Lord save in the first place ye shall pray unto the Father in the name of Christ, that he will consecrate thy performance unto thee, that thy performance may be for the welfare of thy soul."[32]

When we withhold nothing, God withholds nothing, and we thus experience the miracle of consecration.

Premise of Consecration

To enter into this covenant, we acknowledge that all things belong to the Lord and we are stewards.[33] President George Q. Cannon said, "God our Eternal Father has placed all these possessions and blessings—that is, the possessions of the earth and the blessings connected with the earth—He has placed them in our hands merely as stewards, and we hold them subject to Him—in other words, in trust for Him—and if He calls upon us to use them in any given direction He may indicate, it is our duty as His children, occupying the relationship that we do to Him and with the hopes in our breasts that we have, to hold them entirely subject to Him."[34]

Other key principles of consecration are laid out in the scriptures:
- We are to esteem each other as ourselves.[35]
- We practice this law upon the principle of agency.[36]
- We are made equal according to our wants, needs, and family situations.[37]
- We are accountable to the Lord for our stewardships.[38]

Perhaps King Benjamin described best the premise of the law of consecration: "For behold, are we not all beggars? Do we not all depend upon the same Being, even God, for all the substance which we have, for both food and raiment, and for gold, and for silver, and for all the riches which we have of every kind? . . . And now, if God, who has created you, on whom you are dependent for your lives and for all that ye have and are, doth grant unto you whatsoever ye ask that is right, in faith, believing that ye shall receive, O then, how ye ought to impart of the substance that ye have one to another."[39]

---

30   D&C 90:24.
31   D&C 90:23.
32   2 Nephi 32:9.
33   Kimball, *The Teachings of Spencer W. Kimball*, 366.
34   Cannon, *Gospel Truth*, 275.
35   D&C 38:24–27; 51:3, 9; 70:14; 78:6; 82:17.
36   D&C 104:17.
37   D&C 51:3.
38   D&C 72:3; 104:13–18.
39   Mosiah 4:19, 21.

Consecration Is Nonnegotiable

If we make the covenant, we must live the covenant: "And behold, none are exempt from this law who belong to the church of the living God."[40] Nevertheless, as Nephi learned, if we will put forth the effort to live this celestial law in a telestial environment, the Lord will help us, as Nephi asserted: "I will go and do the things which the Lord hath commanded, for I know that the Lord giveth no commandments unto the children of men, save he shall prepare a way for them that they may accomplish the thing which he commandeth them."[41]

Although consecration is described as a celestial law, it is designed so all can live it.[42] Consecration is an "easy," foundational requirement of Zion. Brigham Young said, "No revelation that was ever given is more easy of comprehension than that of the law of consecration."[43] Then he lamented, "It was one of the first commandments or revelations given to this people after they had the privilege of organizing themselves as a Church, as a body, as the kingdom of God on the earth. I observed then, and I now think, that it will be one of the last revelations which the people will receive into their hearts and understand, of their own free will and choice, and esteem it as a pleasure, a privilege, and a blessing unto them to observe and keep most holy."[44]

We risk losing the blessing of eternal life when we postpone or water down the concept of consecration. If we desire exaltation, living this law is nonnegotiable. Earning that supernal gift pivots on our strict adherence to this law that governs the celestial kingdom.

Restoration of the Law of Consecration

As early as 1829, the Lord began to point Joseph Smith toward establishing "the cause of Zion."[45] This single fact should help us realize that the focal point of the Restoration and its end purpose was Zion. After the Church was organized, the Prophet received revelations to lay the foundation of Zion. On January 2, 1831, a significant revelation (D&C 38) linked latter-day Zion with ancient Zion, and suddenly Enoch literature began to emerge.[46] The concept of receiving inheritances from the Lord on the condition of living a specific law was introduced: "I . . . deign to give you greater riches," the Lord promised, "even a land of promise . . . and the land of your inheritance, if you seek it with all your hearts." In that same revelation, the Saints learned that these blessings would be available to them only if they made the associated covenant and lived the law that governed that covenant.[47] The revelation also foretold some of the basic conditions of the law of consecration: "And let every man esteem his brother as himself, and practise virtue and holiness before me. . . . I say unto you, be one; and if

---

40   D&C 70:20.
41   1 Nephi 3:7.
42   Nibley, *Approaching Zion,* 422, quoting Zechariah 14:17–18.
43   Young, *Journal of Discourses,* 2:306.
44   Young, *Discourses of Brigham Young,* 179.
45   D&C 6:6; 11:6; 14:6.
46   D&C 38:4, 32.
47   D&C 38:18–19, 32.

ye are not one ye are not mine." Further, the Lord said, "And ye shall look to the poor and the needy, and administer to their relief that they shall not suffer."[48]

To learn more about Zion and its law, the Prophet was commanded to go to Ohio to receive "the law of the Church,"[49] which is often called the law of Zion. On February 9th of that year, Joseph Smith received what is now Doctrine and Covenants 42. "This revelation presented the laws of the Church government and moral conduct for members and established the basic principles of consecration."[50] Shortly thereafter, at the third general conference of the Church, the law of consecration was formally accepted by the membership, and from that moment until now, the law has never been rescinded.

Bruce Van Orden, professor of Church history and doctrine, wrote:

> A historical misunderstanding arose in the church regarding this early economic application of the Law of Consecration. Most Saints have thought that the united order was widely practiced in Ohio and Missouri. Indeed, the phrases order, united order, and order of Enoch frequently appear in the Doctrine and Covenants, thus adding credence to this assumption. In actuality, these are substitute phrases for "united firm," the original words of the revelations for an organization, which was disbanded 23 April 1834 (see D&C 104). The wording was changed so that enemies of the Church and creditors would not use the printed revelations against the Church. . . .
>
> The united firm was a partnership between a handful of Church leaders, no more than twelve at any time, to consolidate the financial resources and organizational and professional talents of these men to generate profits to be used for the personal living expenses as well as the economic needs of the Church. . . . The main reason for the tremendous indebtedness accrued by the united firm was the destruction of the printing press and the closure of Sidney Gilbert's store by mobs in Independence, Missouri, in July 1831. It is important for modern students of the Doctrine and Covenants to realize that the important revelations that seem to speak of a united order (D&C 78, 82, 92, 96) in actuality give directions about the united firm.[51]

---

48   D&C 38:24, 27, 35.
49   D&C 42, section heading.
50   *Encyclopedia of Mormonism,* 312.
    51 Van Orden, "The Law of Consecration," 85, referencing Cook, *Joseph Smith and the Law of Consecration,* 57–70.

The point we wish to reiterate is that the principles of consecration are a template. In the early days of the Church, this template was applied to a variety of situations and experiments, and it will likely be applied and adapted for future uses.

We find an illustration of the use of this template in Far West, Missouri, on July 9, 1838, in response to the Prophet's plea, "O, Lord! show unto thy servant how much thou requirest of the properties of thy people for a tithing."[52] Then the Lord revealed that henceforth, the Saints were to "pay one-tenth of all their interest annually." Thus tithing qualified as a surplus and became a manifestation of economic consecration. According to the revelation, tithing was to be used specifically "for the building of mine house, and for laying the foundation of Zion and for the priesthood, and for the debts of the Presidency of my Church."[53] Van Orden explained, "The law of tithing, while considered by some commentators in the past as an 'inferior' law to the Law of Consecration, seems to have been merely a new phase of consecration."[54]

LDS historian Lyndon Cook wrote, "Indeed, many hailed it [the law of tithing] as a markedly improved economic plan for obtaining donations and contributions. Admittedly, this program did not provide for the bishop to redistribute the wealth of the members, nor to allocate specific inheritances or personal stewardships. Yet, significantly, the equalizing effect of the 1838 plan on the members was identical to earlier programs."[55] Thus, tithes and offerings (D&C 119) became the official law of consecration, and this law has remained unaltered to this day. The resulting "program" maintained all of the driving principles of consecration without mandating a formal law requiring that all properties be donated to the Church. From 1838 to the present, this economic manifestation of the law of consecration has been the Church's official program: The Saints pay tithing according to a defined amount,[56] and they pay offerings according to choice and personal revelation. The present welfare plan embraces the 1838 revelation.

Does this mean that another official program or programs relating to economic consecration will never be necessary? It is not our prerogative to say. However, numerous prophets' statements indicate that consecration may take on additional forms to fit circumstances and times. Brother Van Orden explained, "Today . . . paying a full and honest tithing in cash of all we earn has proven to be an efficient and productive means of both living the economic side of the Law of Consecration and also with providing the Church with needed operating funds."[57] This is the official program, but perhaps even greater blessings flow from practicing consecration in our personal lives: consecrating time, talents, and resources.

Consecrating Tithes and Offerings

The combination of tithes and offerings provides Saints a unique opportunity to (1) build up the kingdom of God on the earth, which is the primary function of tithing, and

52   Smith, *History of the Church,* 3:87–89.
53   D&C 119:2, 4.
54   Van Orden, "The Law of Consecration," 86.
55   Cook, *Joseph Smith and the Law of Consecration,* 77.
56   D&C 119:4.
57   Van Orden, "The Law of Consecration," 87.

(2) establish the cause of Zion, which is the primary function of offerings. Whereas the revealed use of tithing is "for the building of mine house, and for laying the foundation of Zion and for the priesthood, and for the debts of the Presidency of my Church,"[58] offerings establish the economic base of Zion by providing for the poor.[59]

Together, tithes and offerings allow us to keep the law of consecration and progress in our understanding of that law with ever increasing faith. Because tithing is a defined amount, paying it requires less faith than paying offerings, which is left to our discretion. A person exercises greater faith by yielding to the "enticings of the Holy Spirit"[60] to determine the amount of his offerings. Thus, the payment of offerings provides a vehicle to increase faith, mature in the gospel, and gain the most impressive blessings of the gospel, which are available only to those who approach the ideal of consecration—those who give all that they are and have to the Lord.

Ultimately, every offering we place on the altar represents the only offering that matters: the heart. "Thou shalt offer a sacrifice unto the Lord thy God in righteousness, even that of a broken heart and a contrite spirit."[61] Clearly, the greatest opportunity in consecration lies in giving offerings.

Modern Applications of Consecration

The covenant of consecration was fully revealed during the construction of the Nauvoo Temple. Beginning in 1842, Joseph Smith introduced to trusted associates a sacred ritual, the Endowment of the Holy Priesthood. Total commitment in all things was expected. Complete surrender to the Lord's will was required. Now there could be no doubt that consecration was much more than an economic program; consecration was the complete, freewill offering of one's self.

As we have mentioned, the template of consecration has been laid over a variety of programs that were intended to build the kingdom of God in anticipation of Zion. Most recently, the current welfare plan has steadily grown since its inception in 1936, and it now includes "hundreds of projects, farms, ranches, canneries, and storehouses. This plan, both in theory and in practice, has become the envy of millions of people in public, private, and religious enterprises."[62]

Furthermore, we see consecration's application in LDS Philanthropies, which "serves as the central coordinating agency for all donations to the Church or one of its institutions—beyond tithing and fast offerings—with the goal of helping members and friends of the Church meet the needs of people worldwide."[63] We also see consecration principles at the heart of the Perpetual Education Fund, the Missionary Fund, LDS Humanitarian Services, and other funds that rely on consecrated freewill offerings. We see consecration in action when missionaries give two years of their lives to the Lord,

---

58   D&C 119:2, 4.
59   Malachi 3:8; Smith, *Gospel Doctrine,* 243; McConkie, *Mormon Doctrine,* 277–78.
60   Mosiah 3:19.
61   D&C 59:8.
62   Van Orden, "The Law of Consecration," 89.
63   See mission statement at www.LDSPhilanthropies.org.

and when parents sacrifice to support them. We see the spirit of consecration in the lives of senior missionaries; temple patrons; those who sacrifice to serve in Church callings; those who visit the poor, the needy, and the oppressed; and those who bless the lives of others beyond the bounds of the Church organization. All of these sacrifices are manifestations of consecration by a pure-hearted people whose intention is to build up the kingdom of God and to establish the cause of Zion.

Learning to Better Live the Law of Consecration

Can we become even more consecrated? Of course. We, the covenant, consecrated Saints of God, must apply this law in ever increasing faith until poverty in each of its ugly forms—temporal, emotional, and spiritual—is abolished from among us. Then, when the promised establishment of the priesthood society of Zion is come, the ideal of consecration will shine forth; we will fully be one, and there will be no poor among us. At that day, the poor who have pled to the Lord for relief will find it in Zion.[64]

The Lord said that he is preparing "a feast of fat things . . . for the poor" in "the land upon which the Zion of God shall stand."[65] These humble, impoverished souls who are being nurtured by the pure-hearted of Zion will soon join with those who have blessed them and together come to the "marriage of the Lamb."[66] Safe in Zion, they "shall be provided for,"[67] and "exalted."[68] Clearly, the poor have every reason to "rejoice in the Holy One"[69] and to trust in his Zion.[70]

What an honor it is to establish the cause of Zion!

Sanctified by Consecration: The Law of the Celestial Kingdom

Clearly, consecration is more than a law; it is a way of life. Consecration is a mindset that impacts the heart in such a way that it finally becomes pure. The attitude that signals a change of heart at baptism—"to bear one another's burdens, that they may be light; yea, and . . . to mourn with those that mourn; yea, and comfort those that stand in need of comfort"[71]—is later vitalized with power in the oath and covenant of the priesthood and finally formalized and perfected by the covenant of consecration in the temple.

Upon the law of consecration the Lord can establish Zion in the hearts of individuals, families, wards, stakes, and in the Church. Moreover, with the law of consecration, sanctification increases. According to Doctrine and Covenants 88, this must happen if we are to be cleansed "from all unrighteousness, that [we] may be prepared for the celestial glory." Like the earth, we can fill "the measure of [our] creation" only by abiding the celestial law.

64   D&C 38:16.
65   D&C 58:8, 7.
66   D&C 58:11.
67   D&C 83:6.
68   D&C 104:16.
69   2 Nephi 27:30.
70   Isaiah 14:32.
71   Mosiah 18:8–9.

Ultimately, by abiding that law, we, like the earth, "shall be crowned with glory, even with the presence of God the Father." Clearly, the stakes are high, and consecration seems to be the pivotal point for us. The Lord said, "And they who are not sanctified through the law which I have given unto you, even the law of Christ, must inherit another kingdom, even that of a terrestrial kingdom, or that of a telestial kingdom. For he who is not able to abide the law of a celestial kingdom cannot abide a celestial glory."[72]

If Zion is "the highest order of priesthood society,"[73] and if Zion is founded upon the law of consecration, it behooves us to take seriously this celestial law that governs that priesthood society. Zion can be established in no other way. Inferior choices can result only in inferior blessings and inferior kingdoms. As Elder Neal A. Maxwell reminded us, the terrestrial kingdom will consist of the honorable ones who were not valiant, meaning casually obedient and modestly Christlike. To be valiant is to become like Jesus and to obey him. Elder Maxwell said, consecration helps to create a Christlike character; it is the consecration or surrender of self that defines ultimate victory, because surrender introduces us to God's higher ways.[74]

The Lord has declared in the language of absolutes that the law we are willing to abide sanctifies us to that degree. President Lorenzo Snow said, "[Consecration] is a perfect law,"[75] which concurs with the Savior's injunction to the rich young man who came seeking eternal life: "If thou wilt be perfect, go and sell that thou hast, and give to the poor, and thou shalt have treasure in heaven: and come and follow me."[76] If we ever hope to achieve perfection or Zion-like hearts or an inheritance in the celestial kingdom, we must make and keep the covenant of consecration. President Ezra Taft Benson said, "The law of consecration is a law for an inheritance in the celestial kingdom. God, the Eternal Father, His Son Jesus Christ, and all holy beings abide by this law. It is an eternal law. . . . it will be mandatory for all Saints to live the law in its fulness to receive celestial inheritance."[77]

Familiarity

There could be no principle as foreign to a telestial world or as opposite to Babylon as the law of consecration. But to covenant people who are striving to become pure in heart, consecration feels familiar. The more effort they make to live it, the more their awareness of the beauty and safety of that law. President Lorenzo Snow said, "[The law of consecration] is something that is natural."[78]

As we make efforts to live this law, we become comfortable with consecration because we recognize its benefits; inherently, we understand its blessings. Therefore, we simply need to begin to live it, and its familiar fruits will become evident. Soon we will feel as if we have come home.

---

72   D&C 88:18–22.
73   Kimball, *The Teachings of Spencer W. Kimball,* 125.
74   Maxwell, "Consecrate Thy Performance," 36, quoting D&C 76:75, 79; 3 Nephi 27:27; Isaiah 55:9.
75   Snow, *The Teachings of Lorenzo Snow,* 183.
76   Matthew 19:21.
77   Benson, "A Vision and a Hope for the Youth of Zion," 75.
78   Snow, *The Teachings of Lorenzo Snow,* 184.

Ultimate Consecration—To Sacrifice a Prepared and Purified Heart

Only the pure in heart are able to live the law of consecration. Obedience, sacrifice, and living the laws and ordinances of the gospel, including the celestial lifestyle called *chastity*, prepare us to live this law and to make this ultimate sacrifice. When we finally succeed in living the law to the extent that we can consecrate ourselves unrestrictedly, we will have truly come unto Christ. Then our hearts will finally have become pure. Indeed, consecration is one of the deciding requirements for coming into the presence of the Lord.

Elder Maxwell taught that consecration is so much more than yielding up our possessions when we are directed; ultimate consecration, he said, is yielding up our whole selves to the Lord by choice. That is, we give to him *everything* that is uniquely ours: *our heart, mind, and soul.* This first great commandment, he said, becomes the last test of discipleship and that which identifies the pure in heart. Ultimate consecration—the ideal of consecration—is complete surrender, the total yielding of our thoughts, feelings, words, and actions. When we keep this law, all that we do and all that happens to us, both the good and the bad, work together for our good[79] and for the everlasting welfare of our souls.[80]

Partial consecration could never produce the blessings of eternal reward, and, in one respect, partial consecration is a contradiction of terms. Hugh Nibley wrote:

> By very definition we cannot pay a partial tithe. . . . And if we cannot pay a partial tithe, neither can we keep the law of chastity in a casual and convenient way. . . . We cannot enjoy optional obedience to the law of God, or place our own limits on the law of sacrifice, or mitigate the charges of righteous conduct connected with the law of the gospel. We cannot be willing to sacrifice only that which is convenient to part with, and then expect a reward. The Atonement is everything; it is not to be had "on the cheap." God is not mocked in these things; we do not make promises and covenants with mental reservations. Unless we live up to every covenant, we are literally in Satan's power—a condition easily recognized by the mist of fraud and deception that has enveloped our whole society. . . . The point of all this is that the Atonement requires of the beneficiary nothing less than willingness to part with his most precious possession. . . . The law of consecration . . . has no limiting "if necessary" clause; we agree to it unconditionally here and now. *It represents our contribution to our salvation.*[81]

---

79   D&C 90:24; 98:3; 105:40.
80   Maxwell, "Consecrate Thy Performance," 36, referencing Matthew 22:37; 2 Nephi 32:9.
81   Nibley, *Approaching Zion,* 589–92; emphasis added.

Live Consecration or Lose Eternal Life

How serious is the Lord about our living the law of consecration? President Lorenzo Snow had the answer: "We must dedicate our time, talents, and ability. If we as elders fail to keep the covenants we have made, namely, to use our time, talents, and ability for the upbuilding of the kingdom of God upon the earth, how can we reasonably expect to come forth in the morning of the First Resurrection, identified with the great work of redemption? If we in our manner, habits and dealings, imitate the Gentile world, thereby identifying ourselves with the world, do you think, my brethren, that God will bestow upon us the blessings we desire to inherit? I tell you no, He will not!"[82]

President Kimball spoke of the man who chose to build a kingdom to himself rather than build the kingdom of God: "And now, as life is ebbing out gradually, he finds himself standing alone, forsaken, bitter, unloved, and unsung; and with self-pity, he can still think of only one person, himself. He has sought to save for himself his time, talents, and his means. He has lost the abundant life."[83]

And yet, with all of this prophetic evidence, there are those among us who feel that they are the exception and can have it both ways.

Laying Everything on the Altar

President Kimball explained that consecration is a law that we learn to live by degrees. As we do so, we gain great insight, spiritual maturity, and strength to take consecration to the next level. "We must lay on the altar and sacrifice whatever is required by the Lord. We begin by offering a broken heart and a contrite spirit. We follow this by giving our best effort in our assigned fields of labor and callings. We learn our duty and execute it fully. Finally we consecrate our time, talents, and means as called upon by our file leaders and as prompted by the whisperings of the Spirit. In the Church, as in the welfare system also, we can give expression to every ability, every righteous desire, every thoughtful impulse, and in the end, we learn it was no sacrifice at all."[84]

The concept of laying our all on the altar is a gospel theme that began with Adam and continues to this day. When we think of totally consecrated sacrifices made on an altar, we automatically think of the sacrifice of Abraham, who truly exemplified sacrifice by consecration. We do not individually build altars for sacrifice today, but worshipping and sacrificing at altars remains a central part of our religion. For example, the sacramental table is like an altar, and, of course we find altars in temples.[85] Because we are taught that the body is a temple,[86] we might expect to find an altar therein. Using Abraham as an example, Andrew Skinner explains that the altar of the body is the heart:

---

82   Snow, *The Teachings of Lorenzo Snow,* 44.
83   Kimball, *The Teachings of Spencer W. Kimball,* 251.
84   Kimball, *The Teachings of Spencer W. Kimball,* 364.
85   *Encyclopedia of Mormonism,* 36–37.
86   John 2:21; 1 Corinthians 6:19.

On Moriah Abraham built an altar. The Hebrew word
for altar, *mizbeah,* is derived from the word for sacrifice, *zebah.* Thus, "altar" literally means "the place of
sacrificing." But where did Abraham's sacrifice of Isaac
first occur? In rabbinic and Talmudic times the phrase
"building an altar" was used as a metaphor to mean not
only the observance of the commandments, but also
the total consecration of all one possessed—even the
laying down of one's own life—for the sanctification of
God's name. Some of the ancient rabbinic sages, therefore, coined expressions like "as if an altar was erected
in his heart" to portray those individuals who were willing to do all that God required. Some of them well understood that sacrifice was first made in the mind and
heart of the offerer. Their exemplar was Abraham. He
had erected an altar long before he reached Moriah.
Things are not so different today. We talk about being
ready to lay it all on the altar. We covenant at altars
to sacrifice all we possess to the Lord, and in doing so
we "build altars in our hearts," as the rabbis said. Our
exemplar is also Abraham.[87]

To make the consecrated sacrifice of all that we are and possess on the altar of the heart,
the heart itself must first be prepared and purified through obedience, events requiring
sacrifice, adherence to the law of the gospel, and by living a life of strict chastity. Then
we are ready to climb to our Mount Moriah, build an altar in our heart, and offer everything that we are to God.

Consecration and the Atonement

Because the results of consecration are equality and oneness, consecration becomes immediately connected to the Atonement; the purpose of both is to bring separated things
back into a state of oneness.

We need only survey the condition of Babylon to see that humanity lives in a
constant state of separation, which is common in a telestial world. Misery always results
from separation in its various forms. The continual struggle of telestial residents is to
hold together things that are inclined to drift apart. We suffer the effects of separation in
relationships, in health, and in finances. We often expend enormous effort and resources
to counter the natural tendency of things to wear out, rust, become corrupt, and eventually disintegrate. The telestial world is one of entropy, "the tendency for all matter and

---

87   Skinner: "Genesis 22: The Paradigm for True Sacrifice in Latter-day Israel," 77–78.

energy in the universe to evolve toward a state of inert uniformity. Inevitable and steady deterioration."[88] Whenever we experience entropy or separation, we experience misery to a lesser or greater degree. We sense that life is out of balance; it is lacking, imperfect, spinning out of control, and beyond our ability to reclaim, and when that happens something inside of us says this condition is neither right nor natural.

On the other hand, the Atonement, which is motivated by love, is ever attempting to draw separated things back into a state of unity and perfection with resulting happiness and abundance. Thus we feel the powers of Satan and Christ constantly pulling at us: Satan pulls us toward separation and misery, and Christ pulls us toward unification and happiness.

Mormon called for the urgent employment of the Atonement's unifying capability to ward off Satan's efforts to separate us from God through sin and inequality: "And thus we see how great the inequality of man is because of sin and transgression, and the power of the devil, which comes by the cunning plans which he hath devised to ensnare the hearts of men. And thus we see the great call of diligence of men to labor in the vineyards of the Lord; and thus we see the great reason of sorrow, and also of rejoicing—sorrow because of death and destruction among men, and joy because of the light of Christ unto life."[89]

What does this have to do with consecration and Zion? It is a purpose of the Atonement to correct lack, reverse inequality, bring unequal things back into balance, and unify that which is presently in a state of separation. Therefore, we are called with "a great call of diligence" to labor in the cause of the Atonement. We accomplish that labor through our consecrated effort, which is the giving of who we are and what we have for the purposes of lifting, unifying, equalizing, restoring, and healing whomever or whatever we encounter that is suffering a separated, unequal, or less-than-perfect state of being.

When we draw people into the Atonement through our consecrated sacrifice, their condition vastly improves. Now they begin to achieve balance, abundance, peace, and joy—all of which are described in the scriptures by the words *full* and *fulness*. Consider these verses as they apply to the unifying power of the Atonement:

> And for this cause ye shall have *fulness* of joy; and ye shall sit down in the kingdom of my Father; yea, your joy shall be *full*, even as the Father hath given me *fulness* of joy; and ye shall be even as I am, and I am even as the Father; and the Father and I are one.[90]
>
> For man is spirit. The elements are eternal, and spirit and element, inseparably connected, receive a *fulness* of joy; and when separated, man cannot receive a *fulness* of joy.[91]

---

88   *American Heritage Dictionary*, s.v. "entropy."
89   Alma 28:13–14.
90   3 Nephi 28:10; emphasis added.
91   D&C 93:34; emphasis added.

> Their sleeping dust was to be restored unto its
> perfect frame, bone to his bone, and the sinews and the
> flesh upon them, the spirit and the body to be united
> never again to be divided, that they might receive a
> *fulness* of joy.[92]

For something separated to become one, the Atonement must be applied, and the application of the Atonement is always inaugurated by a consecrated effort.

Consecration—A Temporal Law with Spiritual Implications

Although we must consecrate the things we possess, which is a temporal manifestation of consecration, our consecrated action is a spiritual sacrifice that speaks of who we are. The Lord said, "Wherefore, verily I say unto you that all things unto me are spiritual, and not at any time have I given unto you a law which was temporal; neither any man, nor the children of men; neither Adam, your father, whom I created. Behold, I gave unto him that he should be an agent unto himself; and I gave unto him commandment, but no temporal commandment gave I unto him, for my commandments are spiritual."[93]

David O. McKay made this astute observation concerning temporal consecration as it applies to the spiritual:

> The development of our spiritual nature should concern
> us most. Spirituality is the highest acquisition of the
> soul, the divine in man; "the supreme, crowning gift
> that makes him king of all created things." It is the con-
> sciousness of victory over self and of communion with
> the infinite. It is spirituality alone which really gives
> one the best in life. It is something to supply clothing
> to the scantily clad, to furnish ample food to those
> whose table is thinly spread, to give activity to those
> who are fighting desperately the despair that comes
> from enforced idleness, but after all is said and done,
> the greatest blessings that will accrue from the Church
> are spiritual. Outwardly, every act seems to be directed
> toward the physical: re-making of dresses and suits of
> clothes, canning fruits and vegetables, storing food-
> stuffs, choosing of fertile fields for settlement—all seem
> strictly temporal, but permeating all these acts, inspir-
> ing and sanctifying them, is the element of spirituality.[94]

---

92   D&C 138:17; emphasis added.
93   D&C 29:34–35.
94   McKay, *Gospel Ideals*, 202.

Clearly, it is *temporal* consecration that accomplishes *spiritual* sanctification, and it is sanctification that creates a pure, Zion-like heart. Helaman portrayed this principle—that temporal consecration leads to spiritual sanctification—by describing a faithful group of Saints who grew "firmer and firmer in the faith of Christ . . . even to the purifying and the sanctification of their hearts, which sanctification cometh because of their yielding their hearts unto God."[95] Our willingness to accept and master consecration is central to our becoming sanctified and preparing for the establishment of Zion in our hearts. Ultimately, Zion succeeds or fails in our hearts according to the diligence we give to consecrating our lives to God.[96]

Addressing the reluctance of some Saints to embrace and implement the law of consecration as it pertained to the newly announced welfare plan, President J. Reuben Clark Jr. made this significant statement: "The Church has found that the whole problem is essentially a question of spirituality, rather than of finance or economics. Where the spirituality has been high, the Plan has succeeded; where the spirituality is low, the Plan has lagged. The Church has proved there is no substitute for the great commandments: 'Thou shalt love the Lord thy God with all thy . . . might, mind, and strength, and thy neighbor as thyself.'"[97]

Forty-one years later, in 1980, President Marion G. Romney reported that the Church had made great strides in implementing the welfare plan, but the measurement of its success continued to be reflected in spiritual terms. In the end, he said, consecration can only be measured spiritually by the condition of the hearts of both givers and receivers.[98]

Consecration—A Law That Makes Us Independent from the World

A familiar phrase that distinguishes Zion from Babylon is "in the world but not of the world." This phrase implies independence *from* the world. If Zion cohabits with the world or depends upon Babylon in any degree, it ceases to qualify as Zion.

Zion is independent, unalloyed, wholly separate, distinct, and diametrically opposed to Babylon. Zion does not build a bridge to Babylon and then come and go at will. Zion severs any connection with Babylon and stays on its own side of the chasm. In vision, Lehi saw the three classes of members of the Church who started down the path leading to the tree of life. Sadly, only one group arrived and remained. The select few of that group managed to remain at the tree by clinging to the word of God and ignoring the taunts and temptations of the people who resided in what Lehi described as a "great and spacious building." What was the principle of power that the select few implemented to stay out of and remain independent from the great and spacious building, which of course is a symbol for Babylon? Nephi quoted his father, Lehi, as saying, "We heeded them not." Then as if to punctuate the point, Nephi explained

---

95 Helaman 3:35.
96 Gardner, "Becoming a Zion Society," 31.
97 Clark, *Church Welfare Plan*, 32–33.
98 Romney, "Church Welfare—Temporal Service in a Spiritual Setting," 84.

that it is lethal to venture into Babylon. His concluding statement is sweeping and inclusive: "For as many as heeded them [the people in the building—Babylon], had fallen away."[99]

Consecration is one of the culminating principles in the new and everlasting covenant that allows Zion people to reside in the world but not be of the world—to be wholly independent from the world. To the children of Zion, the Lord said, "Wherefore, a commandment I give unto you, to prepare and organize yourselves by a bond or everlasting covenant that cannot be broken. . . . Behold, this is the preparation wherewith I prepare you, and the foundation, and the ensample which I give unto you, whereby you may accomplish the commandments which are given you; that through my providence, notwithstanding the tribulation which shall descend upon you, that the church may stand *independent* above all other creatures beneath the celestial world."[100] That is to say, the new and everlasting covenant was designed by God to bind us together so that we might more fully keep the commandments. Living the commandments in unison infuses power into our lives. That unifying empowerment prepares us for the tribulation Babylon always heaps upon Zion. But ultimately the covenant keeps us safe and allows us to stand independent of all other creatures or creations. The *Doctrine and Covenants Encyclopedia* states: "In 1832, God revealed his desire to have the Church 'stand independent above all other creatures beneath the celestial world.' The term 'creature' is used here in its widest meaning, to signify all that is created, and refers especially to the various organizations in the world, whether ecclesiastical, political, financial, or industrial. The ultimate destiny of the celestial Saints is to stand above all creatures and creations of lower orders."[101]

The principles that provide the priesthood society of Zion its independence from Babylon are the same principles that afford independence to an individual Zion person. To judge the folly of depending on Babylon, we need only recall that the great and spacious building stood on a foundation of air.[102] With nothing holding it up except pride, its fall was inevitable. On the other hand, when Zion people build their foundation upon the rock of their Redeemer,[103] which foundation is "wide as all eternity,"[104] we are characterized by the Lord as "wise." The Lord's promise to us is that the Zion life we are cultivating in our hearts will neither crumble nor fall.[105] With that knowledge, we will enjoy the resulting feelings of peace and safety: "If ye are prepared, ye shall not fear."[106]

How, then, does consecration contribute to our becoming independent from Babylon? Simply put, Zion takes care of her own, both temporally and spiritually. The following is taken from the *Encyclopedia of Mormonism:*

99   1 Nephi 8:19–34.
100 D&C 78:11, 13–14; emphasis added.
101 Brewster, *Doctrine and Covenants Encyclopedia,* 113.
102 1 Nephi 8:26.
103 Helaman 5:12.
104 Moses 7:41.
105 Matthew 7:24–27.
106 D&C 38:30.

The term "self-sufficiency" refers to a principle underlying the LDS program of Welfare Services, and to an ideal of social experience. Self-sufficiency is the ability to maintain one's self and relates to women and men being agents for themselves. Independence and self-sufficiency are critical keys to spiritual and temporal growth. A situation that threatens one's ability to be self-sufficient also threatens one's confidence, self-esteem, and freedom. As dependence is increased, the freedom to act is decreased.

Church writings often use the terms self-sufficiency and "self-reliance" interchangeably. Teachings pertaining to Welfare Services emphasize and place considerable importance on both individual and family independence. Six principles form the foundation of the infrastructure of the Welfare program. Three of these principles emphasize responsibility to care for one's own needs: work, self-reliance, and stewardship; the other three focus on responsibility to others: love, service, and consecration (Faust, p. 91).

President Spencer W. Kimball defined Welfare Services as the "essence of the Gospel . . . the Gospel in action" (Kimball, p. 77). Within the context of Welfare, the term self-sufficiency also includes an emphasis on prevention, temporary assistance, and rehabilitation. Self-sufficiency is helping oneself to the point of reliance. Welfare, a program based on self-sufficiency, helps individuals to help themselves. Home industry, gardening, food storage, emergency preparedness, and avoidance of debt reflect the applications of self-sufficiency (*Welfare Services Resource Handbook*, p. 21). . . .

As a social ideal, self-sufficiency includes spiritual, intellectual, and emotional dimensions. . . . Self-sufficiency is central to such interdependence and is necessary for one to be in a position to assist others, beginning with one's own family, neighbors, and ward. . . .

New Testament teachings conceive of liberty as a person's relationship to God and others (Buttrick, p. 121). Christ gave his followers sacred charge and opportunity to serve the poor, needy, sick, and afflicted. Rather than looking on God as the only one able to provide, individuals as self-sufficient beings work together in mutual responsibility, compassion, gentleness, and love.

Perspective on the balance between an individual person's being totally self-sufficient and also needing assistance comes from the understanding that everyone is self-reliant in some areas and dependent in others. Latter-day Saints accept the observation that everyone is flawed and imperfect; everyone experiences human limitation or poverty. Scriptures recognize that poverty resides in both temporal or spiritual matters. In fact, all are "beggars" for a remission of sins (Mosiah 4:20). Nevertheless, a certain equality emerges from human interdependence, noted in the counsel to be equal in both heavenly and earthly things: "For if ye are not equal in earthly things ye cannot be equal in obtaining heavenly things" (D&C 78:6). From one's strengths, each should endeavor to help another; on the other hand, one should accept the help of another. "If a man be overtaken in a fault, ye which are spiritual, restore such an one in the spirit of meekness; . . . bear ye one another's burdens, and so fulfill the law of Christ" (Gal. 6:1–2). Interdependence, then, creates the opportunity to participate in the sanctifying experience of giving and receiving (Romney, p. 91).

In a gospel sense, there exists an interdependence between those who have and those who have not. The process of sharing lifts the poor, humbles the rich, and sanctifies both. The poor are released from bondage and limitations of poverty and are able to rise to their full potential, both temporally and spiritually. The rich, by imparting of their surplus, participate in the eternal principle of sharing. A person who is whole or self-sufficient can reach out to others, and the cycle of equality and giving repeats itself.

Without self-sufficiency it is difficult to exercise these innate desires to serve. Food for the hungry cannot come from empty shelves; money to assist the needy cannot come from an empty purse; support and understanding cannot come from the emotionally starved; teaching cannot come from the unlearned. Most important of all, spiritual guidance only comes from the spiritually strong. Indeed, self-sufficiency forms the basis to bear one another's burdens and to live interdependently.[107]

---

107   *Encyclopedia of Mormonism*, 1293–94.

Clearly, Zion people espouse the principle of independence and achieve it by virtue of the law of consecration. Babylon has no efficient program that provides its citizens with true independence. Repeatedly, the prophets have counseled us to guard against worldly substitutes in caring for ourselves and the poor among us. The prophets go so far as to call these government programs ineffective, misleading, and counterfeit.[108] President Marion G. Romney quoted one head of state as saying, "We're going to take all the money we think is unnecessarily being spent and take it from the 'haves' and give to the 'have nots' that need it so much."[109] Then he stated that the difference between taking money from us to administer welfare assistance and voluntarily contributing it out of our love of God and fellowman is the difference between slavery and freedom. On another occasion, he said that no institution that continues to promote forced socialized welfare programs can long endure.[110]

Conversely, Zion people shoulder an obligation to achieve self-sufficiency through consecrated service and offerings, and we must approach self-sufficiency in this way if we ever expect to attain eternal life. Only Zion offers a true and permanent solution for personal and societal independence.

Consecration—An Order That Orders Our Lives

The new and everlasting covenant transforms an undisciplined telestial life into an ordered celestial life. "My house is a house of order," the Lord said.[111] Every law that comprises the Covenant orders our lives so that we might conform to the order of life God enjoys. It should be no surprise, then, that the law of consecration is one of the culminating laws of the Covenant that precedes our receiving an eternal kingdom by means of temple marriage.

Consecration is a way of life—an *ordered* life. Consecration bids us acknowledge that all things belong to God, and that we are stewards.[112] We are accountable to God for the discharge of those stewardships.[113] Although he allows us custody of our property, we recognize that, ultimately, it is his, and he has final say as to the property's use. That he allows us the freedom to manage his property does not exempt us from being accountable to him. This is the celestial order mandated by consecration. President Benson said, "The basic principle underlying [consecration] is that everything we have belongs to the Lord; and, therefore, the Lord may call upon us for any and all of our property, because it belongs to Him."[114]

Consecration orders our relationship with God and his children. First, we are to love "the Lord thy God with all thy heart, with all thy might, mind, and strength," and,

---

108   Kimball, "Becoming the Pure in Heart," 79; Romney, Conference Report, Oct. 1972, 115.
     109   Romney, "Church Welfare Services' Basic Principles," 120, quoting *Congressional Record*, 1964, 6142.
110   Romney, Conference Report, Apr. 1976, 169.
111   D&C 132:18.
112   D&C 38:17; 104:11–14.
113   D&C 72:3; 104:13–18.
114   Benson, *The Teachings of Ezra Taft Benson*, 121.

second, we are to "love thy neighbor as thyself."[115] First one, and then the other—this is the order. With regard to loving others, we are to assume the attitude of esteeming other people as ourselves.[116] This attitude reflects the celestially ordered view of relationships that allows for all men and women to be equal according to their wants, needs, family situations, and access to the Lord's resources.[117] Clearly, at the heart of the celestial order is the law of consecration. When we ignore, rationalize, or modify this order to fit our personal objectives, we step away from the new and everlasting covenant and become a law unto ourselves.[118]

Consecration is a progressive process that begins with repentance and baptism for the remission of sins, which orders our lives in such a way that eventually we can consecrate our hearts. Upon receiving the gift of the Holy Ghost, we begin to experience the ministering of angels, which further helps us to order our lives. The promise of angelic ministration is reconfirmed when we enter the order of the priesthood,[119] which requires a higher standard of righteousness to make the priesthood effectual[120]—which means more order! The path to eternal life is marked with other covenants and ordinances that prepare and point us to the sacrifice of all things, which is ultimate consecration. Elder Bruce C. Hafen wrote, "When we move on to the more mature stage represented by the blessings of the Melchizedek Priesthood and the temple ordinances, we advance to a higher level of religious life. . . . The contrast with the higher law is staggering: '*Love thy wife* with all thy heart'; and '*Be* ye therefore perfect.' (Matthew 5:48.) The higher law asks not only for new behavior; it asks for a new heart."[121] President Benson taught that initial covenants and ordinances prepare us to consecrate our all to the Lord: "Until one abides by the laws of obedience, sacrifice, the gospel, and chastity, he cannot abide the law of consecration, which is the law pertaining to the celestial kingdom. 'For if you will that I give you place in the celestial world, you must prepare yourselves by doing the things which I have commanded you and required of you' (D&C 78:7)."[122]

Consecration orders everything in our lives, and everything we do is based on an eternal perspective. Our attitudes toward property and toward God and his children are brought into order, as are our devotions. For example, we are told that we are not to seek for riches but for wisdom.[123] Notice how the celestial order places first things first, exactly opposite to the order of Babylon. The Book of Mormon prophet Jacob taught: "But before ye seek for riches, seek ye for the kingdom of God. And after ye have obtained a hope in Christ ye shall obtain riches, if ye seek them; and ye will seek them for the intent to do good—to clothe the naked, and to feed the hungry, and to liberate the

---

115   D&C 59:5–6.
116   D&C 38:24–27; 51:3, 9; 70:14; 78:6; 82:17.
117   D&C 51:3.
118   D&C 88:21–35.
119   D&C 84:42.
120   D&C 121:34–46.
121   Hafen, *The Broken Heart*, 158.
122   Ezra Taft Benson, *The Teachings of Ezra Taft Benson*, 121.
123   D&C 6:7.

captive, and administer relief to the sick and the afflicted."[124] Here the celestial sequence is clearly set forth. Nowhere in Babylon would we hear such doctrine; it is not part of that order.

If we would pay the price to live the order of consecration by first loving God and then his children, seeking for the kingdom of God, and hungering for wisdom over every temporal enticement, we would find ourselves aligned with the celestial order. We would achieve an unshakable, faith-filled relationship with God; we would learn to love all of God's creations, including his children;[125] our wisdom and understanding would become great;[126] and we would remain safe from the damning preoccupation with wealth.

The result of the ultimate consecrated effort is the "sacrifice of all things," which is required for eternal life.[127] There is no doubt that this sacrifice is daunting; it is supposed to be. Nevertheless, we are promised that if we will persevere and make this sacrifice, which can be compared to the Savior's comment about losing our lives for his sake, it will lead us to finding our lives.[128] Again, we see a celestial order provided by the order of consecration: "lose" our lives, first, and then "find" our lives, second. Elder Neal A. Maxwell said, "So many of us are kept from eventual consecration because we mistakenly think that, somehow, by letting our wills be swallowed up in the will of God, we lose our individuality. What we are really worried about, of course, is not giving up self, but selfish things—like our roles, time, pre-eminence, and possessions. No wonder we are instructed by the Savior to lose ourselves." Then Elder Maxwell added, "It is not a question of one's losing identity but of finding his true identity!"[129]

In the end, we discover that living the order of consecration has little to do with managing property; consecration has everything to do with managing the condition of the heart.

What Consecration Is Not

President Ezra Taft Benson drew a distinction between Zion's law of consecration, which he referred to as the united order, and Babylon's counterfeits.

> It has been erroneously concluded by some that the united order is both communal and communistic in theory and practice because the revelations speak of equality. Equality under the united order is not economic and social leveling as advocated by some today. Equality, as described by the Lord, is "equal[ity] according to [a man's] family, according to his circumstances and his wants and needs" (D&C 51:3).

---

124   Jacob 2:18–19.
125   McMullin, "Come to Zion! Come to Zion!" 94.
126   D&C 76:2.
127   Smith, *Lectures on Faith,* 6:7.
128   Matthew 10:39.
129   Maxwell, *If Thou Endure It Well,* 51.

Is the united order a communal system? Emphatically not. It never has been and never will be. It is "intensely individualistic." Does the united order eliminate private ownership of property? No. "The fundamental principle of this system [is] the private ownership of property."[130]

Temporal and Spiritual Salvation

The Lord declared, "[Consecration exists] for the benefit of my church, and for the salvation of men," until the Lord comes.[131] On another occasion, he said, "And for your salvation I give unto you a commandment, for I have heard your prayers, and the poor have complained before me, and the rich have I made, and all flesh is mine, and I am no respecter of persons."[132] We enter into the covenant of consecration by agreeing to give our all to the Lord, and in return he covenants to take care of us with his all. By reason of living this covenant, we are protected and saved both temporally and spiritually.

Perhaps the Lord was thinking of consecration's inherent quality of safety when he compared himself to a mother hen under whose wings we children of the Covenant enjoy safety and security: "For, behold, I will gather them as a hen gathereth her chickens under her wings, if they will not harden their hearts."[133] In this covenantal relationship, the Lord assumes the responsibility to supply our needs and wants, provided that we extend our best effort and invoke the law of asking. Hugh Nibley wrote: "The covenant [of consecration] is made by the individual to the Father in the name of the Son, a private and a personal thing, a covenant with the Lord. He intends it specifically to implement a social order—to save his people as a people, to unite them and make them of one heart and one mind, independent of any power on earth."[134]

Equally important, we are saved spiritually by living the law of consecration. Only by making this sacrifice, the sacrifice of all things, which is required for exaltation,[135] can we lay hold on the promise of eternal life. Significantly, before we can receive our eternal kingdom by the ordinance of celestial marriage, we must first covenant to consecrate; then, before our marriage is sealed by the Holy Spirit of Promise[136] and thus *made sure*, we must first accomplish the sacrifice of all things by applying the law of consecration. Consecration, therefore, becomes the point upon which salvation and exaltation are lost or gained. All other covenants and ordinances point us to this singular requirement.

Finally, consecration is the ultimate test of discipleship, the supreme indicator of conversion. President Joseph F. Smith said, "A man who cannot sacrifice his own wishes, who

---

130   Benson, *The Teachings of Ezra Taft Benson*, 122, referencing J. Reuben Clark, Jr., Conference Report, Oct. 1942, 57.
131   D&C 104:1.
132   D&C 38:16.
133   D&C 10:65; see also Matthew 23:37; Luke 13:34; 3 Nephi 10:4–6; D&C 29:2; 43:34.
134   Nibley, *Approaching Zion*, 468.
135   Joseph Smith, *Lectures on Faith*, 6:7.
136   D&C 132:7, 19.

cannot say in his heart, 'Father, Thy will be done, not mine,' is not a truly and thoroughly converted child of God; he is still, to some extent, in the grasp of error and in the shades of darkness that hover around the world, hiding God from the presence of mankind."[137]

Summary and Conclusion

The law of consecration is the law of the celestial kingdom and thus the law of Zion. This law provides that greater beings partner with lesser beings in a covenantal family relationship to allow the lesser beings to rise to a progressively higher stature by giving them the ability to draw upon the resources of the higher kingdom. Heavenly Father lives the law of consecration perfectly. He withholds nothing from us—neither his time, ability, knowledge, power, nor his vast kingdom. He does all of this so that we might become like him—become *one* with him—in attributes, honor, glory, power, might, and dominion. This is his stated work and glory.[138]

This foundational law of Zion is wholly foreign to Babylon. Hence, the Lord declared to Joseph Smith, "Behold, the world at this time lieth in sin, and there is none that doeth good, *no not one*. And mine anger is kindling against the inhabitants of the earth to visit them according to this ungodliness."[139] The universal condition known as ungodliness is this: "But it is not given that one man should possess that which is above another, wherefore the world lieth in sin."[140] Like pride, selfishness and inequality are universal sins. The protective solution is consecration.

The "greatest desire" of prophets "is to see Zion established according to the revelations of God." That desire can happen only upon the principle of consecration. But too many people feel that consecration is a program for the future and that we are living a watered-down version of it today. That assumption is erroneous. The principles of consecration form a template that can be applied successfully to any number of situations, and it can be adapted to the needs of the few or the many. The law of consecration does not lie in some kind of suspended state, waiting for an announcement that the time has come to live it. Consecration is current and in full force today, and it must be lived actively by each of us who makes the covenant; otherwise, we can neither build up the kingdom of God nor establish the principles of Zion in our lives.

Joseph Smith gave the following definition of consecration: "When we consecrate our property to the Lord it is to administer to the wants of the poor and needy, for this is the law of God. . . . Now for a man to consecrate . . . is nothing more nor less than to feed the hungry, clothe the naked, visit the widow and fatherless, the sick and afflicted, and do all he can to administer to their relief in their afflictions, and for him and his house to serve the Lord. In order to do this, he and all his house must be virtuous, and must shun the very appearance of evil."[141]

---

137 Smith, *Teachings of Presidents of the Church,* 192.
138 Moses 1:39.
139 Nibley, *Nibley on the Timely and the Timeless,* 280–81.
140 D&C 49:20; emphasis added.
141 Smith, *Teachings of the Prophet Joseph Smith,* 127.

The present Church welfare plan espouses these principles, both on a Church-wide and a personal basis. This plan describes a consecrated person as someone who does not seek for worldly riches; who esteems his brother as himself; who, through tithes and offerings, helps to build up the kingdom of God by caring for the temporal needs of those General Authorities whom God has called into full-time service; who makes his worldly goods available, over and above his family's necessities, for the Lord's work; and who, with his time, talents, and means, takes care of the temporally and spiritually poor.[142]

The law of consecration requires that we consecrate everything to God, both the good and the bad. In that way, he can transform us into what we must become to inherit the celestial kingdom. The promise is this: "[God] shall consecrate thine afflictions for thy gain."[143]

The law of consecration, which is also a covenant, requires that we acknowledge that all things belong to the Lord and that we are stewards.[144] We are to esteem each other as ourselves.[145] We practice this law upon the principle of free agency.[146] We are made equal according to our wants, needs, and family situations.[147] We are accountable to the Lord for our stewardships.[148] If we make this covenant, we must live the covenant: "And behold, none are exempt from this law who belong to the church of the living God."[149]

Consecration is designed so all can live it.[150] According to Brigham Young, the law of consecration is "easy" to understand and to live.[151] Nevertheless, "it was one of the first commandments or revelations given to this people . . . and I now think, that it will be one of the last revelations which the people will receive into their hearts and understand."[152]

The restoration of the law of consecration began as early as 1829, when the Lord pointed Joseph Smith toward establishing "the cause of Zion."[153] After the organization of the Church, the Prophet was commanded to go to Ohio to receive "the law of the Church,"[154] which is often called the law of Zion. That law is recorded in Doctrine and Covenants 42. Because consecration is a template for living God's law, it was applied to a variety of situations for varying lengths of time, involving either a few people or the entire Church. With regard to the Church, the law of tithes and offerings became the manifestation of the law of consecration and remains in effect to this day. The combination of tithes and offerings provides for (1) building up the kingdom of God on the earth, which is the primary function of tithing, and (2) establishing the cause of Zion, which is the primary function of offerings. Ultimately, every offering we place on the altar represents the only offering that matters: the heart. Most recently, the current welfare plan

---

142   Bowen, *The Church Welfare Plan*, 6.
143   2 Nephi 2:2.
144   Kimball, *The Teachings of Spencer W. Kimball*, 366.
145   D&C 38:24–27; 51:3, 9; 70:14; 78:6; 82:17.
146   D&C 104:17.
147   D&C 51:3.
148   D&C 72:3; 104:13–18.
149   D&C 70:20.
150   Nibley, *Approaching Zion*, 422, quoting Zechariah 14:17–18.
151   Young, *Journal of Discourses*, 2:306.
152   Young, *Discourses of Brigham Young*, 179.
153   D&C 6:6; 11:6; 14:6.
154   D&C 42, section heading.

has become a mainstay of the law of consecration. In addition, we enjoy other programs that are built with the template of consecration. Some of these include LDS Philanthropies, the Perpetual Education Fund, the Missionary Fund, and LDS Humanitarian Services. Those of us who are covenant, consecrated Saints of God must apply this law in ever-increasing faith until poverty in each of its ugly forms, is abolished from among us.

Consecration is more than a law; it is a way of life that feels familiar to us, or, as President Lorenzo Snow said, "something that is natural."[155] Consecration is a mindset that impacts the heart in such a way that it finally becomes pure. By living the law of consecration, sanctification increases. If Zion is "the highest order of priesthood society,"[156] and if Zion is founded upon the law of consecration, it behooves us to take seriously this celestial law that governs that priesthood society. Inferior choices can result only in inferior blessings and inferior kingdoms.

Only the pure in heart are able to live the law of consecration. Obedience, sacrifice, and living the laws and ordinances of gospel, including the celestial lifestyle called *chastity,* prepare us to live this law and to make this ultimate sacrifice. Partial consecration can never produce the blessings of eternal reward. But we need not run faster than we are able. We learn to live a consecrated life by degrees. As we do so, we are enabled to take our consecration to the next level.

Because the results of consecration are equality and oneness, consecration becomes immediately connected to the Atonement; the purpose of both is to bring separated things back into a state of oneness. For something separated to become one, the Atonement must be applied, and the application of the Atonement is always inaugurated by a consecrated effort.

Consecration is often manifested as a temporal sacrifice, but our action has immediate spiritual implications. Consecration speaks of who we are inside, and it vitalizes spiritual sanctification, which creates a pure, Zion-like heart. Therefore, consecration is ultimately measured by the condition of the hearts of both givers and receivers.[157]

Consecration is a law that makes us independent from the world. Our purpose for living in the world is to invite others out of the world and into Zion. Therefore, if we cohabit with the world or depend upon Babylon in any degree, we cease to qualify as Zion people. Zion is distinct, and diametrically opposed to Babylon. Zion people depend upon consecration to remain independent from Babylon. Simply put, Zion people take care of their own, both temporally and spiritually. Zion people do so by espousing the principles of independence that the law of consecration provides. On the other hand, Babylon has no efficient program that can take care of its citizens or truly make them free.

In the end, consecration is an *ordered* way of life. Consecration orders our relationships with God and his children. Consecration orders everything in our lives, and it points us toward celestial goals. Our attitudes toward our possessions, our time and talents, and our attitude toward God and his children are brought into order through

155   Snow, *The Teachings of Lorenzo Snow,* 184,
156   Kimball, *The Teachings of Spencer W. Kimball,* 125.
157   Romney, "Church Welfare—Temporal Service in a Spiritual Setting," 84.

consecration. This law is the vehicle for our making the essential "sacrifice of all things" required for achieving eternal life.[158]

Consecration is not man-made; it is neither a communal nor a communistic experiment. It is a celestial law that governs celestial beings and allows them eternal progression and the expansion of their kingdoms. In this life, consecration is our best opportunity for both temporal and spiritual salvation.

158   Smith, *Lectures on Faith*, 6:7.

Section 2
Consecration Results in Equality and Unity

President Marion G. Romney listed six characteristics of the law of consecration:
1. We must have a belief in God.
2. We must make our freewill offerings voluntarily and not by legislation.
3. We must maintain private ownership and individual management of our property and possessions.
4. The program of consecration is nonpolitical.
5. The prerequisite to our being able to live this law is righteousness.
6. Consecration exalts the poor and humbles the rich.[159]

Undergirding this list are two fundamental principles that define Zion: "Every man seeking the interest of his neighbor, and doing all things with an eye single to the glory of God."[160] Contrasted with Babylon, the results of such an attitude are astonishing. Because of our love for God and his children, we voluntarily choose to abase ourselves so that we might succor those in need of succor, impart of our substance to the poor and the needy, feed the hungry, and suffer "all manner of afflictions for Christ's sake."[161] By so doing, we promote the celestial characteristics of *equality* and *unity*, and thus we our hearts become Zion-like.

Let us examine equality and unity as they pertain to consecration.

Equality—"In Mine Own Way"

President Joseph F. Smith said, "The principles of the Gospel are calculated to make us unselfish, to broaden our minds, to give breadth to our desires for good, to remove

---

159 Romney, "The Purpose of Church Welfare Services," 92.
160 D&C 82:19.
161 Alma 4:13.

hatred, animosity, envy and anger from our hearts, and make us peaceful, tractable, teachable, and willing to sacrifice our own desires, and perchance our own interests, for the welfare of our fellow-creatures, and for the advancement of the Kingdom of God."[162] Upon such fertile ground, the seeds of equality can be planted in the heart; then those seeds sprout and blossom into the bouquet of purity required by Zion.

In the world, the subject of equality troubles people and nations. We see Babylon's attempts to equalize society through counterfeit programs such as forced taxation, communism, and other economic experiments. The results inevitably limit freedom of choice, stifle initiative, hamper prosperity, promote divisiveness, and ultimately level individuals and societies. True equality cannot be legislated, and it can never be achieved in this way. Without the dual motivations of love of God and of mankind, equality will ever need to be mandated rather than chosen, causing both the poor and the rich to feel dissatisfied.

On the other hand, Zion-like equality levels up people and societies. Zion exalts the poor by means of the consecrated freewill offerings of the rich, those who have excess resources. The Lord said, "And it is my purpose to provide for my saints, for all things are mine. But it must needs be done in mine own way; and behold this is the way that I, the Lord, have decreed to provide for my saints, that the *poor shall be exalted,* in that the *rich are made low.*"[163]

"To make low" may sound harsh to those who interpret this phrase as forced socialism or legislated redistribution of wealth. Actually, "to make low" is not a demeaning event at all; it is a safeguard against pride. Jesus himself is described as being "lowly in heart."[164] Therefore, to be "made low" is to be made like Jesus. We are admonished to become lowly in heart to achieve a state of blessedness, and thus we will find rest to our souls.[165] It is no wonder, then, that the lowly in heart are also those who are filled with charity and deemed acceptable to God.[166] Consequently, a lowly-in-heart Zion person allows no poor—monetarily, emotionally, physically, or spiritually poor—within his circle of influence to experience want.[167] Because he is driven by the love of God for his fellowman, a Zion person will attack lack wherever he encounters it. Therefore, it is the love of the lowly in heart that advances equality in Zion. This is Christ's "own way," the consecrated way.

Equality and the Law of Prosperity

In a telestial world, especially one in which the philosophies of Babylon enjoy almost free reign, we struggle when we are confronted with living celestial laws, such as consecration. We can point to nothing in our environment that suggests these laws will work for us if we attempt to live them. For example, how could giving ten percent of our money

162 Smith, *Collected Discourses,* vol. 3, Sept. 3, 1892.
163 D&C 104:15–16; emphasis added.
164 Matthew 11:29.
165 Alma 32:8; 37:33–34.
166 Moroni 7:44.
167 Moses 7:18.

to the Lord return to us blessings beyond our ability to receive?[168] In a telestial world, we can no more make sense of "less is more" than we can of walking on water. So when we survey the laws of Zion, specifically consecration, how do we make sense of giving away progressively more in order to achieve the promised unequalled prosperity of Zion?

We rely on prophets to articulate celestial laws and to urge us to experiment with them. One celestial law is the law of prosperity. King Benjamin summed it up:

> And behold, all that [God] requires of you is to keep his commandments; and he has promised you that if ye would keep his commandments ye should prosper in the land; and he never doth vary from that which he hath said; therefore, if ye do keep his commandments he doth bless you and prosper you. And now, in the first place, he hath created you, and granted unto you your lives, for which ye are indebted unto him. And secondly, he doth require that ye should do as he hath commanded you; for which if ye do, he doth immediately bless you; and therefore he hath paid you. And ye are still indebted unto him, and are, and will be, forever and ever; therefore, of what have ye to boast?[169]

Clearly, we have nothing to boast about. We are in debt to God and will be forever. But whereas telestial debt is a curse, celestial debt propels us toward blessings. Here is how we might portray the celestial "law of prosperity" as it applies to the law of consecration:

- Our love of God motivates us to seek to serve him.
- Because God is not in need, he immediately asks us to transfer our service to his suffering children, who need our help. That is, he asks us to serve him by serving his children, which we do in a spirit of consecration.
- When we do as he asks, God accepts our sacrifice "unto the least of these" as if we had done it unto God.[170]
- Our sacrifice creates something akin to a *credit* in our favor, which credit demands payment.
- God assumes this obligation, which is actually an opportunity to bless us. He rewards us for our service: first, because he loves us; second, because we have obeyed the law upon which the blessing is predicated,[171] and third, because our service has created an implied celestial deficit that needs correcting.
- Because God will not and cannot remain in a real or implied deficit position, "he doth immediately bless [us]; and therefore he hath paid [us]. And [we] are still indebted unto him, and are, and will be, forever and ever."

---

168   Malachi 3:10.
169   Mosiah 2:22–24.
170   D&C 42:38.
171   D&C 130:21.

- Here is where the "hundredfold principle" (discussed earlier in this series) comes in—we are always rewarded beyond our sacrifice. God overpays his obligations, and therefore we find ourselves eternally indebted to him.
- What is the result? Because we are consecrated to God and he is consecrated to us, we live forever in the condition of abundance, the engine of which is driven by celestial debts and credits created and earned by consecrated service and offerings.

New Math

We cannot make sense of the law of prosperity for an obvious reason: The math doesn't work. In a telestial world, ten minus one equals nine; but in a celestial world, because we are dealing with a celestial law and celestial math, ten minus one can equal eleven or fifteen or fifty or "an hundredfold."[172] But never nine. For instance, we recall the example of the kernel of corn. Given the choice of planting or eating it, we chose to exercise faith and plant. Our faith increased when our seed grew into a stalk with several ears of corn. Then we exercised faith again by planting rather than eating the kernels from some of those ears. The result of our faith and sacrifice was a great harvest—all from a single kernel. Elder Boyd K. Packer said, "As you give what you have, there is a replacement, with increase!"[173] That is how consecration works.

We do not have to make sense of the celestial law of prosperity; we just need to know that it works. It has to. Because it is God's law, if it ceased working, God would cease to be God.[174] For now, we must live the law of prosperity by faith, moving forward with the hope that our obedience will always produce an inexplicable miracle that translates into spiritual and temporal abundance. Like the kernel of corn, when that abundance is replanted or consecrated back to the Lord, we experience a harvest of blessings, which allows us to partner with God to "level up" his children.

Esteeming All Flesh in One

Nephi said, "Behold, the Lord esteemeth all flesh in one; he that is righteous is favored of God."[175] Equality governs God's dealings with his children; and righteous Zion people who espouse equality receive God's greatest blessings. What are the "favored of God" supposed to do with their blessings? Clearly, they are supposed to do that which qualified them to be called "righteous" in the first place: use them to bless God's children.

If we desire to become "righteous" Zion-like people and "the favored of God," we cannot treat God's children differently than he does. Rhetorically, Nephi asked, "Behold, hath the Lord commanded any that they should not partake of his goodness?" Then, answering his own question, he said, "Behold I say unto you, Nay; but all men are privileged the one like unto the other, and none are forbidden. . . . He inviteth them all to come unto him and partake of his goodness; and he denieth none that come unto him, black and white, bond and free, male and female."[176] Can we expect to become Zion-like if we adopt inequality?

---

172   Genesis 26:12; 2 Samuel 24:3; Matthew 13:8–23;19:29; Mark 10:30; Luke 8:8; D&C 98:25; 132:55.
173   Packer, "The Candle of the Lord," 51.
174   Alma 42:13, 22, 25.
175   1 Nephi 17:35.
176   2 Nephi 26:28, 33.

The Lord gives each of his children an equal chance and loves them the same, but the this is not always true of us. Nevertheless, the law of consecration stipulates that we shoulder the obligation of the covenant to lift others. It is anti-Zion to exalt ourselves while others languish in poverty. The Apostle Paul wrote, "Let no man seek his own, but every man another's good."[177] What is the divine result of seeking equality? "And the Lord called his people Zion, *because* they were of one heart and one mind, and dwelt in righteousness; and there was no poor among them."[178] Pay particular attention to the word *because* in this scripture. *Because* pure-hearted people strive to lift their neighbors and esteem all of God's children as themselves, Zion flourishes. Zion is established *because* we make a choice to become Zion-like.[179] President Gordon B. Hinckley said, "If we are to build that Zion of which the prophets have spoken and of which the Lord has given mighty promise, we must set aside our consuming selfishness. We must rise above our love for comfort and ease, and in the very process of effort and struggle, even in our extremity, we shall become better acquainted with our God."[180]

Seven Points of Equality

The virtues of equality and love are inseparable. Without divine love, equality could not exist. Without divine love, no redeeming virtue could exist. Indeed, the totality of the gospel is defined by love.[181] The *Encyclopedia of Mormonism* lists various points of equality[182] that flow from consecration and therefore are characterized by divine love. This is the love exemplified by Zion people.

1. **Equal in the sight of God.** All are equal in the sight of God. He is "no respecter of persons."[183] Regardless of race, station, or circumstance, each person is as precious as another. "For none of these iniquities come of the Lord; for he doeth that which is good among the children of men; and he doeth nothing save it be plain unto the children of men; and he inviteth them all to come unto him and partake of his goodness; and he denieth none that come unto him, black and white, bond and free, male and female; and he remembereth the heathen; and all are alike unto God, both Jew and Gentile."[184]

2. **Equal opportunity for eternal life.** God sets the example of equality by evenly offering his children his greatest gift: eternal life. "Remember the worth of souls is great in the sight of God; for, behold, the Lord your Redeemer suffered death in the flesh; wherefore he suffered the pain of *all* men, that *all* men might repent and come unto him. And he hath risen again from the dead, that he might bring

---

177   JST, 1 Corinthians 10:24.
178   Moses 7:18; emphasis added.
179   McMullin, "Come to Zion! Come to Zion!" 94.
180   Hinckley, *Teachings of Gordon B. Hinckley,* 725.
181   Matthew 22:37–40.
182   *Encyclopedia of Mormonism,* 463–64.
183   D&C 38:16; see also D&C 1:35.
184   2 Nephi 26:33; see also Alma 26:37.

all men unto him, on conditions of repentance."[185] "But behold, the resurrection of Christ redeemeth mankind, yea, even *all* mankind, and bringeth them back into the presence of the Lord."[186]

3. **Joint heirs.** Jesus sets the example of equality. Everyone who orders his life in such a way that he qualifies for the celestial kingdom becomes Christ's equal— joint heirs with *the* Heir, possessing all that Christ possesses, which is all that the Father has. Heirs with Christ become equal with him.[187]

4. **Equality in love.** When we love as God requires us to love—love so great that we would sacrifice our life for another—we become Zion-like in our hearts. Then we start to appreciate the equality and love that exists in heaven. We begin to understand the type of equality that defines relationships in the celestial world. "This is my commandment, That ye love one another, as I have loved you. Greater love hath no man than this, that a man lay down his life for his friends."[188] "Verily, verily, I say unto you, ye are little children, and ye have not as yet understood how great blessings the Father hath in his own hands and prepared for you; and ye cannot bear all things now; nevertheless, be of good cheer, for I will lead you along. The kingdom is yours and the blessings thereof are yours, and the riches of eternity are yours."[189]

5. **All things common.** The virtue of equality that is characteristic of Zion allows that the people enjoy "all things common among them."[190] This statement of equality means equal access to the Lord's resources and to the resources consecrated to the Lord; it does not mean, according to President Marion G. Romney, that the Zion is an economic order characterized by commonly owned property.[191] To Joseph Smith the Lord explained the eternal order of common access: "And you are to be equal, or in other words, *you are to have equal claims on the properties,* for the benefit of managing the concerns of your stewardships, every man according to his wants and his needs, inasmuch as his wants are just—and all this for the benefit of the church of the living God, that every man may improve upon his talent, that every man may gain other talents, yea, even an hundred fold, to be cast into the Lord's storehouse, to become the common property of the whole church—every man seeking the interest of his neighbor, and doing all things with an eye single to the glory of God. This order I have appointed to be an everlasting order unto you."[192]

---

185   D&C 18:10–12; emphasis added.
186   Helaman 14:17; emphasis added.
187   D&C 88:107.
188   John 15:12–13.
189   D&C 78:17–18.
190   3 Nephi 26:19; 4 Nephi 1:3.
191   Romney, "The Purpose of Church Welfare Services," 92.
192   D&C 82:17–20; emphasis added.

6. **Equal opportunities to receive and contribute.** Equality means equal opportunity to receive education, to develop talents and abilities, and to engage people in the work of Zion, everyone contributing according to their individual strengths and gifts: "And thus they were all equal, and they did all labor, every man according to his strength."[193]

7. **Equal in fulfillment of needs and wants.** The equality requisite for inheritance in Zion insists that we receive as equals those things we need to survive and that contribute to our well-being. The more we pursue this objective, the more our Zion will have "no poor among them."[194] Does that mean everyone receives the same amount? No. Zion is neither an economic system of communally held property nor a socialistic program that legislates the redistribution of wealth; rather, Zion promotes private ownership, individuality, and incentive, with each individual receiving equal access to the Lord's storehouse of freewill offerings for his unique needs and wants. Zion anticipates and provides for each person's situation, "appoint[ing] unto this people their portions, every man equal according to his family, according to his circumstances and his wants and needs."[195] Nevertheless, in providing equally according to needs and wants, there must be accountability, for the Lord said, "[It is] not given that one should possess that which is above another." Otherwise, Zion would be filled with greed and idleness, which would breed inequality, and where there is inequality "the world lieth in sin."[196] Moreover, "the abundance of the manifestations of the Spirit [would be] withheld."[197] Therefore, the Lord commanded, "And let every man deal honestly, and be alike among this people, and receive alike, that ye may be one, even as I have commanded you."[198]

Taking Equal Responsibility for the Cause of Zion

If we are to become equal in receiving and disseminating the blessings of Zion, we must take an equal part in advancing Zion's cause. Joseph Smith taught, "The cause of God is one common cause, in which the Saints are alike all interested; we are all members of the one common body, and all partake of the same spirit, and are baptized into one baptism and possess alike the same glorious hope. The advancement of the cause of God and the building up of Zion is as much one man's business as another's. The only difference is, that one is called to fulfill one duty, and another another duty; . . . party feelings, separate interests, exclusive designs should be lost sight of in the one common cause, in the interest of the whole."[199]

King Benjamin taught his people this principle of taking equal responsibility for the cause of Zion despite rank and position: "And I, even I, whom ye call your king, am no

193   Alma 1:26.
194   Moses 7:18; 4 Nephi 1:3.
195   D&C 51:3; see also verse 8; D&C 42:33.
196   D&C 49:20; see also Alma 5:53–54.
197   D&C 70:14.
198   D&C 51:9.
199   Smith, *Teachings of the Prophet Joseph Smith*, 231.

better than ye yourselves are."[200] Equality and service, he said, allow us to walk "with a clear conscience before God . . . [and] be found blameless . . . when [we] shall stand to be judged of God."[201] He reminded his people that protection and prosperity follow such a course of action: "Ye shall prosper in the land, and your enemies shall have no power over you."[202]

When we embrace consecration and strive for equality, we draw near unto Zion. The Book of Mormon describes the characteristics of such a blessed people:

> And they did impart of their substance, every man according to that which he had, to the poor, and the needy, and the sick, and the afflicted; and they did not wear costly apparel, yet they were neat and comely. And thus they did establish the affairs of the church; and thus they began to have continual peace again, notwithstanding all their persecutions.
>
> And now, because of the steadiness of the church they began to be exceedingly rich, having abundance of all things whatsoever they stood in need—an abundance of flocks and herds, and fatlings of every kind, and also abundance of grain, and of gold, and of silver, and of precious things, and abundance of silk and fine-twined linen, and all manner of good homely cloth.
>
> And thus, in their prosperous circumstances, they did not send away any who were naked, or that were hungry, or that were athirst, or that were sick, or that had not been nourished; and they did not set their hearts upon riches; therefore they were liberal to all, both old and young, both bond and free, both male and female, whether out of the church or in the church, having no respect to persons as to those who stood in need. And thus they did prosper and become far more wealthy than those who did not belong to their church.[203]

Unity

President Gordon B. Hinckley observed, "When you are united, your power is limitless. You can accomplish anything you wish to accomplish."[204]

---

200 Mosiah 2:26.
201 Mosiah 2:27.
202 Mosiah 2:31.
203 Alma 1:27–31.
204 Hinckley, "Your Greatest Challenge, Mother," 97–100.

This remarkable promise speaks to the power of unity, which flows only from a mutually consecrated effort. Such consecration lies on the bedrock of obedience, sacrifice, observing the law of the gospel, and strictly abiding the celestial lifestyle called chastity. President Daniel H. Wells, former counselor in the First Presidency, taught: "The principles of the Holy Gospel are calculated in their nature to unite the hearts of the people one with another, and to promote faith, union and love towards our fellows."[205] Because we cannot expect the Lord to establish Zion in our hearts without consecrated unity, the Savior commanded us, "I say unto you, be one; and if ye are not one ye are not mine." Prefacing this directive, he made a powerful statement regarding the importance of unity: "It is even as I am."[206]

After Jesus educated his disciples in Jerusalem regarding the power of unity, he taught the principle anew in this dispensation: "Verily, verily, I say unto you, as I said unto my disciples, where two or three are gathered together in my name, *as touching one thing,* behold, there will I be in the midst of them—even so am I in the midst of you."[207] We see in this scripture the means by which President Hinckley's promise is realized. Gathering into one in the name of Christ for a common purpose invites the Savior into our circle. Clearly, unity is a celestial law, and when we obey it, we enjoy its blessings.

The Unifying Power of the At-one-ment

Unity—oneness—is exemplified throughout the gospel. Perhaps the foremost example is the Godhead, which is comprised of three distinct individuals whose united purpose makes them one.[208] They should be our model. Central to their oneness is the At-one-ment. We become *at one* with the Godhead through the Atonement of Jesus Christ, and it is through his At-one-ment that we become one[209] with each other and joint-heirs with Christ.[210]

Oneness is the divinely mandated goal for every covenant relationship; only the Atonement can make and keep such relationships one. The highest order of covenant relationships is a Zion relationship. Wherever such a relationship exists there is oneness, and consequently there is the Lord: "The Lord came and dwelt with his people, and they dwelt in righteousness."[211] Individuals who covenant to enter into any Zion relationship (i.e., marriage, family, quorum, Relief Society, ward, stake, Church), are instructed to become of "one heart and one mind," and, remarkably, when they do so, the resulting unified environment has "no poor among them."[212] Beyond the economic implications, "no poor" also means no poor in spirit—that is, no spiritually or emotionally poor. No lack at all! For instance, in the oneness of a Zion marriage, where the power of the Atonement has made two people one and where the husband and wife have worked to knit their hearts and minds together as one, there is simply no lack.

---

205   Wells, *Journal of Discourses,* 24:314.
206   D&C 38:27.
207   D&C 6:32; emphasis added; see also Matthew 18:20.
208   Hinckley, *Teachings of Gordon B. Hinckley,* 239.
209   McConkie, *The Mortal Messiah,* 1:131.
210   Romans 8:17.
211   Moses 7:16.
212   Moses 7:18.

This is the oneness the Nephites achieved after the visitation of the resurrected Christ. Within a period of only two years, they had managed to reach out to all unbelievers, and soon everyone in the nation was converted to the Lord. Under the umbrella of the Atonement, everyone was unified, and no one lacked for anything. There were no temporally or spiritually poor among them, and all were made one. By the power of the righteous Nephites' oneness, every unbeliever repented and became one with his or her brothers and sisters.[213] Now notice the language that describes their oneness:

> And there were no contentions and disputations among them, and every man did deal justly one with another. And they had all things common among them; therefore there were not rich and poor, bond and free, but they were all made free, and partakers of the heavenly gift. . . . And the Lord did prosper them exceedingly in the land; . . . [they] became an exceedingly fair and delightsome people. And they were married, and given in marriage, and were blessed according to the multitude of the promises which the Lord had made unto them. . . . And it came to pass that there was no contention in the land, because of the love of God which did dwell in the hearts of the people. And there were no envyings, nor strifes, nor tumults, nor whoredoms, nor lyings, nor murders, nor any manner of lasciviousness; and surely there could not be a happier people among all the people who had been created by the hand of God. . . . They were in one, the children of Christ, and heirs to the kingdom of God. And how blessed were they![214]

Other scriptural accounts describe the power of the Atonement and oneness. For example, Alma and Amulek became one and converted thousands of wicked Nephites. The sons of Mosiah became one and converted tens of thousands of wicked people. Alma's grandsons, Nephi and Lehi, became one and converted thousands of wicked people.

The attitude of oneness starts by internalizing the Atonement and allowing its sanctifying effect to make of us a "new creature."[215] That is, Zion begins and flourishes in the heart, and Zion continues as a condition of the heart. Once Zion is firmly rooted there, it wants to find greater expression. Covenant relationships are where Zion thrives. Each time Zion finds a new home, it yields the same unparalleled blessings the Nephites experienced: unity, happiness, abundance, and conversion power.

Understanding this principle is essential to husbands and wives. At the time of their sealing, they are pronounced one. Subsequently, upon their faithfulness, the Holy Spirit

---

213   4 Nephi 1:1–2; emphasis added.
214   4 Nephi 1:2–3, 7, 10, 11, 15–18.
215   2 Corinthians 5:17.

of Promise confirms their sealing[216] and makes their bond *more sure*. Such a marriage is now a celestial marriage, a Zion marriage, and then the blessings of Zion begin to flow: unity, happiness, abundance, and conversion power. President James E. Faust offered one of the clearest statements on the subject: "When the covenant of marriage for time and eternity, the culminating gospel ordinance, is sealed by the Holy Spirit of promise, *it can literally open the windows of heaven for great blessings to flow to a married couple who seek for those blessings.*"[217]

Because every Zion relationship has inherent unifying and conversion power, those who come in contact with Zion people in those Zion relationships (for example, children of Zion-like parents) are leavened by their inherent oneness. Like great suns, they draw people toward them until everyone within their gravitational pull becomes one with them. Thus, in the same way that Jesus Christ and Heavenly Father are one, which oneness enables Jesus to draw all men to him,[218] so we, by our oneness in our covenant relationships, gain power to draw people to us—to Zion—to the At-*one*-ment.

Oneness and Synergy

Oneness has a synergistic effect. *Synergy* refers to the phenomenon in which two or more agents acting together create an effect greater than the sum of the individual agents. For example, if one thread can hold five pounds before it breaks, two threads woven together might be predicted to hold twice as much—ten pounds. But, because of the effect of synergy, the two threads woven together can now hold four times as much—twenty pounds!

The opposite of synergy is antagonism, where two agents work against each other and achieve *less* in combination than the individuals could achieve separately. Adam and Eve are an example both of synergy and antagonism. When God married them, he made them one; but when Satan tempted Eve, she chose to act alone, as if she and Adam were still two. This is antagonism. The antagonistic effect greatly weakened both Adam and Eve. Despite Eve's rationale at the moment of temptation, because she was now married and had been made one with her husband, everything she did affected Adam—as though he had also done the deed. Now Adam was faced with the prospect of eternal division—more antagonism—because Eve would have been cast out of the Garden, and Adam would have been left a lone man there. Therefore, Adam seized the opportunity to change antagonism to synergy. He made the decision to remain one with his wife, and to that end, he also ate the forbidden fruit. He knew that his action would require a fall, but he also knew that he had to act in a way that would rejoin them. Thereafter, we never see Adam and Eve acting separately. We always see them functioning as one, the power of their oneness attracting the promise of an atoning Savior.[219]

Abraham and Sarah are another example of synergy. Their oneness drew down the new and everlasting covenant upon a degenerate and famished world, and by their synergy they secured for their posterity the eternal right to all gospel blessings. Gospel writer E. Douglas Clark has noted:

---

216 D&C 132:19.
217 Faust, "The Gift of the Holy Ghost—A Sure Compass," 2; emphasis added.
218 3 Nephi 27:14–15.
219 Moses 5.

> Abraham had been alone in the world, alone against the
> world, but now [with Sarah] everything changed. . . .
> Sarah had her work, and Abraham had his, but it was all
> part of the same cause. From this point on in Abraham's
> life, to speak of his mission and accomplishments is nec-
> essarily to include Sarah also; for as a modern rabbi has
> observed, she was not merely a strong personality in her
> own right, but, as Abraham's spouse, was "an important
> balancing factor in his life. Abraham and Sarah were
> not just *a married couple* but a team, two people work-
> ing in harmony," as seen in the Genesis portrayal "of
> two as one unit" and "as equals"—"as partners, working
> together for the same goals, walking together along the
> same path, united in thought, word, and deed." Or, as
> told by Philo, "Everywhere and always she was at his
> side, . . . and his true partner in life and life's events,
> resolved to share alike the good and the ill." Theirs was
> the priceless unity of heart and mind that is ever the
> hallmark of Zion.[220]

President Kimball taught that the Spirit of the Lord cannot help us magnify our efforts
without oneness and cooperation in all that we do. Then, quoting Joseph Smith, he said,
"The greatest temporal and spiritual blessings which always come from faithfulness and
concentrated effort, *never attended individual exertion or enterprise.*"[221]

Antagonism—The Opposite of Synergy
The Lord commanded us to be one and to share each other's burdens: "And be you afflicted in all his afflictions, ever lifting up your heart unto me in prayer and faith, for his
and your deliverance."[222] Oneness brings deliverance!

Because we live in a fallen world where we are subject to the temptations of Satan,
duality and conflict retard unity and peace. At such times, we must quickly recognize
and rectify such conditions. Then synergy can replace antagonism, and unity and
strength will reenter the relationship. An antagonistic relationship simply cannot produce the power necessary to create the atmosphere of Zion.

David Whitmer, a close friend of Joseph Smith, related an enlightening experience
that happened while the Prophet was translating the gold plates.

> He [Joseph] was a religious and straightforward man.
> He had to be; for he was illiterate and could do nothing

220   Clark, *The Blessings of Abraham,* 60.
221   Kimball, "Becoming the Pure in Heart," 79, quoting Smith, *Teachings of the Prophet Joseph Smith,* 183; emphasis added.
222   D&C 30:6.

himself. He had to trust in God. He could not translate unless he was humble and possessed the right feelings towards everyone. To illustrate so you can see: One morning when he was getting ready to continue the translation, something went wrong about the house and he was put out about it. Something that Emma, his wife, had done. Oliver and I went upstairs and Joseph came up soon after to continue the translation but he could not do anything. He could not translate a single syllable. He went downstairs, out into the orchard, and made supplication to the Lord; was gone about an hour—came back to the house, and asked Emma's forgiveness and then came upstairs where we were and then the translation went on all right. He could do nothing save he was humble and faithful.[223]

Joseph Smith endeavored to achieve oneness with his wife, with God, and with those of his fellowmen who would purify their hearts in the cause of Zion. Interestingly, in the process of striving for unity, he learned a frightening truth of which every seeker of Zion should become aware. He said, "In relation to the kingdom of God, the devil always sets up his kingdom at the very same time in opposition to God."[224] Imagine, when we were married in the temple and established a new kingdom, Satan simultaneously established an opposing effort to try to destroy us. We simply cannot take the risk of disunity.

Unity and Prayer

In the presence of six elders, the Prophet Joseph Smith received a revelation (D&C 29) that, in part, speaks of the power of multiple voices united in prayer. The Lord prefaced this revelation by reminding those brethren of his power to gather his people "as a hen gathereth her chickens under her wings, even as many as will hearken to my voice and humble themselves before me, and call upon me in mighty prayer."[225] That is, to be gathered together in one is dependent upon obedience, humility, and mighty prayer. The Lord goes on to say, "Behold, verily, verily, I say unto you, that at this time your sins are forgiven you, *therefore ye receive these things.*"[226] Note that the hearts of these brethren were pure and unified, which qualified them to pray for a blessing. This is the power of being gathered into unity as it pertains to praying for blessings.

Because these brethren had gathered in the Lord's name and were united in prayer, the Lord came to them according to celestial law—"where two or three are gathered together in my name, as touching one thing, behold, there will I be in the midst of them."[227]

---

223 Roberts, *History of the Church,* 1:131.
224 Smith, *Teachings of the Prophet Joseph Smith,* 365.
225 D&C 29:2.
226 D&C 29:3; emphasis added.
227 D&C 6:32; Matthew 18:20.

In that setting, the Lord invited them to ask for a blessing, and gave them instructions for how to do so: "Lift up your hearts and be glad, for *I am in your midst,* and am your advocate with the Father; and it is his good will to give you the kingdom. And, as it is written—Whatsoever ye shall ask in faith, *being united in prayer* according to my command, ye shall receive."[228] Then the Lord blessed them with what they were praying for because "it is given unto you that ye may understand, because ye have asked it of me *and are agreed.*"[229]

On December 27, 1832, Joseph Smith received one of the greatest revelations of this dispensation. The Prophet designated it "The Olive Leaf," and in a letter to W. W. Phelps, he said it was "plucked from the Tree of Paradise." The revelation, which is now section 88 of the Doctrine and Covenants, is "the Lord's message of peace to us."[230] Rich in doctrine, the revelation opens a window to the mysteries of God and provides profound details of the events leading up to the Second Coming, including the fall of Babylon and the subsequent thousand years of peace. The episode that paved the way for this revelation is as amazing as the revelation itself.

The Prophet had received a revelation commanding him to organize a "school of the prophets."[231] Just after Christmas, a group of high priests gathered by special invitation to the Prophet's "translating room" in the Gilbert and Whitney store. According to the revelation, these brethren were to attend the school to prepare to better serve one another through increased knowledge and understanding. On the occasion of the revelation, Joseph said, "To receive revelation and the blessings of heaven it [is] necessary to have our minds on God and exercise faith and become of one heart and mind."[232] Of note, Zebedee Coltrin, a member of the School of the Prophets, reported that the brethren would typically come fasting and gather in the morning about sunrise. Before the school began, they would wash, put on clean linen, and partake of the sacrament. Then they would gather to pray.[233] Thus prepared, on the day of the revelation of Doctrine and Covenants 88, the Prophet instructed them "to pray separately and vocally to the Lord for [Him] to reveal His will unto us concerning the upbuilding of Zion and for the benefit of the Saints." The record indicates that each brother "bowed down before the Lord, after which each one arose and spoke in his turn his feelings and determination to keep the commandments of God. And then [Joseph] proceeded to receive a revelation."[234]

The pattern of the School of the Prophets clearly demonstrates the power of prepared, unified voices asking in the prayer of faith for blessings.

How We Achieve Unity

President Marion G. Romney taught us that seeking the Lord and his righteousness is the only avenue to unity.[235] That is, we achieve unity by following the Lord, by learning

---

228 D&C 29:5–6; emphasis added.
229 D&C 29:33; emphasis added.
230 Smith, *Teachings of the Prophet Joseph Smith,* 18.
231 D&C 88:118–41.
232 *Kirtland Council Minute Book,* LDS Church Archives, 3–4.
233 *Salt Lake School of the Prophets Minutes,* Oct. 3, 1883, 56.
234 *Kirtland Council Minute Book,* LDS Church Archives, 3–4.
235 3 Nephi 13:3.

his will, and by doing what he tells us to do. These are basic but essential principles that we must observe; otherwise we can achieve neither unity nor righteousness. The Lord promised that if we will seek him and a more sound understanding of the principles of the gospel, we will come to a state of oneness that will strengthen us beyond anything we have ever known. Therefore, humbling ourselves, keeping the commandments, studying the word of the Lord, following the living prophet without hardening our hearts, applying these teachings to our lives, asking the Lord in faith with the belief that we will receive—these basic principles promote unity.

Is becoming unified essential to our preservation? President Romney said that only a unified people who keep God's commands and live these principles can expect God's protection.[236] President Lorenzo Snow also stated that safety lies only in unity: "I tell you, in the name of the Lord God, that the time is coming when there will be no safety only in the principles of union, for therein lies the secret of our temporal and spiritual salvation."[237]

The End Result of Unity

Moses was given a panoramic vision of the enormity of the universe with its "worlds without number" and its equally numerous inhabitants who reside upon those worlds.[238] With awe, we, too, gaze into the night sky and wonder about the origin of creation and by what power it is upheld.

The gospel offers us an answer.

All the creations, all the inhabitants, and all the seraphic beings that live in this universe can be traced back to two people who made an eternal covenant at a temple altar and unified their hearts in love.

This is the power of oneness.

All Things Common among Them

The astonishing blessings associated with equality and unity are exceeded only by a condition that always describes Zion: "They had all things common among them."[239] Although some gospel authorities and writers have reshaped this phrase as "all things *in* common," it is not scriptural, and it often leads to misunderstanding. Brigham Young University associate professor Clark V. Johnson explained,

> The Lord does not desire his people to have everything the same or all things in common, but to have "all things common among them." (4 Nephi 1:3; see also Moses 7:18.) To have "all things common among them" is to understand that everything a person has is a gift from

---

236 Romney, "Unity," 17–18.
237 Snow, *The Teachings of Lorenzo Snow*, 180.
238 Moses 1:29, 33.
239 3 Nephi 26:19; 4 Nephi 1:3; Acts 2:44; 4:32.

God, which God has given to bless his children. This
attitude does away with superiority complexes and class
structure and allows people to reach a level of equality in
which there are no "rich and poor, bond and free," but all
are "made free, and partakers of the heavenly gift," or life
eternal. (4 Nephi 1:3; see also D&C 42:61.) Joseph Smith
taught that this same attitude must exist on the part of
the destitute, "He that hath not, and cannot obtain, but
saith in his heart, if I had, I would give freely, is accepted
as freely as he that gives of his abundance."[240]

The law of consecration calls for members of the Church to contribute generously to the
Lord's storehouse, upon which the members may draw, when necessary, for their temporal
welfare. That is, we all have *common access* to the resource, thus assuring that there are no
poor among us.[241] Of course, we do not all descend upon the storehouse and take from its
shelves without prior permission and accountability. It is the bishop's stewardship to manage and provide access to the common storehouse.[242] All things must done in order.

But the law of consecration is also a spiritual law that demands we consecrate
our time, talents, and other things the Lord has or will put into our hands for the dual
purposes of building the kingdom and establishing Zion.[243] Because we claim no ownership of these gifts, but rather count them as stewardships, we find ourselves giving service
in the Church, bearing one another's burdens that they might be light, mourning with
those that mourn, comforting those that stand in need of comfort, and standing as
witnesses of God at all times and in all things and in all places "even until death."[244] In
other words, we consecrate what we have and who we are to the common cause of Zion,
which in turn provides us with common claim upon the resources of Zion. Thus, we are
saved both temporally and spiritually.[245]

Consecration and the Law of Offense

Offenses put equality and unity at risk. In the early days of the Church, a number of
attempts to live the law of consecration failed, due, in part, to greed and contention.
Admittedly, this celestial law, which demands our all, can be difficult to live—especially
when we perceive that others might not be as dedicated as we are. Misunderstandings
can arise. The Lord provided for this and gave us the law of offense, which suggests a hierarchy of judgment. At each level, the directive for judgment is this: "Judge not unrighteously, that ye be not judged; but judge righteous judgment."[246]

240   Johnson, "The Law of Consecration," 101.
241   Moses 7:18.
242   D&C 42:30, 34.
243   Benson, *The Teachings of Ezra Taft Benson,* 121.
244   Mosiah 18:8–9.
245   Romney, "Church Welfare—Temporal Service in a Spiritual Setting," 82; see also Kimball, *The Teachings of Spencer W. Kimball,* 366.
246   JST, Matthew 7:2; see also JST, John 7:24.

BYU professor Clark V. Johnson described the law of offense this way:

> Recognizing that differences of opinion and personality clashes might occur among Church members, the Lord also revealed the law of offense to his followers. If someone were offended, he was to go to the person who had offended him and settle the differences. If the differences could not be resolved between the two parties, then the matter was to be taken before the elders. Thus, violators of the commandments and covenants were to be tried by the Church, subject to the "law of God." (D&C 42:81.) The principle set forth by the Savior in this situation is this: "And if thy brother or sister offend many, he or she shall be chastened before many. And if any one offend openly, he or she shall be rebuked openly. . . . If any shall offend in secret, he or she shall be rebuked in secret, that he or she may have opportunity to confess in secret to him or her whom he or she has offended, and to God, that the church may not speak reproachfully of him or her." (D&C 42:90–92.)[247]

Law of Common Consent

To further ensure the equality, unity, and commonality of the Saints, the Lord provided the law of common consent: "All things shall be done by common consent in the church."[248] This law allows each member of the Church equal power[249] in sustaining the governing officers and in supporting decisions that leaders make regarding the policies and management of the kingdom. Beyond these factors, common consent seems to imply a covenantal relationship that paves the way for revelation and guidance. For example, when we sustain the bishop, we raise our arm to the square, which is a sign of covenant making.[250] By that action, we covenant to accept the bishop as the servant of Jesus Christ. Therefore, when we counsel with him and receive his judgments or blessings, it is as though his voice and hands are those of the Lord. This, of course, places a significant burden upon the bishop to live worthy of that trust, and it places a burden on us to accept him as the servant of Christ. When we raise our arm to the square and covenant to sustain the bishop by common consent, we are as obligated to keep that covenant as any other covenant we make. Then it would seem that the Lord also covenants to reveal his mind and will to us through the bishop, and the Lord also confirms the blessings that his servant pronounces upon us: "Unto

---

247   Johnson, "The Law of Consecration," 101.
248   D&C 26:2.
249   *Encyclopedia of Mormonism*, 463.
250   "Abraham's Act of Faith Reflects 'a Soul Like Unto Our Savior,'" *LDS Church News*, Apr. 2, 1994.

him will I confirm all my words, even unto the ends of the earth."[251] "Verily, if a man be called of my Father, as was Aaron, by mine own voice, and by the voice of him that sent me, and I have endowed him with the keys of the power of this priesthood, *if he do anything in my name, and according to my law and by my word, he will not commit sin, and I will justify him."*[252]

Thus, by the covenant of common consent we all enjoy common access to the bishop, the Lord's servant, and we enjoy the totality of the Lord's temporal and spiritual blessings. These are the things that equalize and unify us and make all of the temporal and spiritual resources of the Lord common among us.

Connecting Consecration with the Law of the Gospel and the Law of Sacrifice

Equality and unity are impossible to achieve without the law of consecration. This law stands at the summit of a series of laws to which we must adhere if we expect to conform to and qualify for celestial glory. Hugh Nibley explained, "We have noted that the covenants of the endowment are progressively more binding, in the sense of allowing less and less latitude for personal interpretation as one advances. Thus (1) the law of God is general and mentions no specifics; (2) the law of obedience states that specific orders are to be given and observed; (3) the law of sacrifice still allows a margin of interpretation (this is as far as the old law goes—the Aaronic Priesthood carries out the law of sacrifice and no farther; and it specifies that while sacrifice is a solemn obligation on all, it is up to the individual to decide just how much he will give); (4) the law of chastity, on the other hand, is something else; here at last we have an absolute, bound by a solemn sign; (5) finally the law of consecration is equally uncompromising—everything the Lord has given one is to be consecrated. This law is bound by the firmest token of all."[253]

Although consecration is evident in every gospel covenant, it is most readily connected with the laws of the gospel and of sacrifice. As we have discussed, the law of the gospel is really the fulness of the gospel, which the Savior summed up as the gospel of love: "Thou shalt love the Lord thy God with all thy heart, and with all thy soul, and with all thy mind. This is the first and great commandment. And the second is like unto it, Thou shalt love thy neighbour as thyself. On these two commandments hang all the law and the prophets."[254] This is the higher law, which Jesus came to reveal; it is the law that replaced Moses' preparatory system of lesser sacrifices, laws, performances, and ordinances.

The higher law is characterized by a new heart, one that loves God and his children. To develop such a heart requires preparation, so that eventually it can be sacrificed, that is, "broken"[255] or offered up to God without reservation. From such

---

251   Mormon 9:24–25.
252   D&C 132:59; emphasis added.
253   Nibley, *Approaching Zion*, 441–42.
254   Matthew 22:37–40.
255   D&C 59:8.

a pure and loving heart, righteous actions flow without legislation. Thus, the higher gospel is motivated by love rather than regulated by a system of rules. Elder Bruce C. Hafen writes, "The gospel of the higher law was so simple and so profound that the Pharisees and other learned people of Christ's day missed it completely. They missed the simple part—the core—and they missed everything."[256] The "core" of the higher gospel law is love.

This higher law, which produces higher love—divine love, or charity—is the love that gives God a celestial heart. This is the very attribute that Jesus was trying to reveal to the people about the Father. God is motivated to do what he does because he loves. We can trace his every action, thought, and word back to love. "God is love."[257]

At a BYU Women's Conference, Sister A. D. Sorensen said, "Divine love [God's love] . . . comprehends and fulfills the whole law of the gospel. . . . First, divine love has for its ultimate aim that humankind avoid death and realize everlasting fulness of life. The achievement of that aim represents, as we have observed, the highest possibility of humankind, their ultimate good, and the final purpose of God. But second, divine love also makes possible, indeed literally constitutes, fulness of life."[258]

The law of the gospel provides the miracle of a changed heart and beckons us forward to courageously pursue perfection. Then, when we finally become like God, we, too, will be motivated to act and think because of the love within us. At that point, we could legitimately insert our name into the scripture: "[Our name] is love." When we consider that consecration can be lived only by love, and when we consider how consecration lifts and exalts both the giver and receiver, we begin to understand why the law of consecration, the law of sacrifice, and the law of the gospel are connected. President Joseph F. Smith taught, "I would advise that we learn to love each other, and then friendship will be true and sweet. It has been said by one, that 'we may give without loving, but we cannot love without giving.'"[259]

Love Leads Us to Eternal Life

True equality and unity are motivated by love. This higher gospel law of love defines the pathway leading to eternal life. Because we love God and we desire eternal life, we make a covenant, knowing that only Heavenly Father, Jesus Christ, and the Holy Ghost know the way. Because these three Gods love us, they covenant to help us achieve our goal. For our part, we agree to adopt a new lifestyle conducive to living in the celestial kingdom, where we want to be. As we have learned, this covenant is called the new and everlasting covenant, which is another name for the law of the gospel. Motivated by love, each member of the Godhead effectively "signs" his name to the Covenant at the time of our baptism, doing so with the purpose of leading us to exaltation.

---

256 Hafen, *The Broken Heart*, 1.
257 1 John 4:8, 16.
258 Sorensen, "No Respector of Persons: Equality in the Kingdom," 55.
259 Smith, *Teachings of the Presidents of the Church: Joseph F. Smith*, 192.

Part of our agreement is to follow the designated path to its perfect conclusion. This path, as we have learned, is marked by authorized ordinances; that is, the path is an ordered path with authorized markers that measure our progress and infuse us along the way with celestial power and knowledge. This marked path is the *only* path that will lead us to our divine destination.

To Peter and the Apostles, Jesus said, "Go ye into all the world, and preach the gospel to every creature. He that believeth and is baptized shall be saved; but he that believeth not shall be damned."[260] In this scripture, damnation suggests restricted blessings. According to Jesus' statement, anyone who rejected his teachings and baptism at the hands of the Apostles would be "damned," or unworthy, of further blessings. Clearly, without the order of ordinances we receive along the path leading to eternal life, we would be "damned." This condition is not one of equality, unity, or love.

Is Baptism Sufficient for Exaltation?

No. Baptism and receiving the Holy Ghost only get us on the path. These ordinances can *save* us in the celestial kingdom but will not exalt us there. Exaltation requires our receiving the authority of God (priesthood ordination);[261] specific purification and sanctification to prepare us for our future sacred appointment (temple washing and anointing);[262] protection from Satan, our eternal enemy (the garment of the holy priesthood);[263] an infusion of heavenly power and knowledge (temple endowment);[264] acceptance of the law of the celestial kingdom (consecration);[265] and the promise of an eternal kingdom, given by the Father (celestial marriage).[266] These covenants and ordinances are the markers along the path leading to exaltation. When we make any of these covenants and receive their associated ordinances by the authority of priesthood keys, we are assured, upon our worthiness, that the terms of that covenant will be fulfilled and will endure eternally. We have God's personal seal and guarantee.

Two Purposes of the Law of the Gospel

The two primary purposes of the law of the gospel—the new and everlasting covenant—are: (1) to return us to God, and (2) to help us become like our Heavenly Father. If we follow the path to its conclusion and abide in the law of the gospel to the end, these are the promises:

> And again, verily I say unto you, if a man marry a
> wife by my word, which is my law, and by the new

---

260   Mark 16:15–16.
261   D&C 84:33.
262   *Encyclopedia of Mormonism*, 1551.
263   *Encyclopedia of Mormonism*, 534; Ephesians 6:13; D&C 27:15.
264   *Encyclopedia of Mormonism*, 455.
265   D&C 42; 105:4–5.
266   D&C 132:19–24.

and everlasting covenant, and it is sealed unto them
by the Holy Spirit of promise, by him who is anointed [the prophet], unto whom I have appointed this
power and the keys of this priesthood; and it shall
be said unto them—Ye shall come forth in the first
resurrection; and if it be after the first resurrection,
in the next resurrection; and shall inherit thrones,
kingdoms, principalities, and powers, dominions, all
heights and depths—then shall it be written in the
Lamb's Book of Life, that he shall commit no murder whereby to shed innocent blood, and if ye abide
in my covenant, and commit no murder whereby
to shed innocent blood, it shall be done unto them
in all things whatsoever my servant hath put upon
them, in time, and through all eternity; and shall be
of full force when they are out of the world; and they
shall pass by the angels, and the gods, which are set
there, to their exaltation and glory in all things, as
hath been sealed upon their heads, which glory shall
be a fulness and a continuation of the seeds forever
and ever.

Then shall they be gods, because they have
no end; therefore shall they be from everlasting to
everlasting, because they continue; then shall they be
above all, because all things are subject unto them.
Then shall they be gods, because they have all power,
and the angels are subject unto them.[267]

No Other Way

Can a person obtain these promises in any other way? No. The Lord states, "Verily,
verily, I say unto you, except ye abide my law ye cannot attain to this glory. For strait is
the gate, and narrow the way that leadeth unto the exaltation and continuation of the
lives, and few there be that find it."[268]

Why do only a few find this path? "Because ye receive me not in the world neither
do ye know me."[269]

Does this mean that God condemns these people? No. It usually means that they
have not found him yet, so he will find them. We have to remember that God is our Father and not a condemning judge. No loving parent would withhold the greatest of blessings from his children because of ignorance. We are assured that Heavenly Father will

---

267   D&C 132:19–20.
268   D&C 132:22.
269   D&C 132:22.

use all his resources and work ceaselessly and relentlessly to offer these blessings to his children. Even if his children do not understand at first, he will continue to try until they understand perfectly and can make an informed choice. This is one of the great works of the Church of Jesus Christ, and it is the essence of the law of the gospel. No single issue is more important than this: God loves his children and he never gives up trying to offer them the blessings provided by this law.

What happens when we desire these blessings with all our heart and put forth the effort to obtain them? Here is the Lord's promise: "But if ye receive me in the world, then shall ye know me, and shall receive your exaltation; that where I am ye shall be also."[270]

The Interwoven Covenants

As we have learned, the law of sacrifice and the law of the gospel are connected. Each is motivated by love, and each points to the highest manifestation of love, or consecration. We might say that the law of consecration is the perfect outgrowth of the law of the gospel; that is, consecration is the supernal expression of sacrifice that we agree to when we enter the gospel covenant. This sacrifice culminates with giving our all to God, and we make that sacrifice for the purposes of choosing God over mammon and lifting others and urging them forward toward eternal life. Thus, consecration could have as its mission statement the same that Jesus attached to the gospel itself: "Thou shalt love the Lord thy God with all thy heart, and with all thy soul, and with all thy mind. This is the first and great commandment. And the second is like unto it, Thou shalt love thy neighbour as thyself. On these two commandments hang all the law and the prophets."[271] Herein is equality and unity achieved and perfected.

Perhaps more than any other law, the law of consecration defines the love of God, love of others, and true discipleship; moreover, consecration is the foundational principle of Zion-like equality and unity. Therefore, a consecrated person, by his own choice, liberally imparts of his substance unto the poor and the needy, "according to the law of [the] gospel."[272] As we have said, this attitude cannot be legislated. It is lived by love and choice or not at all. Consecration is the law that creates this ultimate change of heart, which is required for an inheritance in the celestial kingdom. No wonder, then, that consecration is the last law we must agree to live before we can stand in the presence of God. Significantly, it is only after we agree to live the law of consecration that we can pray with enough power (perhaps power that derives from consecration) to approach God and enter his presence. There, in that sacred setting, we see all three members of the Godhead,[273] the same three who symbolically signed their names to the new and everlasting covenant in the first place and agreed to bring us to this point. Now they are here to greet us, as if to signify that they have fulfilled their agreement and are ready to usher us into the presence of God. Equally significant is the fact that it is only after we

---

270   D&C 132:23.
271   Matthew 22:37–40.
272   D&C 104:18.
273   Note: Hebrews 10:20 states that Christ is the veil.

have agreed to accept this last law, consecration, which allows us entrance to celestial glory, that the Father can bless us with our kingdom—eternal marriage.

The Law of Sacrifice

Without the law of sacrifice, we could not achieve equality and unity. Again we emphasize that the law of sacrifice is tied to the law of the gospel in the same way that these two laws are connected with the law of consecration.[274] The Lord said, "Verily I say unto you, all among them who know their hearts are honest, and are broken, and their spirits contrite, and are willing to observe their covenants by sacrifice—yea, every sacrifice which I, the Lord, shall command—they are accepted of me."[275]

Sacrifice can appear to be a negative or a painful principle unless we consider that no good thing is ever accomplished without choice and effort. We are willing to choose between bad, good, better, and best alternatives when we want something badly enough.[276] To implement our choice, we willingly sacrifice all other choices. The same could be said of effort. Once we have made a choice, we are willing to expend effort to achieve that choice; the more essential the choice, the more effort required. To achieve our most important goals, we are willing to gather around us every available resource, fix our minds on our objective, and summon strength to stay the course. It is in the process of making a choice and expending effort that we prove loyal to our goal. We know that a lackluster decision or a mediocre exertion will result in failure. Only dedicated and unrelenting sacrifice will prove our loyalty to our cause and sustain us until we achieve success.

Likewise, we simply cannot prove our loyalty to God, remain obedient to our covenants, and live the law of the gospel without a firm decision and concerted effort—in other words, without *sacrifice*. Our willingness to decide once and for all to choose Zion over Babylon—and to confirm that decision by our offering a freewill sacrifice of time, talents, and all that we have and are to God—is consecration. This is the ultimate manifestation of the law of sacrifice, which finally proves our loyalty to God, the building up of his kingdom, and the establishment of his Zion.

Sacrifice and love

We recall that the law of the gospel is simultaneously called the new and everlasting covenant and the gospel of love. We also recall that the law of the gospel, coupled with sacrifice and love, sets the stage for equality and unity.

True love stands on a three-legged stool of total loyalty, sacrifice, and trust. With that image in our minds, we begin to understand why the law of sacrifice and the law of the gospel go hand in hand. True love cannot exist when loyalties are divided; neither can love exist when either party is selfish or untrustworthy. True love can flourish only when an eternal decision has been made and when continual, strenuous effort

---

274   McConkie, "Obedience, Consecration, and Sacrifice," 50.
275   D&C 97:8.
276   Oaks, "Good, Better, Best," 104–8.

is expended. Then love will grow to its perfect conclusion. Clearly, without sacrifice there can be no love; where there is no love, there is limited obedience to the law of the gospel; and without these things in place, consecration is nonexistent and eternal life forfeited.

On the other hand, if we are willing to obey the law of the gospel, we will be filled with love and anxious to sacrifice anything and everything for eternal life. It has been said that sacrifice is giving up something for something better—and it is certainly that. But sacrifice is much more. To a pure-hearted, covenant person, sacrifices are made in the similitude of Christ, and therefore each sacrifice has proxy characteristics—that is, doing something for someone who cannot do that thing alone or for himself. Therefore, a sacrifice made at a higher level is not a sacrifice we make for our own purposes; rather, this higher sacrifice is made for another person. Consequently, the Lord consecrates our sacrifice for the welfare of our souls.[277]

Such a consecrated, Christlike sacrifice has a redeeming effect upon the recipient and the giver; both are lifted and exalted. This is the essence of the higher law of the gospel. Together, love of God and neighbor and proxy sacrifice form the mechanism that allows us to become Christlike and causes a state of blessedness and purity of heart.

Sacrifice—Our Contribution to Our Salvation

What price must be paid to save and exalt a soul? Hugh Nibley explained: "The . . . Atonement requires of the beneficiary nothing less than willingness to part with his most precious possession. Joined with the law of sacrifice is the law of consecration, which has no limiting 'if necessary' clause; we agree to it unconditionally here and now. It represents our contribution to our salvation."[278] The connection between sacrifice and consecration is obvious, and both are necessary for our salvation. President Gordon B. Hinckley concurred. He also taught that total sacrifice is "our contribution to our salvation." But because of our fallen nature, he said, our sacrifice will ultimately fall short of what is needed. The full price of eternal life can be paid only by our sacrificing "everything that we can give and everything that God can give (His Son) and everything that Jesus can give (His life) and everything that the Holy Ghost can give—their full time, ability and resources. God's work and glory demand his all, and we must give our all."[279]

How much is "our all"? Jesus set the example and described his sacrifice in these words: "How sore you know not, how exquisite you know not, yea, how hard to bear you know not. . . . Which suffering caused myself, even God, the greatest of all, to tremble because of pain, and to bleed at every pore, and to suffer both body and spirit."[280] If he sacrificed for our salvation to the extent of his ability, we likewise must sacrifice to the extent of our ability.

277   2 Nephi 32:9.
278   Nibley, *Approaching Zion,* 590–92.
279   Hinckley, *Teachings of Gordon B. Hinckley,* 147.
280   D&C 19:15–18.

Of this total kind of sacrifice, Joseph Smith said,

> Let us here observe, that a religion that does not require
> the sacrifice of all things never has power sufficient
> to produce the faith necessary unto life and salvation;
> for, from the first existence of man, the faith necessary
> unto the enjoyment of life and salvation never could
> be obtained without the sacrifice of all earthly things.
> It was through this sacrifice, and this only, that God has
> ordained that men should enjoy eternal life. . . . Those,
> then, who make the sacrifice, will have the testimony
> that their course is pleasing in the sight of God; and
> those who have this testimony will have faith to lay hold
> on eternal life, and will be enabled, through faith, to
> endure unto the end, and receive the crown that is laid
> up for them that love the appearing of our Lord Jesus
> Christ. But those who do not make the sacrifice cannot
> enjoy this faith, because men are dependent upon this
> sacrifice in order to obtain this faith: therefore, they
> cannot lay hold upon eternal life.[281]

To gain exaltation, we must pay the price of exaltation, which is our all. That price is consecration—the law of sacrifice in its highest form. Elder Neal A. Maxwell asked, What if Jesus, who performed so many miracles, had stopped short of the miracle of the Atonement? The consequences would have been catastrophic. Just so, we might ask ourselves, What if we live good and decent lives, hoping for exaltation, and yet, when the opportunity presents itself, we shrink when we are faced with the necessary sacrifice for exaltation? We must embrace consecration with faith, Elder Maxwell said. Then our best effort will summon Christ's grace, which is sufficient to make weak things strong. The Lord promises that in the end, we will achieve our hoped-for destination, but in the meantime we have a journey to trek. Along our journey toward eternal life, we will discover that sacrificing our will to God is really not a sacrifice at all. Such a sacrifice leads to receiving all the Father has.[282]

Clearly, consecration is the ultimate manifestation of the law of sacrifice, the law that prepares and purifies the heart so that it can be consecrated and offered to God. On a rudimentary level, sacrifice is giving up something good for something better; but sacrifice on a higher level is *proxy* sacrifice and therefore Christlike in nature—the giving up of something to bless another person. Such a sacrifice is counted by God as doing it unto him.[283] This is the essence of consecration, the sacrifice of the heart. All other sacrifices are shadows of this sacrifice, just as such sacrifices were with Jesus. Every sacrifice that he made led

---

281   Smith, *Lectures on Faith,* 6:7, 10.
282   Maxwell, "Consecrate Thy Performance," 36.
283   Matthew 25:40.

him to Gethsemane and Calvary, where he sacrificed the totality of his heart. Like Jesus, our consecrated sacrifice of all things has the power to usher us into the presence of God.

In the end, we learn that the more our hearts are owned by Zion, the more we will desire to give, and the more we give, the more capable we will become to sacrifice and consecrate our hearts.

Summary and Conclusion

According to President Marion G. Romney, six criteria make up the law of consecration:
1. Belief in God
2. Freewill offerings
3. Private ownership and individual management
4. A nonpolitical program
5. Righteousness as the prerequisite
6. Exalts the poor and humbles the rich.[284]

Moreover, two fundamental principles define Zion: "Every man seeking the interest of his neighbor," and "doing all things with an eye single to the glory of God."[285] This philosophy leads to voluntary unity and equality motivated by love of God and his children. The Babylonian counterparts include forced taxation, communism, and other economic experiments. The results inevitably limit freedom of choice, stifle initiative, hamper prosperity, promote divisiveness, and ultimately "level down" individuals and societies. Conversely, Zion-like equality "levels up" people, exalting the poor by means of the consecrated, freewill offerings of the rich. This is the Lord's "own way."[286]

Equality is a celestial law that provides for the prosperity of all. When we give to one of God's children, our action is counted as though we did it unto God, and, therefore, he recompenses us "an hundredfold," as though he were repaying a debt. Because we are always rewarded beyond our sacrifice, however, we are eternally indebted to God.

The law of consecration requires that we, like the Lord, esteem "all flesh in one."[287] God equally offers us, the "favored of God," access to his blessings, and when we receive them, we must in turn use them to bless others. If we do not, we are anti-Zion; we simply cannot treat God's children differently than he does and expect to become Zion people.

Equality cannot exist except by receiving divine love and exhibiting that love for others. Love is one of several criteria upon which we can become equal. Other criteria include being equal in the sight of God; equal opportunities for eternal life; joint heirs with Christ; having all things common; equal opportunities to contribute and receive education, to develop talents and abilities, and to engage people in the work of Zion; equality in labor, power, and consent; and equality as to fulfillment of needs and wants. By receiving these gifts, we are to use them to take an equal responsibility for the cause of Zion.

---

284   Romney, "The Purpose of Church Welfare Services," 92.
285   D&C 82:19.
286   D&C 104:15–16; emphasis added.
287   1 Nephi 17:35.

As much as consecration is dependent upon equality, it is also dependent upon unity. Unity infuses power into Zion and its people. President Gordon B. Hinckley said that unity gives us the power to accomplish just about anything."[288] An example is unified prayer—multiple voices praying for a common goal. Gathering as one in the name of Christ for a common purpose invites the Savior into our circle. The power to unify is provided only by the At-one-ment, which brings separated things or people back into oneness, the divinely mandated goal for every covenant relationship. Wherever there is oneness, there is the Lord, and, consequently, there is power. Scriptural accounts describe the power of the Atonement and oneness. The Godhead, Alma and Amulek, the sons of Mosiah, and Alma's grandsons Nephi and Lehi are examples of the power of unity. Whenever unity is achieved, happiness, abundance, and conversion power result.

Unity has a synergistic effect; united people have many times more strength than the sum of their individual strengths. The opposite of synergy is antagonism; antagonistic people have less combined strength than the sum strengths of the individuals. President Kimball taught that the Spirit of the Lord cannot help us magnify our efforts without oneness and cooperation in all that we do. We achieve unity only through righteousness; unity is our only safety; unity is the power by which the heavens were made and by which all the seraphic hosts of heaven were created.

Unity, as a celestial principle, meaning that we have "all things common,"[289] gives us common access to the Lord and his resources. This condition assures that there are no poor among us.[290] Although this is a temporal manifestation of the law of consecration, it reflects the spiritual aspects of the law. If we are to be truly equal and unified and have all things common among us, we must consecrate our time, talents, and other things that the Lord has or will put into our hands for the dual purposes of building the kingdom and establishing Zion.[291] We must consecrate our hearts if we are to advance the common cause of Zion and lay claim to the common resources of Zion. Then we are saved both temporally and spiritually.[292]

The Lord provided us a way to handle offenses, which put equality and unity at risk. To counter misunderstandings among the people, the Lord placed major judgments pertaining to the kingdom of God under the auspices of the priesthood. The Lord gave us a directive and provided the law of offense. The directive is: "Judge not unrighteously, that ye be not judged; but judge righteous judgment."[293] Before we make judgments, we must first obtain the mind of the Lord and then act upon the promptings we receive from Him.

To further ensure that equality, unity, and commonality remain intact, the Lord provided the law of common consent. This law allows each member of the Church equal ability to sustain the governing officers, who make decisions that affect the kingdom.

---

288   Hinckley, "Your Greatest Challenge, Mother," 97–100.
289   3 Nephi 26:19; 4 Nephi 1:3; Acts 2:44; 4:32.
290   Moses 7:18.
291   Benson, *The Teachings of Ezra Taft Benson,* 121.
292   Romney, "Church Welfare—Temporal Service in a Spiritual Setting," 84; see also Kimball, *The Teachings of Spencer W. Kimball,* 366.
293   JST, Matthew 7:2; see also JST, John 7:24.

The law of consecration stands at the summit of a series of covenants to which we must adhere if we expect to conform to and qualify for celestial glory. Together, these covenants and laws form the framework of the higher law, which in turn is characterized by each one receiving a new heart, a heart full of love for God and his children. To develop such a heart requires preparation through living the covenants and laws so that eventually the heart can be sacrificed as a "broken" heart,[294] or one that is offered up to God without reservation. Love, not a system of rules, motivates a pure and loving heart. Such a heart approaches the quality of God's heart; "God is love." By following the covenants and laws of the gospel, we can experience the miracle of a changed heart and finally become like God.

When we consider that consecration can be lived only by love, and when we consider how consecration lifts and exalts both the giver and receiver, we begin to understand why the law of consecration, the law of sacrifice, and the law of the gospel are connected. The two primary purposes of the law of the gospel—the new and everlasting covenant—are (1) to return us to God, and (2) to help us become like our Heavenly Father and Mother. The two primary ways to live the law of sacrifice are (1) to give up something for something better, and (2) to give up something for the sake of helping someone who cannot fully help themselves. Consecration addresses both of these criteria by supplying the time, talents, and resources to make this sacrifice, which returns us to God and makes us like him. Moreover, sacrifice is the contribution we make to our own salvation. The full price of eternal life can be paid only by the sacrifice of "everything that we can give and everything that God can give (His Son) and everything that Jesus can give (His life) and everything that the Holy Ghost can give—their full time, ability and resources. God's work and glory demand his all, and we must give our all."[295]

The laws of the gospel, of sacrifice, and of consecration are motivated by love. The law of the gospel is summed up by two laws of love: "Thou shalt love the Lord thy God with all thy heart, and with all thy soul, and with all thy mind. This is the first and great commandment. And the second is like unto it, Thou shalt love thy neighbour as thyself. On these two commandments hang all the law and the prophets."[296] Herein are equality and unity achieved and perfected; consecration is the law that creates this ultimate change of heart, which allows for equality and unity. No wonder, then, that consecration is the last law we must agree to live before we can stand in the presence of God. Significantly, it is only after we agree to live the law of consecration that we can pray with enough power to approach God and enter his presence. Moreover, it is only after we covenant to live the law of consecration that we qualify to receive our own eternal kingdom through temple marriage.

By means of the law of the gospel, the law of sacrifice, and the law of consecration, we prove our loyalty to God once and for all. We remain obedient to our covenants with a firm decision and concerted effort, and we are willing to back up that commitment with all that we are and all that we possess. Only by this ultimate manifestation of obedience and sacrifice can we build up God's kingdom and prepare the way for the establishment of Zion.

---

294   D&C 59:8.
295   Hinckley, *Teachings of Gordon B. Hinckley*, 147.
296   Matthew 22:37–40.

Section 3
The Guiding Principles of
Consecration

Nearly two years after the organization of the Church, Joseph Smith received a revelation from the Lord instructing him to take the next step in establishing the law of consecration. "For verily I say unto you, the time has come, and is now at hand; and behold, and lo, it must needs be that there be an organization of my people, in regulating and establishing the affairs of the storehouse for the poor of my people, both in this place and in the land of Zion." This "order" was to be considered "a permanent and everlasting establishment and order unto my church, to advance the cause, which ye have espoused, to the salvation of man, and to the glory of your Father who is in heaven." Beyond advancing the cause of Zion and providing a means of salvation for us, this order was to make the Saints "equal in the bonds of heavenly things, yea, and earthly things also, for the obtaining of heavenly things." Notice that equality is a constant theme in consecration literature: "For if ye are not equal in earthly things ye cannot be equal in obtaining heavenly things." Obeying the law of consecration cannot be overstated: "For if you will that I give unto you a place in the celestial world, you must prepare yourselves by doing the things which I have commanded you and required of you."[297]

The Prophet learned that disobeying this law carries dire consequences: disloyalty to the truth, blindness to the Source of our blessings, and, perhaps worse, the loss of our standing before God, and subjugation to Satan. The Saints must live this law, the Lord said, "Otherwise, Satan seeketh to turn their hearts away from the truth, that they become blinded and understand not the things which are prepared for them. Wherefore, a commandment I give unto you, to prepare and organize yourselves by a bond or everlasting covenant that cannot be broken. And he who breaketh it shall lose his office and standing in the church, and shall be delivered over to the buffetings of Satan until the day of redemption."[298]

---

297   D&C 78:7.
298   D&C 78:11–12.

Conversely, the order of consecration is the key to our temporal and spiritual salvation. Consecration prepares us against the trials of the last days and sets us apart as independent from this wicked world: "Behold, this is the preparation wherewith I prepare you, and the foundation, and the ensample which I give unto you, whereby you may accomplish the commandments which are given you; that through my providence, notwithstanding the tribulation which shall descend upon you, that the church may stand independent above all other creatures beneath the celestial world."[299]

Guiding Principles of Consecration

In this section, we have already discussed a variety of characteristics of consecration, including equality and unity. In this chapter, we will explore the additional principles of agency, stewardship, accountability, and labor as they appear in the scriptures and as they apply to consecration.

Agency

President Marion G. Romney defined agency as both the liberty and the capability to choose and act. Beyond the gift of life, he said, agency is the most precious gift we receive from God.[300] Speaking of agency, President Brigham Young taught: "This is a law which has always existed from all eternity, and will continue to exist throughout all the eternities to come. Every intelligent being must have the power of choice."[301]

Elder Bruce R. McConkie wrote, "Four great principles must be in force if there is to be agency: 1. Laws must exist, laws ordained by an Omnipotent power, laws which can be obeyed or disobeyed; 2. Opposites must exist—good and evil, virtue and vice, right and wrong—that is, there must be an opposition, one force pulling one way and another pulling the other; 3. A knowledge of good and evil must be had by those who are to enjoy the agency, that is, they must know the difference between the opposites; and 4. An unfettered power of choice must prevail."[302]

Agency and Truth

The measure of our agency increases as we learn and apply truth. For example, a pilot has more agency than a passenger, and a surgeon has more agency than a patient. We cannot exercise agency without information to act upon. Because consecration is perhaps the highest and most demanding exercise of agency, we must become acquainted with its premise and principles. Knowledge of the laws of life helps us to understand their associated blessings and protective punishments. We make better choices (or should), when we are in the possession of knowledge. The scriptures remind us, "And ye shall know the truth, and the truth shall make you free." But freedom of choice carries an obligation: While we are free

299   D&C 78:13–14.
300   Romney, "Church Welfare Services' Basic Principles," 120.
301   Young, *Deseret News,* Oct. 10, 1866, 355.
302   McConkie, *Mormon Doctrine,* 26.

to act, we are not free to define right and wrong. Once we are in possession of the truth, we must choose to act upon it correctly if we hope to obtain the blessings.[303]

Consecration is a choice. That choice can neither be forced upon us nor legislated. However, once we have received light and truth regarding this law, and when we have covenanted to live it, we are faced with an inescapable decision: Will we consecrate or will we not? How we choose will determine whether or not we will receive the highest of blessings or the condemnation.[304] When we become acquainted with this law and covenant to live it, we are still free to consecrate or not, but we are not free to ignore the law, redefine it, or expect that we can achieve celestial glory without abiding it.[305] When we consider that consecration is the ultimate sacrifice and test of will, we might say that God gave us our agency, in part, for the purpose of giving us a choice to live this law so that we could achieve eternal life. Because achieving exaltation pivots on our willingness to consecrate our all to God, and because the sacrifice of all things[306] (defined as a broken heart and a contrite spirit, a sacrifice that answers the end of the law[307]) is *the* criterion, we must be in possession of the "unfettered power of choice" and the capability to act upon that choice.

Agency—A Gift Assured and Protected by the Savior

He who gave us our agency is God.[308] He who opposes our agency is the devil. And he who safeguards our right to this gift is the Savior: "And the Messiah cometh in the fulness of time, that he may redeem the children of men from the fall. *And because they are redeemed from the fall they have become free forever, knowing good from evil, to act for themselves. . . .* Wherefore, men are free according to the flesh; and all things are given them which are expedient unto man. And they are free to choose liberty and eternal life, through the great Mediator of all men, or to choose captivity and death, according to the captivity and power of the devil; for he seeketh that all men might be miserable like unto himself."[309]

Children of God are endowed with the inherent capacity to choose liberty and eternal life or captivity and death—to choose to become a god or a devil. As we have said, without God's gift of agency and the Savior's protection of it, we could not choose to consecrate, which is the singular law that allows us to inherit the celestial kingdom and exaltation.

The Body—The Vehicle for Moral Agency

Just as a pilot (an agent of flight) needs an airplane to give expression to his knowledge, so a spirit (an agent of light) needs a physical body to give ultimate expression to its desires. Think of it this way: A pilot cannot choose to fly without a plane any more than a spirit can choose to act physically without a body.

303 Cannon, "Agency and Accountability," 88–89, quoting John 8:32.
304 Matthew 25:14–30.
305 Cannon, "Agency and Accountability," 88–89.
306 Smith, *Lectures on Faith,* 6:7.
307 2 Nephi 2:7.
308 Moses 7:32.
309 2 Nephi 2:26–27; emphasis added.

Together, spirit and body constitute "the soul of man."[310] To achieve exaltation the soul needs experience in the two major elements that constitute the universe: spirit matter and physical matter. The physical body becomes the great tool of feeling and expression that the spirit can choose to "act upon."[311] The physical body is like the artist's brush; to a spirit, the physical world is its canvas.

With a body we can suddenly choose from and enjoy infinite possibilities. President John Taylor said, "The body was formed as an agent for the spirit."[312] With a body, then, we have both the intellect and the vehicle to imagine and reason, then choose to act out our thoughts. With a body we can give expression to our dreams, desires, and hungers. With a body we have the unlimited potential to reach stratospheric godlike heights or plunge to the hellish depths. With a body, we who are the children of God, and thus have infinite potential, are capable of literally anything—"nothing [would] be impossible."[313] But to become as God, we must learn to control the physical body and discipline it into channels of exalted purposes, the greatest of which, interestingly, are realized only by means of a consecrated effort.

Controlling the body is no small feat. By descending to this planet to take up a fallen, telestial body made of fallen, telestial material, we become "by nature . . . carnal, sensual, and devilish."[314] Consequently, we become subject to the devil.[315] This fallen condition has a name, "natural man," which, by definition, is "an enemy to God." In order to progress toward exaltation, we need to experience a spiritual awakening and press the body to be enticed by "the Holy Spirit and [put] off the natural man and [become] a saint through the Atonement of Christ the Lord." This transformation is preceded by a choice, which means we need our agency. Therefore, to qualify for eternal life, we must choose to suppress our innate carnal, sensual, and devilish natures and become childlike, "submissive, meek, humble, patient, full of love, willing to submit to all things which the Lord seeth fit to inflict upon [us], even as a child doth submit to his father."[316]

Thus, earth life is designed to be a test consisting of choices made possible by our God-given agency. Our mortal test—choosing between the physical and spiritual and between Satan and God—involves learning to "act as an independent being . . . to see what we will do, . . . to be righteous in the dark—to be the friend of God."[317] Our test is to exercise our agency and choose to be faithful, even if our circumstances become "darker than 10,000 midnights."[318]

Our Eternal Destiny Lies within Our Body

With agency and a body, every experience is heightened—we can fall lower or rise higher than anything we had previously known. We can feel more fully, hurt more completely, love more deeply, and, because we now are a complete *soul* comprised of the two building

---

310   D&C 88:15.
311   2 Nephi 2:13.
312   Taylor, "The Government of God," in *Teachings of the Latter-day Prophets,* 15:77–79.
313   Luke 1:37.
314   Alma 42:10.
315   Mosiah 16:3.
316   Mosiah 3:19.
317   Maxwell, *That Ye May Believe,* 194–95.
318   Young, *Journal of Discourses,* 3:207.

blocks of the universe, we have the potential to "receive a fulness of joy."[319] Clearly, our destiny lies within the potential of our bodies.

Satan would expend every effort to persuade us to misuse our bodies. He knows, for example, that with a body we suddenly have the power to reproduce ourselves by procreating other carnate children of God—a powerful and sometimes frightening idea. Satan eagerly zeroes in on this God-defining power and relentlessly tries to influence us to misuse our bodies by experimenting with the sacred powers of procreation. Once we choose badly, we lose agency and give it to him. Another Satanic ploy is to use ignorance as a tool to destroy us—ignorance about who we really are, where we came from, why we are here, and what could be our glorious future. By keeping us ignorant, Satan can more easily tempt us to choose to disobey God. He knows that disobedience cuts a wide gash in the soul and causes us to hemorrhage light and truth.[320] Once that happens, we become weakened and disempowered. We lose agency incrementally; then Satan can gain control over us.[321]

On the other hand, the body, when properly used and understood, according to Joseph Smith, can put us beyond Satan and all of our enemies.[322] He said, "All beings who have bodies have power over those who have not. The devil has no power over us only as we permit him. The moment we revolt at anything which comes from God, the devil takes power."[323] Therefore, "Satan's power over us *always* hinges upon our obedience or disobedience—our willingness or unwillingness to submit to the mind and will of the Father."[324]

The body is designed to be the "tabernacle of God,"[325] a holy, walled fortress to hold the spirit and shield it.[326] We must not forget that the spirit, the actual offspring of God that animates the body, is a powerful being. Our spirit is made of the substance called *truth*, which is also referred to as spirit, light, light of truth, intelligence, glory, power, and, interestingly, "law."[327] Because the body is carnal, sensual, and devilish by nature, it might not perceive the entity of light and truth that resides within it; but the spirit knows who it is. By nature, the spirit is truth-discerning, constructed and instructed so that it can perceive both truth and error.[328] Beyond our limited five physical senses, an ocean of truth exists around us, and although we might try stubbornly to deny it, we are nevertheless drenched in truth.[329] Therefore, within the construct of our souls reside all the necessary tools to allow us to learn and to choose. We are clearly beings of agency.

Agency and Agents

Agents are people who have the power and authority to act.[330] Therefore, agents have agency, which is the ability to "act for themselves,"[331] or the ability to act for themselves

---

319 D&C 93:33–34.
320 D&C 93:39.
321 Mosiah 16:3–5.
322 Smith, *The Words of Joseph Smith*, 208.
323 Smith, *Teachings of the Prophet Joseph Smith*, 181.
324 Yorgason, *I Need Thee Every Hour*, 348.
325 D&C 93:35.
326 Young, *Journal of Discourses*, 9:139–40.
327 D&C 93:23–29, 36; 88:6–13.
328 2 Nephi 2:5.
329 Alma 32:28.
330 *American Heritage Dictionary*, s.v. "agent."
331 2 Nephi 2:26.

with respect to a given responsibility or obligation. Moreover, agents have the capacity to be accountable for their actions. Whereas *freedom* is the power and privilege to exercise our will and act upon it, *agency* is the power, independence of mind, and individual will to choose to act. *Moral agency* describes our ability to act upon and be accountable for spiritual matters.[332] Zion people exercise their God-given agency to choose to make and keep covenants and to reject the enticements of Babylon.

And choose we must.

Posing the choice between Jehovah and Baal, Elijah asked, "How long halt ye between two opinions? if the Lord be God, follow him: but if Baal, then follow him."[333] In our day, he would have been asking us to choose between Zion and Babylon. Remaining lukewarm on celestial issues is not acceptable: "I know thy works, that thou art neither cold nor hot," the Lord said. "I would thou wert cold or hot. So then because thou art lukewarm, and neither cold nor hot, I will spue thee out of my mouth."[334] Consecration is not a lukewarm issue. Everything of eternal consequence rides on our choosing to obey this law. Because we are agents of choice, we have the capacity to choose one way or another. There is no middle ground when it comes to consecration; either we consecrate or we do not.

When the Lord began to establish his people in the land of Zion, he instructed the Saints to consecrate their money for the cause: "And let all the moneys which can be spared, it mattereth not unto me whether it be little or much, be sent up unto the land of Zion."[335] Notice that it did not matter how much the Saints gave as long as they exercised their agency and chose to give all that they could spare. There is an unspoken assumption here that concerns the principle of grace: When we do all we can do, the Lord will make up the difference. As we know, the Lord can take a consecration as small as five loaves and two fishes and bless it so that it can feed thousands.[336] Addressing Newel K. Whitney, the Lord said, "Let him impart all the money which he can impart, to be sent up unto the land of Zion. Behold, these things are in his own hands, let him do according to wisdom."[337] Again, we encounter the principle of choice: "These things are in his own hands, let him do according to wisdom." Brother Whitney and the Saints had received a commandment to consecrate, but the choice and the amount were left up to them. They were agents.

Agency and Self-reliance

The Lord intends that man is to be "an agent unto himself."[338] But it is impossible to be an independent agent if we are not temporally and spiritually self-reliant. When circumstances jeopardize our self-reliance, our agency is also jeopardized. Likewise, the more we are dependent, ignorant, or impoverished, the less we can exercise our agency. According to President Marion G. Romney, our independence and agency to act are inexorably linked to our self-reliance, making self-reliance a critical key to our spiritual development.

---

332   D&C 29:35.
333   1 Kings 18:21.
334   Revelation 3:15–16.
335   D&C 63:40.
336   Matthew 14:13–21.
337   D&C 63:43–44.
338   D&C 29:35.

Spiritual self-reliance depends on our ability, understanding, and willingness to exercise our agency and keep God's commandments. Invariably, the commandments demand that we choose to serve. Without our keeping the commandments, which obedience leads to self-reliance, President Romney said, our ability to serve is limited. We cannot give from empty shelves; we cannot comfort if we are emotionally impoverished; we cannot instruct if we are ignorant; we cannot show others the way if we are spiritually deficient.

As we become more self-reliant, our agency increases; then we can better choose to serve and to help other people to become more self-reliant. President Romney went on to say that there is an interdependence between the rich and the poor. In the process of giving, both parties are sanctified: the impoverished person is freed from poverty and becomes self-reliant, whereupon as a free man he can now rise to his full temporal and spiritual potential; the self-reliant rich person is blessed and multiplied by fulfilling the celestial law of giving. Keep in mind that wealth and poverty are defined in terms of things financial, emotional, educational, physical, and spiritual. A miracle occurs when we rescue an impoverished person. Now he is self-reliant and free to use his agency to rescue others. This is the cycle of Zion, which constantly repeats itself, rescuing, sanctifying, and exalting its participants.[339]

But self-reliance is only the beginning of the blessings of Zion. At an elementary level, our self-reliance allows us to take care of our own, but our agency to serve an increasing number of people may be limited. As we have discussed elsewhere, Zion people practice giving with the assurance that the Lord will subsequently bless them "an hundredfold."[340] If Zion people will advance the process by giving again of the Lord's blessings, abundance will ensue, resulting in enough for Zion people to remain self-sufficient *and* help others to become self-sufficient. This process is the Lord's "own way"[341]— the way he expects us to manage our stewardships.[342]

Therefore, our agency (freedom and ability to choose) is proportional to our self-reliance. When those who have greater resources reach down to lift an impoverished person to a higher degree of self-reliance, that person is then in a position to reach down and lift someone else. In each case, abundance results: the impoverished person is made whole, and those with greater resources are rewarded "an hundredfold." Thus the ever-repeating cycle of Zion exalts its people, increases their agency, ensures their self-reliance, and prospers them. And it all begins with choice.

The Power of Choice

Opposition and opposites are the fuel of agency: "And it must needs be that the devil should tempt the children of men, or they could not be agents unto themselves; for if they never should have bitter they could not know the sweet."[343] Therefore, we are free to

---

339   Romney, "The Celestial Nature of Self-reliance," 61–65.
340   Matthew 19:29.
341   D&C 104:16.
342   Gardner, "Becoming a Zion Society," 31.
343   D&C 29:39.

choose our destiny—we can choose Zion's principles to our salvation, or we can choose Babylon's lack of principles to our condemnation. God provides us enough information to choose between the opposites: "Behold, here is the agency of man, and here is the condemnation of man; because that which was from the beginning is plainly manifest unto them, and they receive not the light."[344]

Agency and freedom flourish in a Zion-like environment. "If the Son therefore shall make you free, ye shall be free indeed."[345] Zion people enjoy the highest degree of both agency and freedom. "And because that they are redeemed from the fall they have become free forever, knowing good from evil; to act for themselves and not to be acted upon."[346]

Whereas agency and freedom exist at their highest levels in a Zion-like environment, they decrease to abysmal levels in Babylon: "And the whole world [Babylon] lieth in sin, and groaneth under darkness and under the bondage of sin."[347] Choosing Babylonian principles always results in fewer choices and less freedom; choosing Zion principles always results in limitless choices and unequalled freedom. If we ever hope to become Zion-like in this life and achieve the celestial kingdom in the life to come, we must exercise our God-given agency and choose to covenant and obey the law—consecration—upon which Zion lives are founded.

Stewardship

In the vocabulary of consecration, an agent is a steward.[348] The trust extended to a steward is a stewardship, which, according to the *Encyclopedia of Mormonism*, is a "responsibility given through the Lord to act in behalf of others." The concept of stewardship reminds us of the principle that "all things ultimately belong to the Lord, whether property, time, talents, families, or capacity for service within the Church organization. An individual acts in a Church calling as a trustee for the Lord, not out of personal ownership or privilege." When we receive a stewardship from the Lord, whether as a calling, a trust, or an inheritance, we are "expected to sacrifice time and talent in the service of others," which builds "a sense of community. When all serve, all may partake of the blessings of service. The ideal attitude toward stewardship suggests that it is not the position held but how well the work is done that counts."[349] One can readily see why stewardship is central to Zion and the law of consecration.

The Riches of the Earth Are the Lord's
When a Zion person exercises his agency to live the law of consecration, he makes a conscious choice to become a steward of the Lord's property. His approach to ownership is that "the earth is the Lord's, and the fulness thereof."[350] Elder Bruce R. McConkie said,

344 D&C 93:31.
345 John 8:36.
346 2 Nephi 2:26.
347 D&C 84:49–50.
348 D&C 104:17.
349 *Encyclopedia of Mormonism*, 1418.
350 Psalm 24:1.

"Underlying this principle of stewardship is the eternal gospel truth that all things belong to the Lord. 'I, the Lord, stretched out the heavens, and built the earth, my very handiwork; and all things therein are mine. . . . Behold, all these properties are mine. . . . And if the properties are mine, then ye are stewards; otherwise ye are no stewards.'"[351] There can be no mistake about who owns what; the Lord emphatically states, "the riches of the earth are mine."[352]

Even in a telestial setting, we constantly encounter the concept of stewardship . For example, a business owner will enter into an agreement to hand over the management of his company to a trusted employee, provided the employee gives his best effort, pursues the mission of the company, is committed to increasing the company's profits, and is accountable to his employer. In return, the employer pays the employee a fair wage, with which the employee takes care of his family. The employee has no right to divide his attention with another interest, change the purpose of the company, use its resources outside his employer's desire, or take the profits for himself. We might ask ourselves, If we understand these principles on a telestial level, why can we not apply them to a celestial situation?

Let us examine the law of consecration in this light. By agreeing to take upon us this covenant, we agree that everything belongs to the Lord and that we are stewards. From this point forward, we cease to lay claim to our time, talents, and possessions. Rather, we essentially enter into a *management agreement* with the Lord, in which we agree to give him our best and undivided effort as we administer the affairs of the stewardship that he places in our hands. We agree to pursue the ordained purpose of that stewardship, the core issue of which is always to assist in bringing to pass the immortality (the *quality* of immortality, whether telestial, terrestrial, or celestial) and the eternal life of man.[353] Moreover, we agree to use and disseminate the stewardship's resources as the stewardship's Owner directs. We agree to magnify the stewardship, to take no more of the surplus than we are entitled to, and to be accountable to the Owner for our management of his resources. For the Lord's part, he agrees to allow us our agency in managing his resources, and he agrees to take care of us and keep us safe while we are on his errand.

In no uncertain terms, we are expressly forbidden to hoard the Lord's property or claim it as our own. Martin Harris learned this lesson: "I command thee that thou shalt not covet thine own property, but impart it freely to the printing of the Book of Mormon."[354] At another time, the Lord commanded William E. McLellin to focus on proclaiming the gospel and to "think not of thy property."[355] Clearly, a Zion person's claim to his property is subordinate to the Lord's claim. But if we view our property as our own and not as a stewardship, we break the law of consecration and step into sin: "Let them repent of all their sins, and of all their covetous desires, before me, saith the Lord; for what is property unto me?"[356] Who can lay claim to property or tempt the Lord with it, especially when we know that everything belongs to him in the first place? We recall that

---

351   McConkie, *Mormon Doctrine*, 767, quoting D&C 104:14, 55–56.
352   D&C 38:39.
353   Moses 1:39.
354   D&C 19:26.
355   D&C 66:6.
356   D&C 117:4.

Satan tried to entice Jesus with property and was soundly condemned: "Again, the devil taketh him up into an exceeding high mountain, and sheweth him all the kingdoms of the world, and the glory of them; and saith unto him, All these things will I give thee, if thou wilt fall down and worship me. Then saith Jesus unto him, Get thee hence, Satan."[357]

On the other hand, as Martin Harris and William E. McLellin learned, our property is a stewardship that must be consecrated for the building up of the kingdom of God and the establishment of Zion. The law of consecration provides that no poor should exist among us. Ultimately we will be held accountable for the diligence we pay to living this law and for the discharge of our stewardships.[358]

God Becomes Our Paymaster

An early attempt to implement the law of consecration required members to deed over their property to the Church.[359] Today, we are asked to figuratively deed over our hearts. We recognize that, ultimately, our time, talents, and property belong to the Lord, and we are stewards assigned to manage his resources under his direction. To appropriately fulfill our assignment, we agree to "live by every word that proceedeth forth from the mouth of God."[360] Furthermore, we agree to become "submissive, meek, humble, patient, full of love," and "willing to submit" to the Lord.[361] Then a remarkable thing happens: God helps us to depart from Babylon, and he becomes our paymaster in Zion. Of course, this miracle is individualized for each person, but it occurs nevertheless.

The Lord takes care of those in his household; he supports the stewards in his employ, and "the laborer is worthy of his hire."[362] What the Lord said to Warren A. Cowdery could be said to every steward in Zion: "[My steward shall] devote his whole time to this high and holy calling, which I now give unto him, seeking diligently the kingdom of heaven and its righteousness, *and all things necessary shall be added thereunto*."[363]

Now that the steward has been extracted and insulated from Babylon, he resides in the safety of his Lord, allowing him to devote his entire effort to his stewardships. In the transition, he ceases to labor for the cause of money and begins to labor for the cause of Zion: "But the laborer in Zion shall labor for Zion; for if they labor for money they shall perish."[364] This does not mean that the steward does not need money or does not receive monetary compensation for his labor; rather, it means that the cause of Zion and managing his stewardship are his focus. The moment he views the stewardship as his own or attempts to accumulate the resources of the stewardship to himself, he is in conflict with the interests of his paymaster. Even in Babylon, such an employee would be considered dishonest and an extortionist; he would be summarily dismissed and cast out. Any employee knows that the surpluses derived from his labor belong to the owner to do with as he pleases. The employee errs when he judges the employer's use and distribution of profits.

357 Matthew 4:8–10.
358 D&C 51:19; 72:3–4; 78:22, 82:3, 11; Matthew 25:14–30; Luke 16:2; 19:17.
359 D&C 42:30.
360 D&C 84:44.
361 Mosiah 3:19.
362 D&C 84:79.
363 D&C 106:3; emphasis added.
364 2 Nephi 26:31.

The righteous steward discovers that his Lord is a very generous paymaster. What Elder Carlos E. Asay said of missionaries' meriting blessings for their labor could be said of any steward:

> The word merit is defined as "reward . . . just deserts" (*Webster's Third New International Dictionary*). Such a definition often turns our minds to temporal gains received for service rendered. It also suggests a dollar return on a dollar invested and nothing more. Another definition, however, refers to merit as "spiritual credit or stored moral surplusage regarded as earned by performance of righteous acts and as ensuring future benefits" (ibid.). This latter definition appeals to me and seems to apply to missionary service because the process of sharing the gospel with others is centered in "righteous acts" and carries "future benefits" for both the giver and the receiver. In fact, the list of spiritual credits or by-products received by those who seek to save souls is endless. *Those who engage in missionary service soon learn that God is a very generous paymaster. We can never place him in our debt* (see Mosiah 2:22–24).[365]

Righteous stewards earn temporal and spiritual credits that may be redeemed in the storehouse of their most generous Paymaster for many times their original value.

Never Turn Back

We must become a righteous steward. Once the Lord has separated us from Babylon, as is exemplified in the temple initiatory ordinances, and when he has placed within our care a stewardship in his kingdom, we must discharge our duty faithfully and never turn back.

Peter taught, "For if after they have escaped the pollutions of the world through the knowledge of the Lord and Saviour Jesus Christ, they are again entangled therein, and overcome, *the latter end is worse with them than the beginning.* For it had been better for them not to have known the way of righteousness, than, after they have known it, to turn from the holy commandment delivered unto them."[366] The implications are sobering. If we have cried unto the Lord to help us escape Babylon, and then he rescues us and gives us a stewardship and *employment* in his kingdom—if, after all that, we weaken and return to Babylon and again become entangled in its charms, our situation will be worse than the first. We will find ourselves left alone with no further claim on the Lord's resources or on him as our paymaster.

---

365   Asay, *The Seven M's of Missionary Service,* 9; emphasis added.
366   2 Peter 2:20–21; emphasis added.

Nephi explained that the journey from Babylon to Zion is the most significant journey in time or eternity. Nothing could be more important than arriving at the tree of life and partaking of its fruit, both of which are symbolic of the love of God.[367] When we finally reach our destination, we must stay. Otherwise, according to Nephi, every person who arrived at the tree and thereafter gave heed to Babylon "had fallen away."[368] Here, then, is the safety and the condemnation of the law of stewardship.

The Law of Stewardship and the Oath and Covenant of the Priesthood

When righteous men (and later righteous men and women at the time of temple marriage) take upon them the oath and covenant of the priesthood, they agree to receive the blessings and obligations of the priesthood "for your sakes, and not for your sakes only, but for the sake of the world."[369] That is, we are under covenant to exercise the priesthood to gain our salvation by helping to save others. Therefore, to fulfill this part of the priesthood covenant, we approach our stewardships with the attitude of caring for our families, caring for others, and caring for the Lord's purposes. Consider the Lord's admonition to the elders who had taken upon them the oath and covenant of the priesthood:

> And behold, thou wilt remember the poor, and consecrate of thy properties for their support that which thou hast to impart unto them. . . .
>
> And inasmuch as ye impart of your substance unto the poor, ye will do it unto me; . . . every man shall be made accountable unto me, a steward over his own property, or that which he has received by consecration, as much as is sufficient for himself and family. And again, if there shall be properties in the hands of the church, or any individuals of it, more than is necessary for their support after this first consecration, which is a residue to be consecrated unto the bishop, it shall be kept to administer to those who have not, from time to time, that every man who has need may be amply supplied and receive according to his wants. Therefore, the residue shall be kept in my storehouse, to administer to the poor and the needy, . . . that my covenant people may be gathered in one in that day when I shall come to my temple. And this I do for the salvation of my people. . . . For inasmuch as ye do it unto the least of these, ye do it unto me. For it shall come to pass, that which I spake by the mouths of my prophets shall be fulfilled; for I will consecrate of the riches of those who

---

367   1 Nephi 11:21–23.
368   1 Nephi 8:34.
369   D&C 84:48.

embrace my gospel among the Gentiles unto the poor of
my people who are of the house of Israel.[370]

Stewardship and Equality

The law of stewardship is the law upon which Zion's equality is achieved. As we have
mentioned, equality is defined as having equal access.[371] In Zion, each person must have
equal opportunity to receive a stewardship, to develop it, and to have equal access to
the Lord and the Lord's resources. To qualify for the celestial kingdom, we must live
the foundational law of stewardship,[372] which stipulates that "every man [must be made]
equal according to his family, according to his circumstances and his wants and needs."[373]

Inequality is wholly telestial in nature; inequality cannot exist in a celestial atmosphere. As we recall, the Lord has stated emphatically that we must become "equal in
the bonds of heavenly things, yea, and earthly things also, for the obtaining of heavenly
things. For if ye are not equal in earthly things ye cannot be equal in obtaining heavenly
things; for if you will that I give unto you a place in the celestial world, you must prepare
yourselves by doing the things which I have commanded you and required of you."[374]

Failing to live the law of stewardship and turning a blind eye to inequality are classified as sins: "But it is not given that one man should possess that which is above another,
wherefore the world lieth in sin."[375] We need only look at the world condition to see the
consequences of selfishness, greed, and using the resources entrusted to us without accountability to God: "And the whole world lieth in sin, and groaneth under darkness and
under the bondage of sin." How can we escape this darkness and bondage? The answer
separates righteous Zion people from the wicked people of Babylon: "And by this you
may know they [the people of Babylon] are under the bondage of sin, *because they come
not unto me.* For whoso cometh not unto me is under the bondage of sin. And whoso
receiveth not my voice is not acquainted with my voice, and is not of me. *And by this you
may know the righteous from the wicked,* and that the whole world groaneth under sin and
darkness even now."[376]

We might ask ourselves this question: Could it be possible to make the covenant of
consecration, then ignore the law of stewardship with its injunction to equalize people—
and still claim that we are acquainted with the voice of the Lord and that we have come
unto him?

Zion people come unto Christ and hearken to his voice by seeking to purify their
hearts; by seeking to equalize the condition of the Lord's children through the giving of their
means; by striving to heal the Lord's children, bolster their faith, and love them. The pure
in heart view themselves as stewards rather than owners, and they seek to bless the Lord's
children with their stewardships, which is the sum of everything that they have and are.

---

370   D&C 42:30–34, 36, 38–39.
371   D&C 82:17.
372   D&C 101:5.
373   D&C 51:3.
374   D&C 78:3–5.
375   D&C 49:20.
376   D&C 84:50–53; emphasis added.

Stewardships in the Scriptures

As we study the standard works, we discover the concept of stewardship throughout. Stewardships are also referred to as callings, trusts, charges, responsibilities, and inheritances or portions.[377] Some stewardships are classified as spiritual while others are temporal.[378] For example, a Church calling is a spiritual stewardship while an individual's business and holdings are a temporal stewardship. Of course, even temporal things are spiritual unto the Lord.[379]

In the early days of the Church, stewardships were also called inheritances or "portions." BYU professor Clark V. Johnson explained that the Lord "required the bishop of the Church to give every man an inheritance. [The Lord] explained that Church members were equal according to their family, circumstances, wants, and needs (D&C 51:4)." Here we see the principles of stewardship and accountability as they apply to an inheritance. We note that it is the bishop who assigns inheritances in Zion, and he is also the one who, in behalf of the Lord, receives an account of their management. Receiving and reporting on Church callings and at tithing settlement are manifestations of these principles. With regard to the management of their stewardships, "the Lord reminded members of the Church that when they had enough to satisfy their needs, they were to give the surplus to the storehouse. Excess gained in the operation of the stewardship was to be used to administer to those who were in need (D&C 42:33–34). The bishop kept all surplus donated from the stewardships in a storehouse he organized (D&C 51:13)."[380]

Even today we might expect to render accountings of our various stewardships to the bishop. For example, we make such an accounting to him when he interviews us for a temple recommend, and, from time to time, when we counsel with him, we also make an accounting of our lives. Because the law of consecration requires that we consecrate our time, talents, and all that we have and are to the kingdom of God, the bulk of our stewardship usually lies outside the Church organization. Nevertheless, we are accountable for them to the Lord and to his servant, the bishop. Perhaps more blessings would flow to us if we lived the law of stewardship more faithfully and felt more accountability on each point of the law.

We would expect that our actual inheritances in priesthood society of Zion would follow the pattern described in Doctrine and Covenants 58: "This is a law unto every man that cometh unto this land to receive an inheritance; and he shall do with his moneys according as the law [of consecration] directs."[381] Although we privately own our inheritances, we must consider them as consecrated stewardships, and thus we are accountable to the Lord for them according to the law of accountability.[382] If we live the

377   Genesis 26:5; Exodus 6:13; Numbers 4:4; 27:23; Matthew 18:23; 20:8; 21:33; 24:45; 25:21; Luke 12:42; 12:48; 16:2; 19:17; 1 Corinthians 4:2; 1 Timothy 4:14; Titus 1:7; 1 Peter 4:10; Jacob 1:19; 2:2; Alma 35:16; D&C 42:32, 70; 51:19; 64:40; 69:5; 70:4, 9; 72:3; 78:22; 82:3, 11; 101:90; 104:11, 55; 124:14; 136:27; JS–H 1:59; see also Genesis 48:22; Deuteronomy 32:9; Psalm 16:5; Isaiah 53:12; Zechariah 2:12; Luke 12:46; D&C 19:34; 51:3; 78:21; 104:18; 132:39.
378   D&C 42:33, "D&C 42:7171.
379   D&C 29:34–35.
380   Johnson, "The Law of Consecration," 100.
381   D&C 58:36.
382   D&C 42:32.

law of stewardship, we are promised safety, for our consecrated effort is "to prepare [us] against the day of vengeance and burning."[383] If we do not live this law, we run the risk of suffering the consequences: "If any man shall take of the abundance which I have made, and impart not his portion, according to the law of my gospel, unto the poor and the needy, he shall, with the wicked, lift up his eyes in hell, being in torment."[384]

Understanding the Order of the Law of Stewardship

In section 104 of the Doctrine and Covenants, the Lord revealed the order by which inheritances (stewardships) are apportioned from the Lord's resources to us, the stewards. We are reminded that "the sacred things" which are "delivered into the treasury" are the Lord's, "and no man among you shall call it his own, or any part of it, for it shall belong to you *all* with one accord." The surplus derived from the management of the stewardship rightly belongs to Lord and must be placed in his sacred repository for the common good: "And thus shall ye preserve the avails of the sacred things in the treasury, for sacred and holy purposes. And this shall be called the sacred treasury of the Lord; and a seal shall be kept upon it that it may be holy and consecrated unto the Lord."[385] The Lord's servant, the bishop, manages the treasury and the Lord's resources. This is the order of the law of stewardship.

In our day, we would call this sacred treasury the bishop's storehouse. Of course, the Church maintains other treasuries—for instance, monetary funds, warehouses of supplies, and service departments. We also read of sacred treasuries in heaven. For example, "Lay up for yourselves a treasure in heaven, yea, which is eternal, and which fadeth not away; yea, that ye may have that precious gift of eternal life."[386] To access that heavenly treasury, we must sacrifice our personal treasures in this world: "Now when Jesus heard these things, he said unto [the rich young man], Yet lackest thou one thing: sell all that thou hast, and distribute unto the poor, and thou shalt have treasure in heaven: and come, follow me."[387]

One definition of treasure is anything that is good. Under this definition, even our testimonies could be considered stewardships. We know that the law of consecration requires that every good thing we receive from the Lord must be returned to him with increase. Interestingly, when we bear sincere testimony, our testimony grows,[388] and that allows us to fulfill the law and return our testimony to the Lord with increase. Our bearing witness of the truth is much like casting our testimony into the treasury of heaven; in return, great blessings are unleashed: "Nevertheless, ye are blessed, for the testimony which ye have borne is recorded in heaven for the angels to look upon; and they rejoice over you, and your sins are forgiven you."[389] "Also I say unto you, Whosoever shall confess me before men, him shall the Son of man also confess before the angels of God."[390] Again, these blessings flow from the order of the law of stewardship.

---

383   D&C 85:3.
384   D&C 104:18.
385   D&C 104:64–66.
386   Helaman 5:8.
387   Luke 18:22.
388   Young, *Discourses of Brigham Young,* 335.
389   D&C 62:3.
390   Luke 12:8.

Upon what principle do consecrated properties flow into the sacred treasuries? "Joseph Smith taught that the consecration of properties must be done by mutual consent. The bishop could not dictate in matters of consecration or he would have 'more power than a king.' The Prophet further explained that there must be a balance of power between the bishop and the people in order to preserve 'harmony and good-will.'"[391] Therefore, the bishop, who is the Lord's steward, is authorized to extend stewardships to his people; the people accept the stewardship and manage and account for it by their freewill choice; the people sustain the bishop in his calling. That sustaining is done by mutual covenant: the people agree to accept the bishop as the voice of the Lord, and he agrees to receive their accountings and judge them righteously in the Lord's name. In his office, the bishop is entrusted to receive freewill offerings from the surpluses of the stewards' stewardships, and he places those offerings in the common treasury. Then the stewards, who have common access to the treasury, may draw upon it, with the bishop's permission, for their needs and wants.

Clearly, the interaction between the stewards and the bishop is one of common consent. The bishop manages the treasury, assigns stewardships, and takes accountings, and the people sustain his actions, and through his ministry he gains access to the Lord's treasury. Such transactions are to be done "only by the voice of the order, or by commandment. . . . And there shall not any part of it [the treasury's resource] be used, or taken out of the treasury, only by the voice and common consent of the order."[392]

We see this law in action in every ward in the Church today. One of the highest manifestations of this law is that the steward receives access to the Lord's resources for the purpose of growing and managing his stewardship: "And this shall be the voice and common consent of the order—that any man among you say to the treasurer: I have need of this to help me in my stewardship."[393] In whatever form the law of consecration and the law of stewardship exist, the order that governs those laws will always apply. By common consent, the bishop, who is sustained by the voice of the people, will always apportion, aid in, judge, and take accounting of all stewardships pertaining to the kingdom of God. This is the order of the law of consecration.

Spiritual Gifts Are Stewardships to Bless Others

The stewardships that the Lord places in our trust are our time, talents and abilities, and everything else that we are or possess. Some of these stewardships are listed in Doctrine and Covenants 46 and are called "spiritual gifts." These gifts include:
- The gift of knowing—"that Jesus Christ is the Son of God, and that he was crucified for the sins of the world."
- The gift of believing—"on their words, that they also might have eternal life if they continue faithful."
- The gift of administration—"the differences of administration."

391   Johnson, "The Law of Consecration," 100, quoting Joseph Smith, *Teachings of the Prophet Joseph Smith*, 23.
392   D&C 104:64, 71.
393   D&C 104:72–73.

- The gift of "the diversities of operations, whether they be of God, that the manifestations of the Spirit may be given to every man to profit withal."
- The gift of "the word of wisdom."
- The gift of "the word of knowledge, that all may be taught to be wise and to have knowledge."
- The gift to have "faith to be healed."
- The gift to have "faith to heal."
- The gift of "the working of miracles."
- The gift of the ability "to prophesy."
- The gift of "discerning of spirits."
- The gift of speaking "with tongues."
- The gift of "the interpretation of tongues."[394]

Why does the Lord give us these gifts as stewardships? The answer echoes the language in the priesthood covenant. We receive gifts from the Lord "for [our] sakes, and not for [our] sakes only, but for the sake of the world."[395] The Lord said, "All these gifts come from God, for the benefit of the children of God."[396] When we consider the Lord's answer, we recall other scriptural injunctions to consecrate our resources for the purpose of blessing other people: "For of him unto whom much is given much is required."[397] "Freely ye have received, freely give."[398] Clearly, we cannot achieve celestial glory without blessing others.

Significantly, Doctrine and Covenants 46 mirrors many of the principles stated in the parable of the talents,[399] signaling to us the parable's latter-day relevance. Talents are gifts and therefore stewardships, and thus are to be used to bless the Lord's children. Because every person receives a gift or gifts from God, we are treated equally—a characteristic of Zion. Thus, the Lord says, "And you are to be equal, or in other words, you are to have equal claims on the properties, for the benefit of managing the concerns of your steward-ships, every man according to his wants and his needs, inasmuch as his wants are just— *and all this for the benefit of the church of the living God, that every man may improve upon his talent, that every man may gain other talents, yea, even an hundred fold, to be cast into the Lord's storehouse, to become the common property of the whole church*—every man seeking the interest of his neighbor, and doing all things with an eye single to the glory of God."[400]

These gifts, or talents, prepare us for the Lord's return; they "are suited to the gifts and needs of the individual to give him or her the maximum opportunity for growth in the King-dom of God."[401] How we manage our talents determines our eventual inheritance in the ce-lestial kingdom. Joseph Smith taught: "Many of our brethren are wise in . . . their labors, and have rid their garments of the blood of this generation and are approved before the Lord."[402]

---

394 D&C 46:13–25.
395 D&C 84:48.
396 D&C 46:13–25.
397 D&C 82:3.
398 Matthew 10:8.
399 Matthew 25:14–30.
400 D&C 82:17–19; emphasis added.
401 Johnson, "The Law of Consecration," 100.
402 Smith, *Evening and Morning Star,* July 1833.

Profitable and Unprofitable Servants

Jesus first introduced the idea of profitable and unprofitable servants in the parable of the talents.[403] Over a century earlier, King Benjamin discussed the concept of serving profitably.[404] Although our present mortal circumstances greatly hamper us from being profitable to the Lord, we must nevertheless make the attempt because profitability is central to our eternal progression and thus to the ever-expanding kingdom of God. When the Lord gives us a trust, we are to magnify it on our watch. Otherwise, as the parable of the talents states, the unprofitable servant is cast into outer darkness, where "there shall be weeping and gnashing of teeth."[405]

At least two criteria lead to profitability: (1) our being "anxiously engaged in a good cause, do[ing] many things of [our] own free will, and bring[ing] to pass much righteousness,"[406] and (2) yielding our hearts and wills to God.[407] Because we are agents with agency, we are endowed with the power of choice and the capability to magnify our stewardships. The goal of our creative effort is to "bring to pass much righteousness."

We also learn that the greater the profitability of the stewardship, the greater the trusts that God will eventually place in our care. Commenting on the teachings of Joseph Smith, Orson Hyde wrote:

> The most eminent and distinguished prophets who have laid down their lives for their testimony (Jesus among the rest), will be crowned at the head of the largest kingdoms under the Father, and will be one with Christ as Christ is one with his Father; for their kingdoms are all joined together, and such as do the will of the Father, the same are his mothers, sisters, and brothers. He that has been faithful over a few things, will be made ruler over many things; he that has been faithful over ten talents, shall have dominion over ten cities, and he that has been faithful over five talents, shall have dominion over five cities, and to every man will be given a kingdom and a dominion, according to his merit, powers, and abilities to govern and control. . . . There are kingdoms of all sizes, an infinite variety to suit all grades of merit and ability. The chosen vessels unto God are the kings and priests that are placed at the head of these kingdoms. These have received their washings and anointings in the temple of God on this earth; they have been chosen, ordained, and anointed kings and priests, to reign as such in the resurrection of the just.[408]

---

403 Matthew 25:14–30.
404 Mosiah 2:20–21.
405 Matthew 25:30.
406 D&C 58:27.
407 Helaman 3:35.
408 Smith, *The Words of Joseph Smith*, 299.

For the present, our maximum effort will not generate the maximum *profit* our stewardship is capable of producing. For that to happen, we must draw upon the principle of grace; we must humbly yield our wills to God, submit to his counsel, and allow him to do for us what we cannot do for ourselves. Only by such a partnership can the stewardship reach the summit of its potential. We are greatly benefitted by such a relationship. Elder Neal A. Maxwell taught that we enhance our individuality by yielding our wills to God; that is, as we are stretched and molded by him, we become more capable of receiving "all that the Father hath."[409] He concluded by saying we simply cannot be entrusted with God's "all" until our wills more closely corresponded to God's will.

Profitable servants improve upon that with which they have been entrusted; they employ sound management principles by reducing waste and insisting that invested resources generate an appropriate return; they are tireless workers and represent well the person to whom they are accountable: "O ye that embark in the service of God, see that ye serve him with all your heart, might, mind and strength."[410] Then, when profits are produced over and above that which the servant needs to care for his family and himself, the servant releases that surplus to the Lord, to whom the surplus rightly belongs: "Nevertheless, inasmuch as they receive more than is needful for their necessities and their wants, it shall be given into my storehouse; and the benefits shall be consecrated unto the inhabitants of Zion, and unto their generations, inasmuch as they become heirs according to the laws of the kingdom. Behold, this is what the Lord requires of every man in his stewardship, even as I, the Lord, have appointed or shall hereafter appoint unto any man. And behold, none are exempt from this law who belong to the church of the living God."[411]

How happy are the profitable servants who can report to God that they have accomplished everything they were charged to do. They will hear: "Well done, thou good and faithful servant: thou hast been faithful over a few things, I will make thee ruler over many things."[412]

Stewardships Prepare Us for Eternal Life

Because the law of consecration is the law of the celestial kingdom,[413] we might expect to receive, develop, and account for stewardships there.[414] This assumption is evidenced in the Lord's promise to righteous couples who are sealed in the temple and keep their marriage covenant. He promises that they "shall inherit thrones, kingdoms, principalities, and powers, dominions, all heights and depths."[415] The fact that this list contains diverse stations stated in the plural suggests that our celestial assignments and inheritances might shift and expand throughout the eternities, as we progress in our Father's kingdom. We also might expect that we will receive these stewardships by consecration, and that we will be held accountable for them. To develop our celestial stewardships,

---

409   D&C 84:38.
410   D&C 4:2.
411   D&C 70:8–10.
412   Matthew 25:21.
413   D&C 105:4–5.
414   D&C 88:107.
415   D&C 132:19.

we might expect that we would draw upon the Father's vast resources to improve and manage our stewardships, and, in turn, we would consecrate the resources thereof back to his higher kingdom to which we belong. If that is the case, if we intend to achieve that exalted state and live in that priesthood society, we must first learn to live the laws of consecration and stewardship here and now.

The Lord said, "And whoso is found a faithful, a just, and a wise steward shall enter into the joy of his Lord, and shall inherit eternal life."[416] And Elder McConkie added, "It is by the wise use of one's stewardship that eternal life is won."[417]

Accountability

As always, Jesus Christ sets the example for stewardship and accountability. We are taught that he is the steward as Creator under the Father's direction.[418] The Father creates everything spiritually; then Jesus creates everything physically as an exact duplicate of the spiritual.[419] Upon completion, he returns to the Father, gives his report, and the Father pronounces his approval. Just so, it behooves every steward to strive to discover the Father's spiritual creation of his stewardship, duplicate it according to the Father's vision, then return to the Father and report. We could receive no greater confirmation from the Father's commendation than that we were good and faithful servants.[420]

We see in Jesus' example all of the guiding principles of consecration. He exercises his agency to do the Father's will; he is given a stewardship in which he duplicates the Father's spiritual creation; he gives accountings to the Father of his management of his stewardship; and he brings to the stewardship his concerted labor. For this, Jesus is exalted on high and receives his Father's throne.

Accounting in Time and Eternity

All stewards ultimately receive their stewardships from the Father, and they must account for their stewardships to him. The Father delegates the giving of stewardships and the receiving of accountings to Jesus Christ, who is the Father's representative. It is Jesus Christ who will judge our efforts.[421]

In addition to our being accountable to the Father and the Son, we are also accountable to the Lord's representative. Clark V. Johnson wrote, "The Lord reminded his prophet, who subsequently reminded Church members, that they were the Lord's stewards and therefore, had to account for their stewardship 'both in time and in eternity.' (D&C 72:3; see also 70:4, 9.) The accounting procedures were quite clear. First, members accounted to the bishop for their stewardship as well as for their personal conduct. (D&C 72:5, 16–17; 104:12–13.) And second, they will ultimately account to their Father

---

416   D&C 51:19.
417   McConkie, *Mormon Doctrine,* 767.
418   Moses 7:29; John 1:1–3; Colossians 1:16–17; Hebrews 1:1–3; D&C 38:1–4; 76:22–24; Abraham 3:22–24.
419   McConkie, *Mormon Doctrine,* 170.
420   Matthew 25:21, 23.
421   Luke 16:2; 19:17.

in heaven."[422] The scripture states: "And an account of this stewardship will I require of them in the day of judgment."[423]

At the time of accounting, at least three things are certain in both time and eternity:

1. Diligence in lesser stewardships results in receiving greater stewardships: "And he that is a faithful and wise steward shall inherit all things."[424] "For he who is faithful and wise in time is accounted worthy to inherit the mansions prepared for him of my Father."[425]

2. The greater the stewardship, the greater the accountability: "To whom much is given, much is required."[426]

3. While the faithful and wise steward is rewarded, the unjust or slothful steward gains but little and may even lose what he has: "Take therefore the talent from him, and give it unto him which hath ten talents."[427] The stewardship continues, but the slothful steward loses the opportunity to work with it.

A stewardship that is extended through a Church calling is reported to the Lord's representative, who is the steward's immediate superior.[428] "For example, a ward Relief Society president reports to the bishop of her ward. A bishop reports to his stake president."[429] Zion people are under covenant to account for their earthly stewardships to the Lord's servant, the bishop: "Verily I say unto you, the elders of the church in this part of my vineyard shall render an account of their stewardship unto the bishop, who shall be appointed of me in this part of my vineyard. These things shall be had on record, to be handed over unto the bishop in Zion."[430] For this reason, we report our financial stewardship regarding our tithes and offerings to the bishop each year.

On the Day of Judgment, each of us will be required to render our report to Jesus Christ, who will give a report to the Father: "The primary accounting is with the Lord. He knows a person's heart, intentions, and talents."[431]

Accountability and Agency

In Galatians we read, "Be not deceived; God is not mocked: for whatsoever a man soweth, that shall he also reap."[432] That is, we are free to choose, but we are responsible for how we choose, and because our agency is a stewardship, we are accountable to God for our use of this gift.[433]

The principle of agency applies to how we manage the resources the Lord places in our hands. Mormon foresaw the latter-day abandonment of the concept of stewardship,

---

422   Johnson, "The Law of Consecration," 100.
423   D&C 70:4.
424   D&C 78:22.
425   D&C 72:3–4.
426   Luke 12:48; D&C 82:3.
427   Matthew 25:28.
428   Clarke, "Successful Welfare Stewardship," 81.
429   *Encyclopedia of Mormonism,* 1418.
430   D&C 72:5–6.
431   *Encyclopedia of Mormonism,* 1418.
432   Galatians 6:7.
433   Cannon, "Agency and Accountability," 88–89.

our contrary choices with regard to the Lord's resources, and our present abysmal lack of accountability: "Why do ye adorn yourselves with that which hath no life, and yet suffer the hungry, and the needy, and the naked, and the sick and the afflicted to pass by you, and notice them not? Yea, why do ye . . . cause that widows should mourn before the Lord, and also orphans to mourn before the Lord?"[434]

Our freedom to choose is a stewardship that carries accountability we cannot escape. When we receive any stewardship from the Lord, whether it be in the form of time, talents, resources, property, or any other good thing, we will render an accounting both in time and eternity. How we report will determine our receiving additional trusts, and our report will determine whether we qualify to receive all that the Father has or instead forfeit our stewardship and inherit little to nothing.

Labor

Consecration demands all that we have and are, including our effort. When we are given a stewardship from God, we magnify it by our labor. Elder Bruce R. McConkie wrote, "Work is the great basic principle which makes all things possible both in time and in eternity. Men, spirits, angels, and Gods use their physical and mental powers in work."[435]

Work, like other principles, exists in degrees ranging from telestial to celestial. Adam was commanded to work to support his family in this telestial world.[436] He made his labor a celestial endeavor by his attitude toward his work. He clearly understood that he was to use his stewardship to support his family and to support the kingdom of God for the establishment of Zion. He was not to use his stewardship, as did Cain, for empire building, plundering, extorting, leveraging, competing, augmenting his balance sheet, or amassing personal wealth on the backs of the poor, all of which are telestial approaches to labor. Rather, Adam worked to create the first Zion-like society upon the earth: Adam-ondi-Ahman. W. W. Phelps captures that idea in his hymn: "And men did live a holy race and worship Jesus face to face in Adam-ondi-Ahman."[437] There he labored to sustain his immediate family and to bless the lives of others.

Likewise, Enoch labored to support his family and to establish Zion, as did Melchizedek. Nephi is another example: "And it came to pass that I, Nephi, did cause my people to be industrious, and to labor with their hands."[438] Nephi's people worked together for the benefit of all. They labored to establish righteousness. They worked in unity to raise crops, smelt ore to create weapons for defense, and fashion objects of beauty. Together, they built buildings and a temple. Because of their celestial level of labor they were blessed with prosperity and familial strength: "And it came to pass that we began to prosper exceedingly, and to multiply in the land."[439] Things began to fall apart when the Nephites became selfish and began to work on a telestial level. Jacob chastised them for searching "for gold, and for silver,

---

434   Mormon 8:39–40.
435   McConkie, *Mormon Doctrine,* 847.
436   Genesis 3:19.
437   Phelps, "Adam-ondi-Ahman," *Hymns,* no. 49.
438   2 Nephi 5:17.
439   2 Nephi 5:10–16.

and for all manner of precious ores" for the purpose of obtaining riches "more abundantly
than that of your brethren," causing some errant Nephites to be "lifted up in the pride
of your hearts, and . . . suppose that ye are better than they."[440] This kind of labor is not
justified in Zion; it is condemned. President Kimball said, "As I understand these matters,
Zion can be established only by those who are pure in heart, and who labor for Zion, for the
'laborer in Zion shall labor for Zion; for if they labor for money [riches] they shall perish.'"[441]

Jacob taught the celestial law of labor and its underlying motivation: "Think of
your brethren like unto yourselves, and be familiar with all and free with your substance, that they may be rich like unto you. But before ye seek for riches, seek ye for
the kingdom of God. And after ye have obtained a hope in Christ ye shall obtain
riches, if ye seek them; and ye will seek them for the intent to do good—to clothe the
naked, and to feed the hungry, and to liberate the captive, and administer relief to
the sick and the afflicted."[442] Clearly, we must work, but what we work for determines
whether the work is telestial or celestial.

Idleness Condemned

"Idleness has no place [in Zion]," said President Benson, "and greed, selfishness, and covetousness are condemned. [Zion] may therefore operate only with a righteous people."[443]

When the Lord revealed the "law of the Church" (D&C 42), which sets forth the
law of consecration, he condemned the idler—both the poor and the rich idlers: "Thou
shalt not be idle; for he that is idle shall not eat the bread nor wear the garments of the
laborer."[444] The Lord insists that Zion be founded upon the principle of industry: "Behold, they have been sent to preach my gospel among the congregations of the wicked;
wherefore, I give unto them a commandment, thus: Thou shalt not idle away thy time,
neither shalt thou bury thy talent that it may not be known."[445]

The Idle Poor

The Lord denounces wanton idleness, its attendant pride, and the attitude of entitle-
ment: "Wo unto you poor men, whose hearts are not broken, whose spirits are not
contrite, and whose bellies are not satisfied, and whose hands are not stayed from laying
hold upon other men's goods, whose eyes are full of greediness, and who will not labor
with your own hands!"[446]

On the other hand, the Lord opens his storehouse to the poor who are trying their
best.[447] Beyond his agreeing to help the poor in their present circumstance, he promises to
compensate them for their suffering with rich abundance in the future: "But blessed are
the poor who are pure in heart, whose hearts are broken, and whose spirits are contrite, for

440 Jacob 2:12–14.
441 Kimball, *The Teachings of Spencer W. Kimball*, 363.
442 Jacob 2:17–19.
443 Benson, "A Vision and a Hope for the Youth of Zion," 74.
444 D&C 42:42.
445 D&C 60:13.
446 D&C 56:17.
447 Deuteronomy 15:7–11; 24:19; 2 Thessalonians 3:10.

they shall see the kingdom of God coming in power and great glory unto their deliverance; for the fatness of the earth shall be theirs. For behold, the Lord shall come, and his recompense shall be with him, and he shall reward every man, and the poor shall rejoice."[448]

On the other hand, the idle poor need to beware. To shirk one's familial duties or to approach a stewardship apathetically is akin to apostasy: "But if any provide not for his own, and specially for those of his own house, he hath denied the faith, and is worse than an infidel." Such people tend to perfect the skill of idleness by roaming here and there and preying on the goodhearted laborers: "And withal they learn [to be] idle, wandering about from house to house."[449]

The Lord warns that such idleness sets a bad example and will condemn the idlers and spill over into the next generation: "And the inhabitants of Zion also shall remember their labors, inasmuch as they are appointed to labor, in all faithfulness; for the idler shall be had in remembrance before the Lord. Now, I, the Lord, am not well pleased with the inhabitants of Zion, for there are idlers among them; and their children are also growing up in wickedness; they also seek not earnestly the riches of eternity, but their eyes are full of greediness. These things ought not to be, and must be done away from among them."[450]

Our mandate is to cease to be idle and expend exerted effort in all our stewardships—family, Church callings, time, talents, and everything that the Lord has given and all that we are. Our eternal salvation depends upon how well we labor: "Behold, I say unto you that it is my will that you should go forth and not tarry, neither be idle but labor with your might. . . . And again, verily I say unto you, that every man who is obliged to provide for his own family, let him provide, and he shall in nowise lose his crown; and let him labor. . . . Let every man be diligent in all things. And the idler shall not have place in the church, except he repent and mend his ways."[451]

However, when the legitimate poor need help, the Lord has provided a means of assistance. The Lord's stewards are to use the resources and surpluses of their stewardships to help the poor become self-reliant and independent as much as possible. Often, this aid comes through the bishop. The Lord has revealed a hierarchy of aid to the poor. When a person has done all he can temporally and spiritually, he should go first to his family for help and then the Church.[452] It makes sense. Both the family and the Church are Zion organizations charged with helping the poor.

But help does not stop there. Because we are "agents," who are commanded to "be anxiously engaged in a good cause, and do many things of [our] own free will, and bring to pass much righteousness,"[453] we must attack poverty and suffering wherever we encounter them, stretching forth a helping hand, lifting up the impoverished person and placing him in a situation where his labor will sustain him.

448   D&C 56:18–19.
449   1 Timothy 5:8, 13.
450   D&C 68:30–32.
451   D&C 75:3, 28–29.
452   "Statement of the Presiding Bishopric," 20.
453   D&C 58:27–28.

The Idle Rich

The rich who hold people in poverty, who living a life of luxury and idleness from the efforts of the poor people's labor, are also condemned by the Lord. An article in the 1936 *Improvement Era* reads: "'Suspended animation' is the prerogative of no man. . . . The fact that the man of comparative wealth needs no food or comfort or service does not excuse him from producing needful goods or services for those who are in want."[454]

Hugh Nibley offered this insight regarding the scripture about the idler: "'The idler shall not eat the bread of the laborer,' which means that the idle rich shall not eat the bread of the laboring poor. That's the way it has been throughout history; the poor have been ground down supporting the rich. Brigham said, 'Man has become so perverted as to debar his fellows as much as possible from these blessings, and constrain them by physical force or circumstances to contribute the proceeds of their labor to sustain the favored few.'"[455]

Hugh Nibley defined idlers as those who neglect laboring for Zion. He also denounced wealthy people whose riches allow them a life of pleasure while the poor suffer:

> An idler in the Lord's book is one who is not working for the building up of the kingdom of God on earth and the establishment of Zion, no matter how hard he may be working to satisfy his own greed. Latter-day Saints prefer to ignore that distinction as they repeat a favorite maxim of their own invention, that the idler shall not eat the bread or wear the clothing of the laborer. And what an ingenious argument they make of it! The director of a Latter-day Saint Institute was recently astounded when this writer pointed out to him that the ancient teaching that the idler shall not eat the bread of the laborer has always meant that the idle rich shall not eat the bread of the laboring poor, as they always have. "To serve the classes that are living on them," Brigham Young reports from England, "the poor, the laboring men and women are toiling, working their lives out to earn that which will keep a little life in them. Is this equality? No! What is going to be done? The Latter-day Saints will never accomplish their mission until this inequality shall cease on the earth." But the institute director was amazed, because he had always been taught that the idle poor should not eat the bread of the laboring rich, because it is perfectly obvious that a poor man has not worked as hard as a rich man. With the

---

454   Editorial, "The Right to Labor," *Improvement Era*, Sept. 1936.
    455   Nibley, *Teachings of the Book of Mormon*, Semester 1, 233, quoting Brigham Young, *Millennial Star* 17:673–74.

> same lucid logic my Latter-day Saint students tell me
> that there were no poor in the Zion of Enoch because
> only the well-to-do were admitted to the city.[456]

Clearly, the rich people in Zion are to labor alongside the poor for the cause of Zion. The rich are to lift the poor rather than suppress or ignore them. They are to increase their stewardships for the Lord's purposes and not their own, and those purposes, according to the covenant of consecration, are for the building up of God's kingdom on the earth and the establishment of Zion. Beyond these points, an idler is anyone, poor or rich, who is under covenant to advance the cause of Zion and does not.

The Virtue of Labor

President David O. McKay said, "Work brings happiness, and that happiness is doubled to him who initiates the work."[457] President Spencer W. Kimball concurred: "Work brings happiness, self-esteem, and prosperity. It is the means of all accomplishment; it is the opposite of idleness. We are commanded to work. Attempts to obtain our temporal, social, emotional, or spiritual well-being by means of a dole violate the divine mandate that we should work for what we receive. Work should be the ruling principle in the lives of our Church membership."[458]

On the day the Church was organized, the Lord linked labor with significant rewards. He declared, "I will bless all those who labor in my vineyard with a mighty blessing."[459] Later he said to Amos Davies the same thing he would say to each of us: "Let him . . . labor with his own hands that he may obtain the confidence of men."[460] Clearly, to qualify for double happiness, as President McKay said, along with self-respect, prosperity, gaining the confidence of our fellowmen, and receiving the Lord's mighty blessing, we must labor and consecrate that labor to the Lord.

Labor for What?

An intriguing verse concerning labor is found in 2 Nephi 26:31: "But the laborer in Zion shall labor for Zion; for if they labor for money they shall perish."[461] Obviously, we cannot be compensated with money for laboring in our Church callings. But this verse could also mean that laboring for money as a priority is unacceptable to Zion people. As we consider the hierarchy of compensation in a Zion person's life against the hierarchy of compensation that exists in Babylon, we realize that we might want to change our priorities. For example, a father in Zion must selflessly labor to support his family, provide for the education of his children, save for a rainy day, and build up the kingdom of God, but he is forbidden to step into Babylon and selfishly accumulate wealth for himself. The Lord has warned us: "Thou shalt not covet thine own property."[462]

---

456   Nibley, *Approaching Zion*, 240–41.
457   McKay, *Gospel Ideals*, 204.
458   Kimball, "Welfare Services," 76; referencing Genesis 3:19; D&C 42:42; 56:17; 68:30–32; 75:29.
459   D&C 21:9.
460   D&C 124:112.
461   2 Nephi 26:31.
462   Gardner, "Becoming a Zion Society," 31, quoting D&C 19:26.

Achieving balance can be challenging.

We are taught that laboring for money is strictly prohibited as we fulfill Church callings, but it is allowed when we labor to support our family and provide for their future needs. When we begin to view our responsibilities as stewardships, we begin to see where the delineation comes between providing for and selfishly accumulating. Stewards are under covenant to manage their stewardships and receive fair compensation according to the rules that govern those stewardships. As a test, we might ask ourselves if we recognize that everything we have belongs to the Lord and that we are merely stewards over our property. Are we doing with his money and resources what he has mandated, or do we seldom discuss with him his desires concerning them?

Speaking of labor in Zion, Hugh Nibley said: "The whole emphasis in the holy writ is not on whether one works or not, but what one works for: 'The laborer in Zion shall labor for Zion; for if they labor for money they shall perish' (2 Nephi 26:31). 'The people of the church began to wax proud, because of their exceeding riches . . . precious things, which they had obtained by their industry' (Alma 4:6) and which proved their undoing, for all their hard work. *In Zion you labor, to be sure, but not for money, and not for yourself.*"

Then, quoting Brigham Young, Brother Nibley said,

> "If we lust . . . for the riches of the world, and spare no pains [hard work] to obtain and retain them, and feel 'these are mine,' then the spirit of the anti-Christ comes upon us. This is the danger . . . [we] are in." Admirable and indispensable in themselves, hard work, ingenuity, and enterprise become an evil when they are misdirected, meaning directed to personal aggrandizement: "A man says, 'I am going to make iron, and I will have the credit of making the first iron in the Territory. I will have the credit of knowing how to flux the ore that is found in these regions, and bringing out the metal in abundance, or no other man shall.' Now, the beauty and glory of this kind of proceeding is the blackest of darkness, and its comeliness as deformity." An act, good in itself, becomes a monstrous deformity when thus misdirected.[463]

Building up the kingdom of God for the establishment of Zion should be the one and only reason a covenant Zion person labors. When he sees his family, career, time, talents, interests, Church callings, and everything good through the lens of Zion, he is approaching his labor according to the covenant of consecration. As Zion people, we must exert as much effort as possible in the cause of Zion; this is our calling and our stewardship: "Therefore, O ye that embark in the service of God, see that ye serve him

---

463   Nibley, *Approaching Zion,* 48–49; emphasis added.

with all your heart, might, mind and strength, that ye may stand blameless before God at the last day."[464]

A Zion person who has entered the new and everlasting covenant by baptism, who has thereafter been charged by the holy commission of the priesthood to draw out from Babylon the Lord's children, who has been washed clean and separated from the world, who has been anointed to receive a kingdom and a crown, who has been endowed with keys of knowledge and power, and who, finally, has been placed in an eternal kingdom— such a person can never again return to Babylon and labor as do the people of the world, laboring for the sake of money and claiming it as their own. To the laborers in Zion, the Lord said, "I give unto you a commandment, that every man, both elder, priest, teacher, and also member, go to with his might, with the labor of his hands, to prepare and accomplish the things which I have commanded."[465] What has he commanded? To labor to build up the kingdom of God for the establishment of Zion.

Augmenting the Effect of Labor

Perhaps one of the greatest discoveries we make in this life is that we can do very little of ourselves. What we might label genius or extraordinary ability has been given to us as a stewardship by God. He is the one who created us, who preserves us, who lends us breath, and who makes it possible for us to live and move and do according to our will from moment to moment.[466] He is our paymaster. Should he ever withdraw his Spirit from us, our fortunes would simultaneously collapse. Therefore, if we hope to support ourselves or prosper, we must always give thanks to God, obey him, and live according to his laws that govern consecration and stewardship. By doing so, we will augment the effects, effectiveness, and the rewards of our labor.

Jacob gave us the doctrine and the priorities of labor: "Think of your brethren like unto yourselves, and be familiar with all and free with your substance, that they may be rich like unto you. But before ye seek for riches, seek ye for the kingdom of God. And after ye have obtained a hope in Christ ye shall obtain riches, if ye seek them; and ye will seek them for the intent to do good—to clothe the naked, and to feed the hungry, and to liberate the captive, and administer relief to the sick and the afflicted."[467] That is, when we labor within the stipulations of the laws of consecration and stewardship, we place ourselves in a position to call upon the Lord to help us augment our labor to bless the lives of others, which is our covenant. In return, the Lord will answer our sincere petition and give us the resources to help us fulfill our consecration covenant.

An example of partnering with the Lord to augment our labor is the law of tithes and offerings. This law prospers, protects, and exalts its adherents. Malachi lists the stipulations and blessings of this law:
- *Prosperity.* From the fruits of our labors, we are to "bring . . . all the tithes into the storehouse, that there may be meat in mine house, and prove me now

464   D&C 4:2.
465   D&C 38:40.
466   Mosiah 2:21.
467   Jacob 2:17–19.

herewith, saith the Lord of hosts, if I will not open you the windows of heaven, and pour you out a blessing, that there shall not be room enough to receive it."

- *Protection.* "And I will rebuke the devourer for your sakes, and he shall not destroy the fruits of your ground; neither shall your vine cast her fruit before the time in the field, saith the Lord of hosts."
- *Exaltation.* "And all nations shall call you blessed: for ye shall be a delightsome land, saith the Lord of hosts."[468]

Because tithes and offerings are part of the law of consecration, and because stewardships are tithed, we may rely on the Lord's promises. He will augment our labors for our support, prosperity, protection, and exaltation. Then we are to use those blessings for the Lord's purposes: to bless our families and to bless the children of God.

Labor and Judgment

We read in the Doctrine and Covenants that we will give accountings to and receive rewards from the Lord in the Day of Judgment: "[When the Lord comes he will] recompense unto every man according to his work."[469] We determine our eternal status by our attitude toward labor and how we prioritize our efforts with regard to our stewardships.

Brigham Young said our achieving the celestial or a lower kingdom and our becoming a god or a servant will depend upon the quality of and our attitude toward labor. President Young compared many Saints in his day to the Savior's parable of the unprofitable servant: "'How shall I get this or that; how rich can I get; or, how much can I get out of this brother or from that brother?' and dicker and work, and take advantage here and there—no such man ever can magnify the priesthood nor enter the celestial kingdom. Now, remember, they will not enter that kingdom; and if they happen to go there, it will be because somebody takes them by the hand, saying, 'I want you for a servant'; or, 'Master, will you let this man pass in my service?' 'Yes, he may go into your service; but he is not fit for a lord, nor a master, nor fit to be crowned'; and if such men get there, it will be because somebody takes them in as servants."[470]

President Marion G. Romney taught that our salvation depends on our laboring to do all we can, whereupon we receive the Lord's grace to make up the difference. Further, he said, we cannot expect to achieve exaltation on the work of someone else. Exerting our own labor is the key to achieving exaltation as long as our labor is consistent with the laws of the celestial kingdom. From the days of Adam, the Lord has said that individual effort is the foundation of his spiritual and temporal economy. That economy demands "that the poor shall be exalted, in that the rich are made low."[471] By adhering to the Lord's economy, both the poor and the rich labor, and both are blessed: the poor are exalted by the rich and helped to become self-reliant, assuming that the poor are doing all they can do; the rich are made low (lowly in heart) when they help the poor by living the second commandment—"Thou

468   Malachi 3:10–12.
469   D&C 1:10; see also D&C 112:34.
470   Young, *Journal of Discourses*, 11:297.
471   D&C 104:16.

shalt love thy neighbour as thyself"[472]—and impart of their substance "according to the law of [the] gospel, unto the poor and the needy."[473] If we will prioritize our labor according to the law of consecration and strive with all our "heart, might, mind and strength" to labor for Zion and not for money, we will be able to "stand blameless before God at the last day."[474]

Summary and Conclusion

The guiding principles of the law of consecration are agency, stewardship, accountability, and labor. By abiding by these principles, we achieve equality, which is a characteristic of the celestial kingdom. That is, we are given equal access to the stewardships, inheritances, and resources of the Lord. The "order" this celestial system creates is to be considered "a permanent and everlasting establishment and order unto my church, to advance the cause, which ye have espoused, to the salvation of man, and to the glory of your Father who is in heaven."[475] Additionally, these guiding principles of consecration prepare us for the trials of the last days and the coming of the Savior.

Agency, stewardship, accountability, and labor form an unbreakable foundation upon which consecration thrives. God gives us both the liberty and the capability to choose and to act. By exercising our agency, we can choose to escape Babylon and flee to the safety of Zion and its covenants. There, we choose to enter into the new and everlasting covenant and follow the path to exaltation by receiving the oath and covenant of the priesthood, then the temple covenants and ordinances, which culminate with the law of consecration, one of the final covenants we must make in order to enter into God's presence and thereafter receive our eternal kingdom.

Now we are a Zion person. Now we choose to view everything we have and are as a stewardship, and thus we qualify to approach God so that he might make us independent and self-reliant, both temporally and spiritually. Now we are accountable stewards. As such, we have (1) freedom to use the proceeds of our stewardship to provide for our personal needs, and (2) the charge to consecrate the surplus of our stewardship to bless God's needy children. Moreover, we stewards agree to apply our diligent labor to our stewardship, striving always to create a physical manifestation of our stewardship according to what God has already created spiritually.

As we righteously discharge our stewardship, we enter into a system of celestial compensation; God becomes our paymaster. However our living is provided, we realize God is source of it.

The law of consecration stipulates that we be given agency to choose and act, but that we then consecrate our agency back to God in the form of a broken heart and a contrite spirit, allowing our will to be swallowed up in the will of the Father. In return, God agrees to take care of us and guide us as we manage the affairs of our stewardship. Furthermore, we agree to "live by every word that proceedeth forth from the mouth of

---

472   Matthew 22:39.
473   Romney, "'In Mine Own Way,'" 123.
474   D&C 4:2.
475   D&C 78:4.

God"[476] and become "submissive, meek, humble, patient, full of love," and "willing to submit" to the Lord.[477] Our effort allows him to bless "every man according to his wants and his needs, inasmuch as his wants are just—and all this for the benefit of the church of the living God, that every man may improve upon his talent, that every man may gain other talents, yea, even an hundred fold, to be cast into the Lord's storehouse, to become the common property of the whole church—every man seeking the interest of his neighbor, and doing all things with an eye single to the glory of God."[478] By doing these things, we are called profitable and just stewards.

Through choosing to live the covenant of consecration, we gain valuable skills that will benefit us in the celestial kingdom. There we "shall inherit thrones, kingdoms, principalities, and powers, dominions, all heights and depths."[479] Clearly, our celestial stewardships within our Father's kingdom will be vast; therefore we must choose to learn and live the principles of stewardship here and now. This is the promise: "And whoso is found a faithful, a just, and a wise steward shall enter into the joy of his Lord, and shall inherit eternal life."[480]

Because all stewardships originate with the Lord, we are accountable to him both in time and in eternity for our performance. While we are free to choose how we manage the Lord's resources, we are not free from being accountable to him. How we choose to handle our stewardships will determine our receiving additional trusts. Our eventually receiving all things or forfeiting our stewardship and inheriting nothing pivot on that choice.

Stewardships are invigorated by our labor. Upon the principle of labor we have another choice for which we are accountable: We can either choose to labor and build up the Lord's stewardship to ourselves, pillage its resources for our selfish benefit, claim the property as our own, and take credit for its performance—or we can choose to build up our stewardship for the support of the kingdom of God and the establishment of Zion, use the surplus resources to bless the lives of his children, acknowledge that our stewardship and all we have and are belong to the Lord, and give him all the glory. The question before us is always this: Are we laboring for ourselves or for God? For Babylon or for Zion?

Labor augments our stewardship. "Work is the great basic principle which makes all things possible both in time and in eternity. Men, spirits, angels, and Gods use their physical and mental powers in work."[481] To achieve the celestial kingdom our labor must mirror the celestial law of labor and its underlying motivation: "Think of your brethren like unto yourselves, and be familiar with all and free with your substance, that they may be rich like unto you. But before ye seek for riches, seek ye for the kingdom of God. And after ye have obtained a hope in Christ ye shall obtain riches, if ye seek them; and ye will seek them for the intent to do good—to clothe the naked, and to feed the hungry, and to liberate the captive, and administer relief to the sick and the afflicted."[482] Furthermore,

---

476   D&C 84:44.
477   Mosiah 3:19.
478   D&C 82:17–19; emphasis added.
479   D&C 132:19.
480   D&C 51:19.
481   McConkie, *Mormon Doctrine*, 847.
482   Jacob 2:17–19.

we can augment our labor and improve our stewardship by the principle of grace: we do all we can do then draw upon the Lord's help. The law of tithes and offerings is just such an augmenting principle: by giving a little and doing our best, this law returns us "an hundredfold" prosperity, protection, and exaltation.

Building up the kingdom of God for the establishment of Zion is the one and only reason that a covenant Zion person labors. Seen through the lens of Zion, this attitude permeates every manifestation of labor.

Idleness cannot land us in the celestial realm: "Thou shalt not be idle; for he that is idle shall not eat the bread nor wear the garments of the laborer.[483] The idle poor have no claim upon the Lord's resources; the idle rich are rebuked when they live from the efforts of the working poor. Any covenant person who does not labor for Zion is termed "idle," and thus is under condemnation. Only a celestial effort and attitude toward labor will transport us to where we want to be.

These guiding principles of the law of consecration prepare us for the Final Judgment. "[When the Lord comes he will] recompense unto every man according to his work."[484] Within the law of consecration, God has given us all that we need to qualify for the highest reward. Our agency allows us to choose and to act; our stewardship provides us a means of self-reliance and a way to fulfill our obligation to care for the Lord's children; our accountability gives us means to progress within the Lord's kingdom and to gain trust after trust, until we obtain exaltation; our labor bestows upon us double happiness, self-respect, prosperity, the confidence of our fellowmen, and the Lord's mighty blessing. Such is the genius of the law of consecration and its guiding principles.

---

483   D&C 42:42.
484   D&C 1:10; see also D&C 112:34.

Section 4
The Ultimate Test: God or Mammon

Jesus said we cannot serve God and mammon.[485] *Mammon* is "the standard Hebrew word for any kind of financial dealing."[486] Mammon is defined as riches,[487] or, we would say, love of riches. Serving both God and mammon is as impossible as simultaneously walking east and west.[488] The two are polar opposites, like love and hate. To the degree that we give our affection to one, we withhold our affection from the other: "Either [we] will hate the one, and love the other; or else [we] will hold to the one, and despise the other."[489] Neither can we choose to participate in both God's and Satan's economies: Zion and mammon. According to Hugh Nibley, "Every step in the direction of increasing one's personal holdings is a step away from Zion."[490]

The harshness and absoluteness of these statements is troubling. Of necessity, these statements spawn difficult questions. We hope sincere questioners will pursue answers until they discover the principles upon which a Zion life is built. We are saddened when other questioners disbelieve the statements, rationalize their mammon-seeking, or say that present-day realities discount the practicality of avoiding mammon. Almost all of us struggle with how to live this law. The quick answer, as we shall see, centers on the condition and the priorities of our hearts. There is no sin in wealth; there is sin only in setting our hearts on it and seeking it before seeking the kingdom of God; there is sin only in hoarding it rather than regarding it as a stewardship and disseminating it as the law of stewardship demands: to build up the kingdom of God for the establishment of Zion and to bless God's children. When we see wealth through the filter of Zion, we set ourselves up to become very prosperous, for Zion is always described as a place and condition of no lack and exceeding abundance. But that prosperity comes only when we have the right heart, the right motivations.

---

485 Matthew 6:24; Luke 16:13; 3 Nephi 13:24.
486 Nibley, *Approaching Zion,* 37.
487 Bible Dictionary, "Mammon," 728.
488 Hunter, Conference Report, Apr. 1964, 35.
489 Matthew 6:24.
490 Nibley, *Approaching Zion,* 37.

The Test of Riches

The harsh reality is this: life is a test. At the center of that test is money. Our attitude toward our financial dealings proves the condition of our hearts, as well as our loyalty, character, willingness to sacrifice, and trustworthiness. We can no more avoid this financial test than we can avoid choosing between the relentless opposing forces that try to influence our financial dealings. But choose we must. If we fool ourselves into believing that we can succeed in choosing *both* God and mammon, we are deceived. But that has not deterred many people from trying. Most of humanity has attempted to combine God and mammon, but not one person has ever succeeded. The moment we make the attempt, we have already chosen Satan and his economy. Jesus' words are perennially true: "No man can serve two masters."[491]

So what should we do? Should we take the concept to extremes, take a vow of poverty, shun money, and live lean like medieval monks? Of course not. "You always do have to handle things," Hugh Nibley says.

> But in what spirit do we do it? Not . . . by renunciation,
> for example. . . . If you refuse to be concerned with
> these things at all, and say, 'I'm above all that,' that's
> as great a fault. The things of the world have got to be
> administered; they must be taken care of, they are to be
> considered. We have to keep things clean, and in order.
> That's required of us. This is a test by which we are being proven. This is the way by which we prepare, always
> showing that these things will never captivate our
> hearts, that they will never become our principal concern. That takes a bit of doing, and that is why we have
> the formula 'with an eye single to his glory' (Mormon
> 8:15). Keep first your eye on the star, then on all the
> other considerations of the ship. You will have all sorts
> of problems on the ship, but unless you steer by the star,
> forget the ship. Sink it. You won't go anywhere.[492]

The test of wealth determines whether or not we can be trusted with God's resources—those things he has placed in our hands for safekeeping and prudent management. As accountable stewards, some pointed questions are always before us: Will we choose to remain within the guidelines of stewardship? Will we manage the stewardship according to God's desires, or will we "cheat" the Lord?[493] Will we redefine the terms of stewardship, claim ownership of the Lord's property, then enlarge and indulge ourselves with the proceeds rather than use the surplus for its intended use, which is to take care of God's

---

491   Romney, Conference Report, Oct. 1962, 94, quoting Matthew 6:24.
492   Nibley, *Approaching Zion*, 336.
493   Nibley, *Approaching Zion*, 426.

children and build up the kingdom of God for the establishment of Zion? Our answers to these questions determine our passing or failing the mortal test of riches.

Only the Pure in Heart Can Pass This Test

Without divine intervention, we cannot have the power to choose God over mammon. Babylon simply has too great a hold on the hearts of men. Consequently, only the pure in heart who receive a spiritual endowment can make this choice and thereafter live the law of consecration. The pure in heart alone receive spiritual help to view money for what it is and to put it in its proper place. They are children of Zion who do not venture into Babylon and partake of its philosophies. Rather, they enter the temple and make an informed, resolute covenant to receive and manage the Lord's property in an ordered way; then they return to the world and implement that covenant as the Lord directs. Clearly, this test is too hard for the natural man. Only those who know and love God can do it. Hence, *God or mammon* is the ultimate test that determines the condition of the heart and lands us in or out of the celestial kingdom. Nibley writes:

> God has always given his people the same choice of either living up to the covenants made with him or being in Satan's power; there is no middle ground (Moses 4:4). True, we spend this time of probation in a no-man's-land between the two camps of salvation and damnation, but at every moment of the day and night we must be moving toward the one or the other. Progressive testing takes place along the way in either direction; the same tests in every dispensation and generation mark the progress of the people of God.
>
> (1) Do you, first of all, agree to do things his way rather than your way—to follow the law of God? (2) If so, will you be obedient to him, no matter what he asks of you? (3) Will you, specifically, be willing to sacrifice anything he asks you for? (4) Will you at all times behave morally and soberly? (5) Finally, if God asks you to part with your worldly possessions by consecrating them all to his work, will you give his own back to him to be distributed as he sees fit, not as you think wise?
>
> That last test has been by far the hardest of all, and few indeed have chosen that strait and narrow way. The rich young man was careful and correct in observing every point of the law—up to that one; but that was too much for him, and the Savior, who refused to compromise or make a deal, could only send him off

sorrowing, observing to the apostles that passing that
test was so difficult to those possessing the things of the
world that only a special dispensation from God could
get them by.[494]

The Lord's Willingness to Be Tested

Perhaps because this test requires so much faith, the Lord both promises and offers evidence that if we will live the law of consecration, he will take care of us and even prosper us. The law of tithing, as we have observed, is one of his proofs: "Bring ye all the tithes into the storehouse, that there may be meat in mine house, *and prove me now herewith,* saith the Lord of hosts, if I will not open you the windows of heaven, and pour you out a blessing, that there shall be room enough to receive it."[495] Paying tithing is always an act of faith. The math doesn't make sense. Ten minus one is supposed to equal nine, but somehow when we pay our tithing the product is always more than ten. Clearly, celestial math is baffling in a telestial setting, and only faith can urge us on. But if we will persevere and apply the principle of tithing then experience the pouring out of blessings, we will be prepared to employ that principle in other consecrated offerings, which will require even greater faith.

Alma taught that faith grows like a seed.[496] First, faith takes root in our hearts as we hear the word of God.[497] Then it sprouts and blossoms by continual nourishing, which we are willing to do because we observe incremental proofs that the plant is growing.[498] Over time, the seed becomes a great, fruit-bearing tree.[499] Tithing is such a tree, and it provides us a way to test the Lord on the principle of consecration; tithing allows us and the Lord to get to know each other. Once we discover that the Lord will not let us down and that he will prosper us, we are willing to take the next step and pay offerings. Once again we discover the Lord's care and abundance, and, as we do, we grow in our appreciation of the principle of consecration until we can live the law according to its ideal. But every step of the way, between initial tithing and eventual total consecration, requires our venturing into the darkness of uncertainty, hoping and anticipating that the light will appear. Each step demands giving before we receive, and every time we take another step, it will make absolutely no mathematical sense. The laws in Babylon that govern finance will scream at us to hold back: "It won't work!" Only our testimony of the celestial laws of tithing and consecrated offerings can provide us the confidence that all will be well and that the outcome will result in safety and abundance. Nibley wrote:

> In giving his children the law, God repeatedly speci-
> fies that he is placing before them two ways, the ways

---

494   Nibley, *Approaching Zion,* 342.
495   Malachi 3:10; emphasis added.
496   Alma 32:28.
497   Romans 10:17.
498   Alma 32:28–37.
499   Alma 32:37–42.

of life and death, light and darkness. For parallel to the one law runs another. It is part of the plan that Satan should be allowed to try us and to tempt us to see whether we would prove faithful in all things: Who does not live up to every covenant made with the Lord will be in his power (cf. Moses 4:4, 5:23). So we find ourselves drawn in two directions (Moroni 7:11–13). *Thus this life becomes a special test of probation set before us in this world—it is an economic one. If the law of consecration is the supreme test of virtue—the final one—money is to be the supreme temptation to vice;* sex runs a poor second, but on both counts, this is the time and place for us to meet the challenge of the flesh. It is the weakness of the flesh in both cases to prove our spirits stronger than the pull of matter, to assert our command over the new medium of physical bodies before proceeding onward to another state of existence. As Brigham Young often repeats, "God has given us the things of this world to see what we will do with them." The test will be whether we will set our hearts on the four things that lead to destruction. Whoever seeks for (1) wealth, (2) power, (3) popularity, and (4) the pleasures of the flesh—anyone who seeks those will be destroyed, says the Book of Mormon (1 Nephi 22:23; 3 Nephi 6:15). Need we point out that those four things compose the whole substance of success in the present-day world. They are the things that money will get you.[500]

Tithing, therefore, is the *preparation* to become Zion-like; offerings are the *opportunity* to become Zion-like. In each case, God is willing to be put to the test. The only question remaining is, Are we? Do we really want to become Zion people or not?

Consecration Is All about Love

Certainly, the test of life centers on money, but it has more to do with proving the heart. Consecration is all about relationship: either we love God or we love mammon. If we give God our hearts, giving him our money is easy.

Think of a marriage. All lesser sacrifices are simple if we have offered our spouse our heart. But if we are selfish in any way, the marriage will be damaged and possibly fail. We recall that Ananias and Sapphira held back a portion of their consecration and lost

---

500   Nibley, *Approaching Zion*, 434–35; emphasis added.

their lives as a consequence of their selfishness.[501] Our covenant relationship with Christ is like a marriage. He is the Bridegroom, and we are his bride.[502] If both parties do not place their all on the altar and agree to live thereafter as *one*, meaning complete sacrifice, loyalty, and trust, the relationship will crumble, leaving the two with hollow words and pitiful, surface-level acts of devotion. A husband who will not share his money with his wife is selfish and abusive; if he cannot give his wife his money, he cannot give his wife his heart. The same could be said of a wife who selfishly withholds anything from her husband. Just so, the sacrifice of our money for the purposes of God provides singular *proof* that we love God above every other consideration. Consecration is how we prove our love for God and his children.

A Change of Orders

At the outset of the Doctrine and Covenants, the great Jehovah declared that the order of Babylon, which has oppressed God's people for millennia, was all but used up. "The Lord insists that the whole history of the world is about to turn on its hinges," said Hugh Nibley. "It will change; this is not an order with which he is pleased."[503] Now a new order—*Zion*—is about to burst upon the stage of human history. Zion's advent will be an act of mercy for the salvation of all mankind.[504]

From the moment of the First Vision, Christ drew a line in the sand: Babylon on one side, and Zion on the other. His call for the Saints to flee Babylon is the same call he has issued in past dispensations: "Come out of her, my people, that ye be not partakers of her sins, and that ye receive not of her plagues."[505] Once escaped from Babylon, we are not to turn back; rather, we are to embrace a new way of life: "Ye shall not live after the manner of the world."[506] Forevermore, mammon-seeking is strictly forbidden in Zion: "Touch not the evil gift, nor the unclean thing."[507] From the moment we make that decision, we will feel like and be viewed as "strangers"[508] in the earth. But that should not be a concern for Zion people. The world as it presently exists is not our home; someday Babylon and its citizenry will fall,[509] and we, the children of Zion, will inherit the earth.[510] Until then, we are to live among the people of Babylon with the charge to call as many of them out as possible. But in no case are we to be absorbed by them; rather, we are to be the "light of the world" as our ruler, the King of Zion,[511] is *the* Light of the world.[512]

A first step toward Zion is to recognize where we live. When Adam and Eve "found" themselves in the lone and dreary world—a discovery all of us must make—they

---

501 Acts 5:1–5.
502 Isaiah 61:10; 62:5; Jeremiah 7:34; 16:9; 25:10; 33:11; Joel 2:16; John 3:29; Revelation 18:23.
503 Nibley, *Approaching Zion*, 331.
504 D&C 1.
505 Revelation 18:4.
506 D&C 95:13.
507 Moroni 10:30.
508 D&C 45:13.
509 Revelation 18:2.
510 Matthew 5:5; 3 Nephi 12:5; D&C 59:2.
511 Moses 7:53.
512 Matthew 5:14; John 8:12.

immediately sought heavenly help to get back home.[513] This world is not our home, and we must not set up camp here. Our movement should be away and up, and, in the process of going, we must take with us as many people as possible.

Love of Money Is the Root of *All* Evil

Few statements are as sweeping as Paul's denunciation of covetousness: "For the love of money is the root of all evil."[514] In one sentence he identifies the origin of all sin: "the love of money." The implications of this statement are huge. Lying, sexual transgression, taking God's name in vain, breaking the Sabbath day, pride—every transgression that grows on the tree of sin can be traced to its root cause: a covetous attitude about money and possessions. Those who embrace this attitude are caught in Satan's snare, from which there is little hope of escape: "But they that will be rich fall into temptation and a snare, and into many foolish and hurtful lusts, which drown men in destruction and perdition." Paul warns that those who persist in pursuing wealth "have erred from the faith, and pierced themselves through with many sorrows." This condition is one from which we must run: "But thou, O man of God, flee these things; and follow after righteousness, godliness, faith, love, patience, meekness." In the economy of God, Paul explains, "great gain" is defined as "godliness with contentment."[515]

The Book of Mormon prophet Jacob listed the love of money as one of the foremost offenses against God. Hugh Nibley wrote:

> It is at the climax of his great discourse on the Atonement that Jacob cries out, "But wo unto the rich, who are rich as to the things of the world. For because they are rich they despise the poor." This is a very important statement, setting down as a general principle that the rich as a matter of course despise the poor, for "their hearts are upon their treasures; wherefore, their treasure is their God. And behold, their treasure shall perish with them also" (2 Nephi 9:30). Why does Jacob make this number one in his explicit list of offenses against God? Because it is the number-one device among the enticings of "that cunning one" (2 Nephi 9:39), who knows that riches are his most effective weapon in leading men astray. You must choose between being at one with God or with Mammon, not both; the one promises everything in this world for money, the other a place in the kingdom after you have "endured the crosses of the world, and despised the shame of it," for only so can you "inherit the kingdom of God, which was prepared for them from the

---

513   Moses 5:4–12.
514   1 Timothy 6:10.
515   1 Timothy 6:6–11.

foundation of the world," and where your "joy shall be full forever" (2 Nephi 9:18). Need we point out that the main reason for having money is precisely to avoid "the crosses of the world, and . . . the shame of it"?[516]

The counsel given by President Anthon H. Lund in 1903 is applicable today:

> The Lord, in one of His revelations given very early in the Church, says: "Seek not for riches, but for wisdom and, behold, the mysteries of God shall be unfolded unto you, and then shall you be made rich; behold he that hath eternal life is rich." The riches of eternal life we ought to seek, not the riches of the world. There is a raging thirst for riches in this land. The love of money is growing, even in our midst. We do not look upon wealth in itself as a curse. We believe that those who can handle means rightly can do much to bless their fellows. But he who is ruled by the love of money is tempted to commit sin. The love of money is the root of all evil. *There is hardly a commandment but is violated through this seeking for riches.*[517]

Covetousness—The Last Law

"Thou shalt not covet," Jehovah commanded Israel.[518] This was the last law given in the Ten Commandments. In our day, the Lord repeated the injunction: "I command thee that thou shalt not covet thy neighbor's wife. . . . I command thee that thou shalt not covet thine own property, but impart it freely [for the building up of the kingdom of God]."[519] Joseph Smith expanded on the subject of the last law: "God cursed the children of Israel because they would not receive the last law from Moses. . . . The Israelites prayed that God would speak to Moses and not to them; in consequence of which he cursed them with a carnal law." The Prophet then went on to apparently connect the law of covetousness with the fulness of the priesthood: "Abraham gave a tenth part of all his spoils and then received a blessing under the hands of Melchizedek *even the last law or a fulness of the law or priesthood* which constituted him a king and priest after the order of Melchizedek or an endless life."[520]

Whether or not the Prophet intended a dual meaning here is not known, but the noticeable connection is sobering. A review of history substantiates that the Israelites rejected the last law—"Thou shalt not covet"—and simultaneously they rejected the last law "or a fulness of the law" of the priesthood, which would have made them kings and priests after

---

516   Nibley, *Approaching Zion*, 592–93.
517   Lund, Conference Report, Apr. 1903, 97.
518   Exodus 20:17.
519   D&C 19:25–26.
520   Smith, *Words of Joseph Smith*, 245–46; emphasis added.

the order of Melchizedek, which same order would have brought them to an endless life: "Now this Moses plainly taught to the children of Israel in the wilderness, and sought diligently to sanctify his people that they might behold the face of God; but they hardened their hearts and could not endure his presence; therefore, the Lord in his wrath, for his anger was kindled against them, swore that they should not enter into his rest while in the wilderness, which rest is the fulness of his glory. Therefore, he took Moses out of their midst, and the Holy Priesthood also."[521] We simply cannot break this last law, *avoiding covetousness,* and expect to receive the fulness of the priesthood along with its attendant blessings.

As the prohibition against covetousness was the last law given in the lesser law, the law of consecration is the last law given in the higher law. Consecration protects us from covetousness and idolatry by prescribing the usage of our surpluses. If we keep this last law, we will prosper and experience abundance beyond any telestial effort we might make to enrich ourselves.

The Higher and Lower Laws of Prosperity

Mormon describes the two systems of prosperity. Beginning with the higher law, he said:

> And now, because of the steadiness of the church they began to be exceedingly rich, having abundance of all things whatsoever they stood in need—an abundance of flocks and herds, and fatlings of every kind, and also abundance of grain, and of gold, and of silver, and of precious things, and abundance of silk and fine-twined linen, and all manner of good homely cloth.
>
> And thus, in their prosperous circumstances, they did not send away any who were naked, or that were hungry, or that were athirst, or that were sick, or that had not been nourished; and they did not set their hearts upon riches; therefore they were liberal to all, both old and young, both bond and free, both male and female, whether out of the church or in the church, having no respect to persons as to those who stood in need.
>
> *And thus they did prosper and become far more wealthy than those who did not belong to their church.*
>
> For those who did not belong to their church did indulge themselves in sorceries, and in idolatry or idleness, and in babblings, and in envyings and strife; wearing costly apparel; being lifted up in the pride of their own eyes; persecuting, lying, thieving, robbing, committing whoredoms, and murdering, and all manner of wickedness.[522]

521   D&C 84:23–25.
522   Alma 1:29–32; emphasis added.

When the Lord determines to enrich us, we become rich indeed. But when we attempt to enrich ourselves, our abundance will subsist only for a season, and in the end we will be left impoverished, temporally, emotionally, and spiritually.

The More Weighty Matters

The Lord's invitation to us is always the same: renounce mammon and choose God; flee Babylon and come to Zion. We hear his voice crying, "Therefore, come up hither unto the land of my people, even Zion." Our success in arriving in Zion depends upon our attitude toward money: "Let them repent of all their sins, and of all their covetous desires, before me, saith the Lord; for what is property unto me? saith the Lord." That is, the things of the world are but a drop in the vast ocean of possible blessings—"the weighty matters"—and those weighty blessings await those who will make the effort: "Is there not room enough on the mountains of Adam-ondi-Ahman, and on the plains of Olaha Shinehah, or the land where Adam dwelt, that you should covet that which is but the drop, and neglect the more weighty matters?"[523] Obviously, weighty blessings flow from our attending to weighty matters and not from coveting "the drop."

Those who insist on remaining in Babylon or trying to keep one foot there and the other in Zion may expect the Lord's cursing: "Ye are cursed because of your riches, and also are your riches cursed because ye have set your hearts upon them, and have not hearkened unto the words of him who gave them unto you." This despicable condition is evidence of breaking our oath of obedience; it is a manifestation of disloyalty to God and the abandonment of our lawful affections. We are under covenant to always remember the Lord,[524] his gifts,[525] and the poor,[526] but we too often remember and love our riches: "Ye do not remember the Lord your God in the things with which he hath blessed you, but ye do always remember your riches, not to thank the Lord your God for them; yea, your hearts are not drawn out unto the Lord, but they do swell with great pride, unto boasting, and unto great swelling, envyings, strifes, malice, persecutions, and murders, and all manner of iniquities." In this condition, we sometimes wonder why we are not receiving the Lord's favor. His answer is an indictment of our covetous behavior: "For this cause hath the Lord God caused that a curse should come upon the land, and also upon your riches, and this because of your iniquities."[527]

Who could blame him? Our affections are elsewhere, and we hardly give him a second thought. Clearly, covetousness is akin to adultery.

Trying to Mix Mammon and Zion

With an eye on our day, Mormon apparently searched Nephite history to find a parallel to describe the consequences of the latter-day epidemic of wealth-seeking. He discovered

---

523   D&C 117:4, 8.
524   D&C 20:77, 79.
525   D&C 46:10.
526   D&C 42:30; 52:40.
527   Helaman 13:21–23.

a perfect example in the Zoramites. Nibley wrote about the Zoramites' sin of combining God and mammon:

> Alma found them [the Zoramites] to be the wicked-est people in the world. He couldn't believe that people could be so evil. . . . With all their [supposed] virtues, they set their hearts upon riches (Alma 31:24–38). Alma couldn't stand it. He couldn't look at it anymore. It hurt too much. How could people be so wicked? This is what was wrong: "Behold, O my God, their costly apparel, and their ringlets, and their bracelets, and their ornaments of gold, and all their precious things which they are orna-mented with; and behold, their hearts are set upon them, and yet they cry unto thee and say—We thank thee, O God, for we are a chosen people unto thee, while others shall perish" (Alma 31:28). "O, how long, O Lord, wilt thou suffer that thy servants shall dwell here below in the flesh, to behold such gross wickedness among the children of men? Behold, O God, they cry unto thee, and yet their hearts are swallowed up in their pride. Behold, O God, they cry unto thee with their mouths" (Alma 31:26–27). Remember, they went to church once a week, and they bore their testimony, and they were very strict in dress regulations, and so forth. They were brave and courageous and enterprising and prosperous and all those other things—but this was what was wrong: . . . "They cry unto thee with their mouths, while they are puffed up, even to greatness, . . . [with] their ringlets; . . . and behold, their hearts are set upon them, and yet they cry unto thee and say [at the same time], We thank thee, O God, for we are a chosen people unto thee" (Alma 31:27–28). And that was what the great crime was. *Don't try to combine the two.*[528]

The Zoramites had fallen into a snare. In order to justify laying claim to their wealth, they pointed to their pretended piety, "supposing gain is godliness."[529] Of course, we are taught that true godliness is tied to the covenants and ordinances of the temple, not to money.[530] In this account, the two economies suddenly become clear: On the one hand, we see hypocrites, the worst of sinners according to Jesus, they who insist "on proper dress and grooming, their careful observance of all the rules, their precious concern for

---

status symbols, their strict legality, their pious patriotism,"[531] they who appear to be good and blessed because they are rich,[532] all the while turning a blind eye to the poor; and on the other hand, we see the penitent, meek folk, who are poor in heart, seeking the word of God, and ultimately being pronounced by the prophet as "blessed."[533] Some of the greatest teachings found in the Book of Mormon were given to these humble followers of Christ, and, as we know, they finally received as a reward an inheritance in a land of promise,[534] symbolizing that they had achieved Zion.

In this dispensation, the early Saints' attempt to mix Zion with mammon broke Joseph Smith's heart. Speaking to the Saints in Far West, Missouri, concerning covetousness, he said:

> Brethren, we are gathering to this beautiful land to build up Zion; Zion, which is the pure in heart. But since I have been here I have perceived the spirit of selfishness. Covetousness exists in the hearts of the Saints which is not becoming to those who have received the gospel. Here are those who begin to spread out buying up all the land they are able to [get] to the exclusion of the poor ones who are not so much blessed with this world's goods, thinking to lay foundations for themselves, only looking to their own individual families and those who are to follow them. *Now I want to tell you that Zion cannot be built up in any such way.* We are called out from this world to learn God's ways, to become one, looking each to his brother's interest and his welfare, the widow, the fatherless, and poor without distinction. I see signs put out, beer signs, speculative schemes are being introduced. This is the way of the world, Babylon indeed, and I tell you in the name of the God of Israel, if there is not repentance with this people and a turning from ungodliness, covetousness, and self-will, you will be broken up and scattered from this choice land to the four winds of heaven. For the Lord will have a people who will serve him and keep his commandments humbly, each one seeking his neighbor's welfare, to preach the gospel, gather the poor, and aid them, and build up a holy city unto our God.[535]

531   Nibley, *Approaching Zion*, xvi.
532   Nibley, *Approaching Zion*, xxi.
533   Alma 32:2–8.
534   Alma 35:9.
535   Stevenson, *Life and History of Elder Edward Stevenson*, 40–41; emphasis added.

Covetousness broke the heart of Brigham Young, too.

> What does the Lord want of us up here in the tops of
> these mountains? He wishes us to build up Zion. What
> are the people doing? They are merchandizing, trafficking
> and trading . . . making [the merchants] immensely rich.
> We all have our pursuits, our different ways of supplying
> ourselves with the common necessaries of life and also its
> luxuries. This is right and the possession of earthly wealth
> is right, if we follow our varied pursuits, and amass the
> wealth of this life for the purpose of advancing righteous-
> ness and building up the kingdom of God on earth. But
> how easy it is to wander from the path of righteousness.
> We toil days and months to attain a certain degree of per-
> fection, a certain victory over a failing or weakness, and
> in an unguarded moment slide back again to our former
> state. How quickly we become darkened in our minds
> when we neglect our duties to God and each other, and
> forget the great objects of our lives."[536]

On another occasion, he said:

> [The Saints] do not know what to do with the revela-
> tions, commandments and blessings of God. Talking, for
> instance about everyday things, how many do we see here
> that know what to do with money and property when
> they get it? Are their eyes single to the building up of
> the kingdom of God? No; they are single to the building
> up of themselves. . . . There are few who understand the
> principles of the kingdom and whose eyes are single to the
> building of it up in all respects; but their eyes are like the
> fool's eye—looking to the ends of the earth. They want
> this and that, and they do not know what to do; they lack
> wisdom. By-and-by, perhaps, their wealth will depart from
> them, and when left poor and penniless, they will humble
> themselves before the Lord that they may be saved.[537]

Warnings against Compromise

As we've said, we cannot embrace Zion and mammon simultaneously. Hugh Nibley wrote:
"Brigham Young and Joseph often warned the Saints about subsiding into this telestial

---

536   Young, *Journal of Discourses*, 12:155.
537   Young, *Journal of Discourses*, 11:325.

order. Even though the Lord said that Zion could not be built up unless it is in the principle of the law (otherwise I cannot receive her unto myself), the Latter-day Saints still wanted to compromise and say, 'We will not go up unto Zion, and will keep our moneys' (D&C 105:8). But as long as that was their plan, there could be no Zion, they were told."[538]

The Lord rhetorically asked, "For shall the children of the kingdom pollute my holy land?" Then, answering his own question, he said, "Verily, I say unto you, Nay."[539] We have a clear choice to make if we truly desire Zion over all other affections: either we forsake the world and come to the Lord's marriage or we languish in Babylon to tend our property and peddle our merchandise; but we cannot do both.[540] "'Israel, Israel, God is calling,' we often sing, 'Babylon the great is falling,' But we have taken our stand between them; Brigham Young speaks of Latter-day Saints who want to take Babylon by one hand and Zion by the other—it won't work."[541]

Making Mammon Holy

We try to legitimize our desiring mammon by trying to find something holy about pursuing it. Brigham Young describes such people: "Elders of Israel are greedy after the things of this world. If you ask them if they are ready to build up the kingdom of God, their answer is prompt—'Why, to be sure we are, with our whole souls; but we want first to get so much gold, speculate and get rich, and then we can help the Church considerably. We will go to California and get gold, go and buy goods and get rich, trade with the emigrants, build a mill, make a farm, get a large herd of cattle, and then we can do a great deal for Israel.' When will you be ready to do it? 'In a few years, Brother Brigham, if you do not disturb us.'"[542]

In our desperation to continue to seek mammon while still retaining our standing in Zion, we sometimes grasp for scriptural comfort. Often we point to the parable of the talents.[543] We say to ourselves, "Surely we are to increase our holdings if we are to be nominated as good stewards." But, according to the scriptures, there is a vast difference between expanding our stewardship for the kingdom's sake and expanding it for the sake of personal wealth. Jacob gives us the key: "But before ye seek for riches, seek ye for the kingdom of God." First the kingdom, then riches! "And *after* ye have obtained a hope in Christ [notice the sequence] ye shall obtain riches, if ye seek them; and ye will seek them for the intent to do good—to clothe the naked, and to feed the hungry, and to liberate the captive, and administer relief to the sick and the afflicted."[544] Clearly, we are not justified in seeking riches *before* (or even *simultaneously*) we seek the kingdom of God; but *after* we obtain a hope in Christ, we may ask for riches with the intent to "level people up." Jacob says, "Think of your brethren like unto yourselves, and be familiar with

538   Nibley, *Approaching Zion*, 331.
539   D&C 84:59.
540   Matthew 22:2–14.
541   Nibley, *Approaching Zion*, 279.
542   Young, *Journal of Discourses*, 1:164–65.
543   Matthew 25:14–30.
544   Jacob 2:18–19; emphasis added.

all and free with your substance, that they may be rich like unto you."[545] It is this attitude toward money that brings us to a hope in Christ, and it is this attitude that places us in a position to make a request for more resources to bless more people.

We can become rich by following either Zion's way or Babylon's way. But before we decide which way to go, we ought to at least know where the two ways will lead us. The Zion way will land us in heaven, while the Babylon way will land us elsewhere—not in heaven. We might try to convince ourselves otherwise, but in the end it will not make a difference. We can no more make mammon holy than we can possess it and Zion, too. We cannot have it both ways.

Mormon's View of the Last Days

Few condemnations of mammon are harsher than Moroni's. Understanding our day perhaps better than we do, the last Nephite prophet described a latter-day scene of unequalled depravity, rivaling the days of Noah.[546] "Behold, I speak unto you as if ye were present, and yet ye are not. But behold, Jesus Christ hath shown you unto me, and I know your doing. And I know that ye do walk in the pride of your hearts; and there are none save a few only who do not lift themselves up in the pride of their hearts, unto the wearing of very fine apparel, unto envying, and strifes, and malice, and persecutions, and all manner of iniquities; and your churches, yea, even every one, have become polluted because of the pride of your hearts. *For behold, ye do love money, and your substance, and your fine apparel, and the adorning of your churches, more than ye love the poor and the needy, the sick and the afflicted."*[547]

We often read these verses and congratulate ourselves that we are not part of that wretched group . . . until Moroni points his finger at the hypocritical Saints who have polluted the holy church of God: "O ye pollutions, ye hypocrites, ye teachers, who sell yourselves for that which will canker, why have ye polluted the holy church of God? Why are ye ashamed to take upon you the name of Christ? Why do ye not think that greater is the value of an endless happiness than that misery which never dies—because of the praise of the world? Why do ye adorn yourselves with that which hath no life, and yet suffer the hungry, and the needy, and the naked, and the sick and the afflicted to pass by you, and notice them not?"[548]

Moroni's question hangs answerless. We have no excuse. The prophet saw us as we really are. Our actions indict us. They are, and always have been, in open prophetic view.

The First Commandments of This Dispensation

A full year before the organization of the Church, the Lord gave Joseph Smith and Oliver Cowdery the first two commandments pertaining to his latter-day kingdom: (1) "Seek

---

545 Jacob 2:17.
546 Joseph Smith–Matthew 1:41.
547 Mormon 8:35–37; emphasis added.
548 Mormon 8:38–39.

to bring forth and establish the cause of Zion"; (2) "Seek not for riches but for wisdom." The promised blessings would eclipse anything Babylon could offer: "And behold, the mysteries of God shall be unfolded unto you, and then shall you be made rich. Behold, he that hath eternal life is rich."[549] Then, one month later, as if to accomplish the law of witnesses,[550] the Lord repeated these commandments verbatim to Hyrum Smith.[551] Thus, the initial witnesses of the Restoration (Joseph and Oliver), and the ultimate witnesses (Joseph and Hyrum) who would seal their testimony with blood, were given the first two commandments that would define all commandments that would follow.

These first commandments stand in stark contrast to Satan's first commandment: *Everything shall have a price.* "Satan's first article of faithlessness has been repeated with creedal clarity since the beginning: One can buy anything in this world for money. It is a hellish philosophy, and those who operate in harmony with it sell that which is priceless for a paltry sum."[552] From the earliest moment in the Garden of Eden, Hugh Nibley wrote:

> [Satan] flares up in his pride and announces what his program for the economic and political order of the new world is going to be. He will take the resources of the earth, and with precious metals as a medium of exchange he will buy up military and naval might, or rather those who control it, and so will govern the earth—for he is the prince of this world. He does rule: he is king. Here at the outset is the clearest possible statement of a military-industrial complex ruling the earth with violence and ruin. But as we are told, this cannot lead to anything but war, because it has been programmed to do that. It was conceived in the mind of Satan in his determination 'to destroy the world' (Moses 4:6). The whole purpose of the program is to produce blood and horror on this earth.[553]

The central issue contained in these first two commandments concerns the definition and use of treasure. Consider the results of the two philosophies:

Zion: "Lay not up for yourselves treasures upon earth, where moth and rust doth corrupt, and where thieves break through and steal: But lay up for yourselves treasures in heaven, where neither moth nor rust doth corrupt, and where thieves do not break through nor steal: For where your treasure is, there will your heart be also."[554]

Babylon: "But wo unto the rich, who are rich as to the things of the world. For because they are rich they despise the poor, and they persecute the meek, and their

---

549   D&C 6:6–7.
550   Deuteronomy 19:15.
551   D&C 11:6–7.
552   McConkie and Millet, *Doctrinal Commentary on the Book of Mormon,* 1:302.
553   Nibley, *Approaching Zion,* 92.
554   Matthew 6:19–21.

hearts are upon their treasures; wherefore, their treasure is their God. And behold, their treasure shall perish with them also."[555]

No Security in Mammon

The quest for riches is a powerful opiate and Satan's most "deadly and effective" weapon.[556] Seeking security in mammon was detected by Nephi as a latter-day Satanic strategy to destroy the Latter-day Saints: "And others will he pacify, and lull them away into carnal security, that they will say: All is well in Zion; yea, Zion prospereth, all is well—and thus the devil cheateth their souls, and leadeth them away carefully down to hell."[557] President Spencer W. Kimball drew a distinction between the economies of Babylon and Zion: "Zion can be built up only among those who are the pure in heart, not a people torn by covetousness or greed, but a pure and selfless people. Not a people who are pure in appearance, rather a people who are pure in heart. Zion is to be in the world and not of the world, not dulled by a sense of carnal security, nor paralyzed by materialism. No, Zion is not things of the lower, but of the higher order, things that exalt the mind and sanctify the heart."[558] Seeking mammon and attempting to find security in it is an illusion and a cheap trick of the devil.

Brigham Young had much to say against worshiping mammon for security: "I would as soon see a man worshipping a little god made of brass or of wood as see him worship his property. . . . Does this congregation understand what idolatry is? The New Testament says that covetousness is idolatry; therefore, a covetous people is an idolatrous people."[559] President Young focused the last year of his life on preaching against the folly of idolatry: "We wish the wealth or things of the world; we think about them morning, noon and night; they are first in our minds when we awake in the morning, and the last thing before we go to sleep at night."[560] And at another time he said: "One man has his eye on a gold mine, another is for a silver mine, another is for marketing his flour or his wheat, another for selling his cattle, another to raise cattle, another to get a farm, or building here and there, and trading and trafficking with each other, just like Babylon. . . . Babylon is here, and we are following in the footsteps of the inhabitants of the earth, who are in a perfect sea of confusion. Do you know this? You ought to, for there are none of you but what see it daily. . . . The Latter-day Saints [are] trying to take advantage of their brethren. There are Elders in this Church who would take the widow's last cow, for five dollars, and then kneel down and thank God for the fine bargain they had made."[561]

At one point the Lord allowed the Saints in wisdom to associate prudently with mammon: "And now, verily I say unto you, and this is wisdom, make unto yourselves friends

---

555   2 Nephi 9:30.
556   Nibley, *Approaching Zion*, 39, 332.
557   2 Nephi 28:21.
558   Kimball, *The Teachings of Spencer W. Kimball*, 363.
559   Young, *Journal of Discourses*, 6:196–97.
560   Young, *Journal of Discourses*, 18:239.
561   Young, *Journal of Discourses*, 17:41–42.

with the mammon of unrighteousness, and they will not destroy you."[562] So that we do not see in this scripture a ticket to depart Zion and enter Babylon, Hugh Nibley clarifies, "This was only to save their lives in an emergency."[563] Wisdom demands that when we read this verse, we cross-reference it with Zenos's allegory of the olive tree. We recall that the tree's natural branches temporarily needed crucial nourishing from the wild trees, but only to preserve them for a season. Their destiny was always to be grafted back into their mother tree, and the destiny of the wild branches was always to be clipped and burned.[564]

Slippery Treasures

There is no security in mammon. Riches are hard to hold and manage—they are "slippery." They can collapse under the instability of financial markets, a dishonest or incompetent partner, or one bad personal decision. Riches are built on the same foundation as the great and spacious building—a foundation of air.[565] Helaman warned his people of the folly of seeking security in mammon:

> And behold, the time cometh that he curseth your riches, that they become slippery, that ye cannot hold them; and in the days of your poverty ye cannot retain them.
>
> And in the days of your poverty ye shall cry unto the Lord; and in vain shall ye cry, for your desolation is already come upon you, and your destruction is made sure; and then shall ye weep and howl in that day, saith the Lord of Hosts. And then shall ye lament, and say:
>
> O that I had repented, and had not killed the prophets, and stoned them, and cast them out. Yea, in that day ye shall say: O that we had remembered the Lord our God in the day that he gave us our riches, and then they would not have become slippery that we should lose them; for behold, our riches are gone from us.
>
> Behold, we lay a tool here and on the morrow it is gone; and behold, our swords are taken from us in the day we have sought them for battle.
>
> Yea, we have hid up our treasures and they have slipped away from us, because of the curse of the land.
>
> O that we had repented in the day that the word of the Lord came unto us; for behold the land

---

562   D&C 82:22.
563   Nibley, *Approaching Zion*, 20.
564   Jacob 5.
565   1 Nephi 8:26.

is cursed, and all things are become slippery, and we cannot hold them.

Behold, we are surrounded by demons, yea, we are encircled about by the angels of him who hath sought to destroy our souls. Behold, our iniquities are great. O Lord, canst thou not turn away thine anger from us? And this shall be your language in those days.

But behold, your days of probation are past; ye have procrastinated the day of your salvation until it is everlastingly too late, and your destruction is made sure; yea, for ye have sought all the days of your lives for that which ye could not obtain; and ye have sought for happiness in doing iniquity, which thing is contrary to the nature of that righteousness which is in our great and Eternal Head.

O ye people of the land, that ye would hear my words! And I pray that the anger of the Lord be turned away from you, and that ye would repent and be saved.[566]

Cursed are they who set their hearts on mammon and trust in its security; their riches are programmed to become slippery. Nevertheless, despite the Lord's warning, these people will try to hoard their riches; but they hide them in vain. One day these people will awaken, and that which they loved so much will be gone. Then they will mourn, to no avail. They will be faced with the stark reality that they chose mammon over God; they rejected the words of the true prophets, and they honored flatterers as if they were prophets. Then Satan and his angels will rejoice.

On the other hand, Zion people are commanded to hide their treasures unto the Lord: "For I will, saith the Lord, that they shall hide up their treasures unto me; and cursed be they who hide not up their treasures unto me; for none hideth up their treasures unto me save it be the righteous; and he that hideth not up his treasures unto me, cursed is he, and also the treasure, and none shall redeem it because of the curse of the land."[567] The only reasons to hide a treasure are to safeguard it from an enemy and to preserve it for its intended purpose. Therefore, a Zion person might say that he hides, or *consecrates,* his treasure unto the Lord to keep it safe from unholy hands and to preserve it for its sacred purpose.

Lazarus and the Rich Man

The tragedy of choosing God over mammon and thus sacrificing one's soul is stated powerfully in Jesus' parable of the rich man and Lazarus.

---

566   Helaman 13:31–39.
567   Helaman 13:19.

There was a certain rich man, which was clothed in
purple and fine linen, and fared sumptuously every day:
And there was a certain beggar named Lazarus, which
was laid at his gate, full of sores, and desiring to be fed
with the crumbs which fell from the rich man's table:
moreover the dogs came and licked his sores.

And it came to pass, that the beggar died, and
was carried by the angels into Abraham's bosom: the
rich man also died, and was buried; and in hell he lift
up his eyes, being in torments, and seeth Abraham afar
off, and Lazarus in his bosom. And he cried and said,
Father Abraham, have mercy on me, and send Lazarus,
that he may dip the tip of his finger in water, and cool
my tongue; for I am tormented in this flame.

But Abraham said, Son, remember that thou in
thy lifetime receivedst thy good things, and likewise
Lazarus evil things: but now he is comforted, and thou
art tormented. And beside all this, between us and you
there is a great gulf fixed: so that they which would pass
from hence to you cannot; neither can they pass to us,
that would come from thence.

Then he said, I pray thee therefore, father, that
thou wouldest send him to my father's house: For I have
five brethren; that he may testify unto them, lest they
also come into this place of torment.Abraham saith
unto him, They have Moses and the prophets; let them
hear them. And he said, Nay, father Abraham: but if
one went unto them from the dead, they will repent.

And he said unto him, If they hear not Moses and
the prophets, neither will they be persuaded, though
one rose from the dead.[568]

The parable is indeed frightful. A dramatic change of status may await the righteous
poor and the selfish rich. Then the once-selfish rich will look up and cry out to the once-
humble poor for relief as the poor had once cried out for help and found none. James, the
Lord's brother, expounded on this subject by saying that the poor who are faithful in this
life are destined to become heirs of celestial glory.[569] Then the tables will be turned, and
the rich will be the ones to cry out for relief and find none. They will cry out to the poor
as the poor had once cried out to them. They will neither enjoy the sweet association of
the blessed nor be at rest; rather, they will be in torment with a great gulf dividing them
from the righteous.

---

568   Luke 16:19–31.
569   James 2:5.

It is telling that the rich man in the parable was in agony; he pled that Abraham would send Lazarus to his brothers who were still on earth, hoping, we suppose, that there might be the tiniest chance that they could escape his fate. But Abraham knew the lure of mammon. Such people who are taken in that snare, he said, would no more respond to an angel than they would to the prophets, who constantly warn about such behavior.

Nothing Compares to the Danger

"Wealth is a pleasant and heady narcotic that gives the addict an exhilarating sense of power accompanied by a growing deadening of feeling for anything of real value," wrote Hugh Nibley. "Wealth is a jealous mistress: she will not tolerate any competition; rulers of business are openly contemptuous of all other vocations; and all those 'how-to-get-rich' books by rich men virtuously assure us that the first and foremost prerequisite for acquiring wealth is to think of nothing else—the aspirant who is guilty even of a momentary lapse in his loyalty, they tell us, does not deserve the wealth he seeks."[570]

Mammon is a decoy, a trap, a lure, a snare; it dangles its bait to capture our attention long enough to grasp us in its jaws and devour us. Quoting Brigham Young, Hugh Nibley said, "[Material things] 'decoy . . . [our] minds' away from the real values of things." Then Nibley added: "They are irresistible. The merchants do research: they know what we'll take and what we'll not. They know what will sell, and they know the line that nobody can resist. This is the very real thing we are being tempted by. By these deceptions—through public relations, the skill of advertising, and people who devote their lives to nothing else than trying to entice—the devil tries to entice and tempt us, 'by sorceries and witchcraft that deceive the nations' (cf. Revelation 18:23)."[571]

On a number of occasions, Brigham Young expressed his fears concerning the Saints' pursuit of wealth over seeking the things of God: "I am more afraid of covetousness in our Elders than I am of the hordes of hell. . . . Those who are covetous and greedy, anxious to grasp the whole world, are all the time uneasy, and are constantly laying their plans and contriving how to obtain this, that, and the other. . . . [But] riches of themselves cannot produce permanent happiness; only the Spirit that comes from above can do that. . . . How the Devil will play with a man who so worships gain!"[572]

As we have discussed, Jesus was once confronted by a rich young man who asked him concerning eternal life. "Keep the commandments" was the Lord's reply. When the rich man said that he had done this, he asked the Lord what else he lacked. "Now when Jesus heard these things, he said unto him, Yet lackest thou one thing: sell all that thou hast, and distribute unto the poor, and thou shalt have treasure in heaven: and come, follow me. And when he heard this, he was very sorrowful: for he was very rich. And when Jesus saw that he was very sorrowful, he said, How hardly shall they that have riches enter into the kingdom of God!" It is *hard* for a rich man to enter into heaven: "It is easier for a camel to go through a needle's eye, than for a rich man to enter into the

---

570   Nibley, *Approaching Zion*, 39–40.
571   Nibley, *Approaching Zion*, 330–31.
572   Young, *Discourses of Brigham Young,* 306.

kingdom of God." It requires special intervention from heaven: "The things which are impossible with men are possible with God."[573]

We would have to be blind to miss the point: We cannot achieve eternal life as long as our heart is set upon mammon. It is dangerous to think otherwise. Mammon and Zion do not mix. We cannot have them both. If we hold to one, we will despise the other. If we love one, we hate the other. The message is clear and scriptural: We must give up mammon to obtain God. Joseph Smith said eternal life is bought with a price: the sacrifice of all things.[574] That is the essence of consecration. Only then are we truly safe.

When someone tried to lure Jesus into a conversation about money, he rebuked him soundly. "Man, who made me a judge or a divider over you?"[575] The Savior's mission had nothing to do with mammon. Satan had once tried and failed to draw him into the distraction of wealth.[576] Now here was another person expecting the Lord to take an interest in financial affairs: "Master, speak to my brother, that he divide the inheritance with me." It was an insult, and Jesus told him as much: "Take heed, and beware of covetousness: for a man's life consisteth not in the abundance of the things which he possesseth."[577] The parable that followed spoke plainly of the folly of building up possessions on earth only to end up destitute in the next life.

> And he spake a parable unto them, saying, The ground of a certain rich man brought forth plentifully: And he thought within himself, saying, What shall I do, because I have no room where to bestow my fruits? And he said, This will I do: I will pull down my barns, and build greater; and there will I bestow all my fruits and my goods· And I will say to my soul, Soul, thou hast much goods laid up for many years; take thine ease, eat, drink, and be merry.
>
> But God said unto him, Thou fool, this night thy soul shall be required of thee: then whose shall those things be, which thou hast provided? So is he that layeth up treasure for himself, and is not rich toward God.[578]

We are ever moving in the direction of our treasure, and we are investing in that treasure right now. Should we concentrate soley on filling our barns, we will most certainly abandon God and his children in the process. Jesus asks each of us two questions when we contemplate our loyalties: "For what shall it profit a man, if he shall gain the whole world, and lose his own soul? Or what shall a man give in exchange for his soul?"[579]

---

573   Luke 18:18–27.
574   Smith, *Lectures on Faith*, 6:7.
575   Luke 12:14.
576   JST, Luke 4:5–8.
577   Luke 12:13, 15.
578   Luke 12:16–21.
579   Mark 8:36–37.

Lessons in the Scriptures Concerning Wealth

The mantra of Babylon might be summed up by one scripture: "Money answereth all things."[580] But in no uncertain terms the Lord forbids wealth-seeking: "Seek not after riches nor the vain things of this world; for behold, you cannot carry them with you."[581] Wealth is a fleeting fancy that does not make a good eternal investment: "Riches are not forever."[582] Satan is he who tempts us to seek for riches, knowing their inherent danger: "Now the cause of this iniquity of the people was this—Satan had great power, unto the stirring up of the people to do all manner of iniquity, and to the puffing them up with pride, tempting them to seek for power, and authority, and riches, and the vain things of the world."[583]

The scriptures contain many descriptions, cautions, and denunciations concerning our attitude toward wealth. We are clearly warned that "he that trusteth in riches shall fall."[584] How we obtain riches is even more damning: "He that oppresseth the poor to increase his riches shall surely come to want."[585]

Seeking and withholding riches blights the soul with a terminal spiritual disease: "Wo unto you rich men, that will not give your substance to the poor, for your riches will canker your souls; and this shall be your lamentation in the day of visitation, and of judgment, and of indignation: The harvest is past, the summer is ended, and my soul is not saved!"[586]

As evidenced in the scriptures below, when people begin to prosper, the bells of Hades begin to ring, and consequently the Church starts to fail. Notice in each of these scriptures the downward sequence of events:

- "But they grew proud, being lifted up in their hearts, because of their exceedingly great riches; therefore they grew rich in their own eyes, and would not give heed to their words, to walk uprightly before God."[587]

- "And it came to pass that the fifty and second year ended in peace also, save it were the exceedingly great pride which had gotten into the hearts of the people; and it was because of their exceedingly great riches and their prosperity in the land; and it did grow upon them from day to day."[588]

- "Now this great loss of the Nephites, and the great slaughter which was among them, would not have happened had it not been for their wickedness and their abomination which was among them; yea, and it was among those also who professed to belong to the church of God. And it was because of the pride

---

580   Ecclesiastes 10:19.
581   Alma 39:14.
582   Proverbs 27:24.
583   3 Nephi 6:15.
584   Proverbs 11:28.
585   Proverbs 22:16.
586   D&C 56:16.
587   Alma 45:24.
588   Helaman 3:36.

of their hearts, because of their exceeding riches, yea, it was because of their oppression to the poor, withholding their food from the hungry, withholding their clothing from the naked, and smiting their humble brethren upon the cheek, making a mock of that which was sacred, denying the spirit of prophecy and of revelation, murdering, plundering, lying, stealing, committing adultery, rising up in great contentions, and deserting away into the land of Nephi, among the Lamanites—and because of this their great wickedness, and their boastings in their own strength, they were left in their own strength; therefore they did not prosper, but were afflicted and smitten, and driven before the Lamanites, until they had lost possession of almost all their lands."[589]

- "And in the commencement of the sixty and seventh year the people began to grow exceedingly wicked again. For behold, the Lord had blessed them so long with the riches of the world that they had not been stirred up to anger, to wars, nor to bloodshed; therefore they began to set their hearts upon their riches; yea, they began to seek to get gain that they might be lifted up one above another; therefore they began to commit secret murders, and to rob and to plunder, that they might get gain."[590]

Clearly, the scriptures are replete with warnings about mammon-seeking. If we think that we are somehow exempt or that we have a special dispensation to receive other than the universal and eternal reward for mammon-seeking, we are deceived and are destined to become sorely disappointed.

Scriptural Description of the Last Days

Quoting Isaiah, Nephi paints a picture of latter-day idolatry that is chilling: "Their land also is full of silver and gold, neither is there any end of their treasures; their land is also full of horses, neither is there any end of their chariots. Their land is also full of idols; they worship the work of their own hands, that which their own fingers have made." Isaiah foresaw that the resulting pride and lack of humility would challenge the Lord's forgiveness and would be answered with a harsh turn of events: "And the mean man boweth not down, and the great man humbleth himself not, therefore, forgive him not. O ye wicked ones, enter into the rock, and hide thee in the dust, for the fear of the Lord and the glory of his majesty shall smite thee. And it shall come to pass that the lofty looks of man shall be humbled, and the haughtiness of men shall be bowed down, and the Lord alone shall be exalted in that day."[591]

In the latter days, the Lord prescribed an antidote for such spiritual sickness: "See that ye love one another; cease to be covetous; learn to impart one to another as the gospel requires."[592]

---

589   Helaman 4:11–13.
590   Helaman 6:16–17.
591   2 Nephi 12:7–11.
592   D&C 88:123.

Scriptures about Idolatry and Wealth

The scriptures have much to say about the ugly sisters, covetousness and idolatry, which seem to define the last days. Covetousness is idolatry, Paul taught.[593] A "wo" is pronounced upon those whose "eyes are full of greediness."[594] It is through greediness and idolatry that many break "the covenant through covetousness."[595]

Alma was faced with an idolatrous, selfish people who were ripening for destruction. His words to them could be just as well delivered today as a sermon at general conference:

> And also the Spirit saith unto me, yea, crieth unto me with a mighty voice, saying: Go forth and say unto this people—Repent, for except ye repent ye can in nowise inherit the kingdom of heaven. And again I say unto you, the Spirit saith: Behold, the ax is laid at the root of the tree; therefore every tree that bringeth not forth good fruit shall be hewn down and cast into the fire, yea, a fire which cannot be consumed, even an unquenchable fire. Behold, and remember, the Holy One hath spoken it.

And now my beloved brethren, I say unto you, can ye withstand these sayings; yea, can ye lay aside these things, and trample the Holy One under your feet; yea, can ye be puffed up in the pride of your hearts; *yea, will ye still persist in the wearing of costly apparel and setting your hearts upon the vain things of the world, upon your riches?*

Yea, will ye persist in supposing that ye are better one than another; yea, will ye persist in the persecution of your brethren, who humble themselves and do walk after the holy order of God, wherewith they have been brought into this church, having been sanctified by the Holy Spirit, and they do bring forth works which are meet for repentance—*yea, and will you persist in turning your backs upon the poor, and the needy, and in withholding your substance from them?*

And finally, all ye that will persist in your wickedness, I say unto you that these are they who shall be hewn down and cast into the fire except they speedily repent.[596]

Scriptures about Seeking Wealth and Forgetting God

Seeking wealth and becoming idolatrous is so very dangerous because it causes us to forget God. In the process of pursuing wealth, mammon becomes our god.

Nephi, the son of Helaman, described the downward spiral of sins that results from setting our hearts on mammon and thus forgetting God. Nephi challenged his people: "O, how could you have forgotten your God in the very day that he has delivered you? But be-

593 Colossians 3:5.
594 D&C 56:17.
595 D&C 104:4, 52.
596 Alma 5:51–56; emphasis added.

hold, it is to get gain, to be praised of men, yea, and that ye might get gold and silver. And ye have set your hearts upon the riches and the vain things of this world, for the which ye do murder, and plunder, and steal, and bear false witness against your neighbor, and do all manner of iniquity. And for this cause wo shall come unto you except ye shall repent."[597]

Centuries earlier, Moses struggled with his people who had forgotten the God who had preserved them. Moses found them boasting in their own strength and worshipping their riches. Moses denounced them and promised destruction for their haughty attitude:

> Who led thee through that great and terrible wilderness, wherein were fiery serpents, and scorpions, and drought, where there was no water; who brought thee forth water out of the rock of flint; who fed thee in the wilderness with manna, which thy fathers knew not, that he might humble thee, and that he might prove thee, to do thee good at thy latter end; *and thou say in thine heart, My power and the might of mine hand hath gotten me this wealth. But thou shalt remember the Lord thy God: for it is he that giveth thee power to get wealth,* that he may establish his covenant which he sware unto thy fathers, as it is this day.
>
> And it shall be, if thou do at all forget the Lord thy God, and walk after other gods, and serve them, and worship them, I testify against you this day that ye shall surely perish.[598]

Clearly, if we seek mammon, we risk forgetting God.

Scriptures about Mammon, Inequality, and Divisiveness

No redeeming quality comes from seeking mammon. Satan programs this process to cause widespread misery: for the poor man, misery occurs by the rich man's unwillingness to part with his goods to help provide for the poor man's necessities and the opportunity to rise above the condition of poverty; for the rich man, misery happens by losing his soul to mammon-seeking and hoarding. In 3 Nephi, Mormon chronicles the cycle of misery:

> And thus passed away the twenty and eighth year, and the people had continual peace.
>
> But it came to pass in the twenty and ninth year there began to be some disputings among the people;

---

597   Helaman 7:20–22.
598   Deuteronomy 8:15–19; emphasis added.

> and some were lifted up unto pride and boastings
> because of their exceedingly great riches, yea, even unto
> great persecutions;
>> For there were many merchants in the land, and
> also many lawyers, and many officers.
>> And the people began to be distinguished by
> ranks, according to their riches and their chances for
> learning; yea, some were ignorant because of their
> poverty, and others did receive great learning because
> of their riches.
>> Some were lifted up in pride, and others were
> exceedingly humble; some did return railing for railing,
> while others would receive railing and persecution and
> all manner of afflictions, and would not turn and revile
> again, but were humble and penitent before God.[599]599

Take note of Mormon's description of the perils of mammon-seeking:
- Within a short period of time, peace can devolve to disputations driven by pride.
- Then riches lead to more pride, boasting, and persecution;
- Then merchandising becomes prominent as a distinguishing element of society;
- Then riches define rank and opportunity.
- The resulting oppression of the poor shackles them to their low station.

Frighteningly, only a few righteous people manage to remain uninfected by the growing sickness.

Mormon explained that these conditions lead to inequality and divisiveness, the offspring of Babylon and the antithesis of Zion. The sickness that had infected the Nephite nation, he said, quickly infiltrated the Church, and soon the Saints were crushed under the weight of mammon-seeking. Only a small number managed to climb to high ground and remain safe from the tsunami about to drown the nation. Mormon reports: "And thus there became a great inequality in all the land, insomuch that the church began to be broken up; yea, insomuch that in the thirtieth year the church was broken up in all the land save it were among a few of the Lamanites who were converted unto the true faith; and they would not depart from it, for they were firm, and steadfast, and immovable, willing with all diligence to keep the commandments of the Lord."

How had this insanity happened? Mormon had the answer: "Now the cause of this iniquity of the people was this—Satan had great power, unto the stirring up of the people to do all manner of iniquity, and to the puffing them up with pride, tempting them to seek for power, and authority, and riches, and the vain things of the world. And thus Satan did lead away the hearts of the people to do all manner of iniquity; therefore they had enjoyed peace but a few years."

599   3 Nephi 6:9–13.

If that news were not bad enough, the subsequent scene was even worse: "And thus, in the commencement of the thirtieth year—the people having been delivered up for the space of a long time to be carried about by the temptations of the devil whithersoever he desired to carry them, and to do whatsoever iniquity he desired they should—and thus in the commencement of this, the thirtieth year, they were in a state of awful wickedness. *Now they did not sin ignorantly, for they knew the will of God concerning them, for it had been taught unto them; therefore they did wilfully rebel against God.*"[600]

They knew better! The members of the Church had been warned against seeking wealth by every prophet, including Nephi and Moses, all the way back to Adam, and they did it anyway. They thought they could serve both God and mammon, but in the end they ended up hating God, just as Jesus had predicted: "No man can serve two masters: for either he will hate the one, and love the other; or else he will hold to the one, and despise the other."[601] The Nephites were living proof.

Scriptural Evidence That the Lord Despises the Selfish Rich

Our ability to access the Lord and receive his blessings is linked to our attitude toward money. Jacob distinguishes between those to whom the Lord responds and those whom he despises: "And whoso knocketh, to him will he open; and the wise, and the learned, and they that are rich, who are puffed up because of their learning, and their wisdom, and their riches—yea, they are they whom he despiseth; and save they shall cast these things away, and consider themselves fools before God, and come down in the depths of humility, he will not open unto them."[602]

Nephi ends his book with a scathing rebuke, pronouncing three woes upon the prideful rich: "O the wise, and the learned, and the rich, that are puffed up in the pride of their hearts, and all those who preach false doctrines, and all those who commit whoredoms, and pervert the right way of the Lord, wo, wo, wo be unto them, saith the Lord God Almighty, for they shall be thrust down to hell!"[603] The Lord adds another woe: "Wo unto you rich men, that will not give your substance to the poor."[604] Another woe is pronounced by King Benjamin, who reminds us that we can lay no legitimate claim on our wealth, and if we attempt to do so, our withholding will cement our condemnation.

> And now, if God, who has created you, on whom you
> are dependent for your lives and for all that ye have and
> are, doth grant unto you whatsoever ye ask that is right,
> in faith, believing that ye shall receive, O then, how ye
> ought to impart of the substance that ye have one to

---

600 3 Nephi 6:9–18; emphasis added.
601 Matthew 6:24.
602 2 Nephi 9:42.
603 2 Nephi 28:15.
604 D&C 56:16.

> another. And if ye judge the man who putteth up his
> petition to you for your substance that he perish not,
> and condemn him, how much more just will be your
> condemnation for withholding your substance, which
> doth not belong to you but to God, to whom also your
> life belongeth; and yet ye put up no petition, nor repent
> of the thing which thou hast done. I say unto you, wo
> be unto that man, for his substance shall perish with
> him; and now, I say these things unto those who are
> rich as pertaining to the things of this world.[605]

Few things could cause the Lord to despise someone. But seeking and hoarding wealth, assuming ownership of that which is rightfully the Lord's, and selfishly holding back when God's children are in need will most certainly summon divine anger and trigger heavenly disgust. Choosing mammon over God is always listed among the darkest of deeds. Moreover, choosing mammon over God is to abandon covenantal loyalty, shift affection, totally disregard sacred covenants, and forget the One who gave us our blessings in the first place. By choosing mammon, we are sending God a message that we despise and hate him and that we have found another love to serve and adore. Again, "No man can serve two masters: for either he will hate the one, and love the other; or else he will hold to the one, and despise the other. Ye cannot serve God and mammon."[606] According to King Benjamin, one significant way to love and serve God and to obtain eternal life is to serve God's children: "When ye are in the service of your fellow beings ye are only in the service of your God."[607]

Persecuting the Poor

Poverty takes many forms—temporal, emotional, spiritual—but in the end, poverty always is defined by a lack. Every prophet has looked upon the condition of the poor who are oppressed by Babylon, and grieved. In his day, Ezekiel mourned, "The people of the land have used oppression, and exercised robbery, and have vexed the poor and needy: yea, they have oppressed the stranger wrongfully."[608] Mistreating the poor has always been indicative of the most depraved people: "Behold, this was the iniquity of thy sister Sodom, pride, fulness of bread, and abundance of idleness was in her and in her daughters, *neither did she strengthen the hand of the poor and needy.*"[609]

The human tendency toward meanness is beyond comprehension. A disfigured child whose condition should invite pity is often teased, taunted, and otherwise cruelly mistreated by his peers. Likewise, the Psalmist laments of the poor, "The wicked in his

605   Mosiah 4:21–23.
606   Matthew 6:24.
607   Mosiah 2:17.
608   Ezekiel 22:29.
609   Ezekiel 16:49; emphasis added.

pride doth persecute the poor."[610] To persecute is to "systematically subject a race or group of people to cruel or unfair treatment; to make somebody the victim of continual pestering or harassment."[611] The scriptures use extreme language when describing our turning away from impoverished souls. Consider the verbs *persecute, rob, hate, pollute, despise*. Sadly, the poor often search in vain for mercy: "The poor is hated even of his own neighbor."[612] If we turn our backs on one of God's children, he takes it personally: "Whoso mocketh the poor reproacheth his Maker."[613] Such a person cannot be classified as a follower of Christ: "And remember in all things the poor and the needy, the sick and the afflicted, for he that doeth not these things, the same is not my disciple."[614]

On the other hand, the Lord loves and generously recompenses those who care for his disadvantaged children: "He that hath pity upon the poor lendeth unto the Lord; and that which he hath given will he pay him again."[615]

Wo unto the Rich Who Despise the Poor

Nephi, speaking prophetically, pronounced ten woes on those to whom the Atonement is proffered and who neglect or reject the Savior who wrought it. As we shall see, these woes eventually settle on the issue of mammon-seeking.

The first of these woes condemns an attitude of disregard for and rebellion against the laws of God. A careful reading reveals the troubling fact that Nephi was speaking to members of the Church, those who have received "all the laws of God." Nephi said, "But wo unto him that has the law given, yea, that has all the commandments of God, like unto us, and that transgresseth them, and that wasteth the days of his probation, for awful is his state!" This depraved condition is inspired by Satan and embraced by vain, foolish, and spiritually frail individuals: "O that cunning plan of the evil one! O the vainness, and the frailties, and the foolishness of men! When they are learned they think they are wise, and they hearken not unto the counsel of God, for they set it aside, supposing they know of themselves, wherefore, their wisdom is foolishness and it profiteth them not. And they shall perish."

We might ask ourselves, What could cause a situation so awful that even the covenant people would perish? Nephi answered by listing his set of woes, and, significantly, he began with mammon and its impact on the poor: "But wo unto the rich, who are rich as to the things of the world. For because they are rich they despise the poor, and they persecute the meek, and their hearts are upon their treasures; wherefore, their treasure is their God. And behold, their treasure shall perish with them also."[616]

We hear echoes of idolatry in these verses. Treasure had captured the hearts of the Saints. They worshipped their treasure adoringly, as if it were their god, and they were paying for their treasure with their souls.

---

610 Psalm 10:2.
611 *Encarta Dictionary*, s.v. "persecute."
612 Proverbs 14:20.
613 Proverbs 17:5.
614 D&C 52:40.
615 Proverbs 19:17.
616 2 Nephi 9:27–28, 30.

They Rob the Poor

Elsewhere Nephi continues to use the imagery of worship to describe our latter-day adulation of money. In the following verse, he accuses people in the latter days of robbing the poor by using the *Lord's* money for our personal luxuries and building "sanctuaries," that is, "shrines," or "temples," wherein our god can reside: "They rob the poor because of their fine sanctuaries; they rob the poor because of their fine clothing; and they persecute the meek and the poor in heart, because in their pride they are puffed up."[617] While Nephi may have been referencing actual places of worship, he might also have been speaking metaphorically of places or things that are not of God, which places and things we worship. Do we consider such places and things as "holy" because they represent to us that which we hold most sacred?

Such "sanctuaries" may take all sorts of forms: elegant homes, expensive cars, excessive leisure, "fine clothing," and other luxuries—anything we worship, anything we can point to as evidence of our industry, ingenuity, and genius. When it comes to devotion, we are devout worshipers; we are completely loyal to our false *god*. We can always be found in our "sanctuary" paying homage to the deity of mammon. And in the shadows of our sanctuaries, the poor languish and suffer.

Nephi's choice of phrase, "they rob the poor," links our withholding assistance to the poor with thievery. A person can be robbed only of something that rightfully belongs to him. We have no right to cling to or withhold that which does not rightfully belong to us. "The riches of the earth are mine to give," the Lord states emphatically. And to whom does he intend to give those riches as an inheritance? "The poor and the needy." For what purpose? To "administer to their relief that they shall not suffer."[618] We are stewards of the Lord's property, not owners. We are under covenant to do with the Lord's money as he has directed. But if we claim or hoard the resources of our stewardship, pamper ourselves with the Lord's goods, and withhold these things from the poor, whom the goods could help, we are thieves.

Building Sanctuaries

Moroni scolded the people of the latter-days: "Ye love money more than ye love the poor. For behold, ye do love money, and your substance, and your fine apparel, and the adorning of your churches [sanctuaries], more than ye love the poor and the needy, the sick and the afflicted." Once again we hear the reference to money being used to pamper and adorn rather than helping the Lord's impoverished children. Once again we see money being wrongfully claimed and used in an unordained manner; and once again we see the poor being robbed and suffering for it. Moroni couldn't stand it. Again we read: "O ye pollutions, ye hypocrites, ye teachers, who sell yourselves for that which will canker, why have ye polluted the holy church of God? Why are ye ashamed to take upon you the

617   2 Nephi 28:13.
618   D&C 38:39, 35.

name of Christ? Why do ye not think that greater is the value of an endless happiness than that misery which never dies—because of the praise of the world?" Our eternal happiness is at stake, and certain misery is looming if we do not change our attitude toward the poor.

Moroni continued by asking us questions as if he were our judge. We note here that the rich neither have answers for these questions now nor will they have answers at the Day of Judgment: "Why do ye adorn yourselves with that which hath no life, and yet suffer the hungry, and the needy, and the naked, and the sick and the afflicted to pass by you, and notice them not? Yea, why do ye build up your secret abominations to get gain, and cause that widows should mourn before the Lord, and also orphans to mourn before the Lord, and also the blood of their fathers and their husbands to cry unto the Lord from the ground, for vengeance upon your heads?"[619] Divine retaliation is the only answer to personal pampering with the Lord's resources and the resultant neglect and abuse of the needy.

Wealth-Seeking—The Sin That Hinders and Destroys the Church

Alma's experience with the plague of wealth-seeking set him on a mission of reclamation.

Alma, "seeing all their inequality, began to be very sorrowful."[620] The people whom he had loved so much were waxing "proud because of their exceeding riches, and their fine silks, and their fine-twined linen, and because of their many flocks and herds, and their gold and their silver, and all manner of precious things, which they had obtained by their industry; and in all these things were they lifted up in the pride of their eyes, for they began to wear very costly apparel."[621] The prophet knew where this condition would lead; therefore, he relinquished the judgment seat so that "he might preach the word of God unto them, to stir them up in remembrance of their duty, and that he might pull down, by the word of God, all the pride and craftiness and all the contentions which were among the people."[622] The call of a prophet is to warn the people, cry repentance, and declare the truth.

Alma's task was daunting. The Nephites had enjoyed a season of peace and abundance. Many had joined the Church and had now grown prosperous. As we so often learn in the Book of Mormon, prosperity is a trial that few people can handle. Now Alma and his companions "saw and beheld with great sorrow that the people of the church began to be lifted up in the pride of their eyes, and to set their hearts upon riches and upon the vain things of the world, that they began to be scornful, one towards another, and they began to persecute those that did not believe according to their own will and pleasure."

The results of this condition were serious and included "great contentions among the people of the church; yea, there were envyings, and strife, and malice, and persecutions, and pride, even to exceed the pride of those who did not belong to the church of

---

619   Mormon 8:37–40.
620   Alma 4:15.
621   Alma 4:6.
622   Alma 4:19.

God." Moreover, the work of the Church had all but stopped because of the bad example of the members: "The wickedness of the church was a great stumbling-block to those who did not belong to the church; and thus the church began to fail in its progress." Alma knew that this situation could only lead to a disastrous end: "Alma saw the wickedness of the church, and he saw also that the example of the church began to lead those who were unbelievers on from one piece of iniquity to another, thus bringing on the destruction of the people."[623]

The Ugliness of Inequality Contrasted with the Beautiful Work of Angels

The scene worsens: "Yea, [Alma] saw great inequality among the people, some lifting themselves up with their pride, despising others, turning their backs upon the needy and the naked and those who were hungry, and those who were athirst, and those who were sick and afflicted." Where there had been happiness, prosperity, and peace, there was now misery: "Now this was a great cause for lamentations among the people." Only a few members of the Church had remained true to their covenants. Alma found these few humble, faithful souls doing the right things: "Abasing themselves, succoring those who stood in need of their succor, such as imparting their substance to the poor and the needy, feeding the hungry, and suffering all manner of afflictions, for Christ's sake, who should come according to the spirit of prophecy; looking forward to that day, thus retaining a remission of their sins; being filled with great joy because of the resurrection of the dead, according to the will and power and deliverance of Jesus Christ from the bands of death." Here we note with interest that these humble followers of Christ, who were administering to the poor, were "retaining a remission of their sins."[624]

The Lord never intended for inequality to exist among his children: "And again I say unto you, let every man esteem his brother as himself. For what man among you having twelve sons, and is no respecter of them, and they serve him obediently, and he saith unto the one: Be thou clothed in robes and sit thou here; and to the other: Be thou clothed in rags and sit thou there—and looketh upon his sons and saith I am just? Behold, this I have given unto you as a parable, and it is even as I am. I say unto you, be one; and if ye are not one ye are not mine."[625]

Commenting on this parable, Brigham Young said, "Now the object is to improve the minds of the inhabitants of the earth, until we learn what we are here for, and become one before the Lord, that we may rejoice together and be equal. Not to make all poor, no. The whole world is before us. The earth is here, and the fulness thereof is here. It was made for man; and one man was not made to trample his fellow man under his feet, and enjoy all his heart desires, while the thousands suffer."[626]

God created the earth to support his children equitably: "For the earth is full, and there is enough and to spare." There is enough as long as we do not hoard! "Therefore, if

623   Alma 4:8–11.
624   Alma 4:12–14.
625   D&C 38:25–27.
626   Young, *Discourses of Brigham Young*, 286.

any man shall take of the abundance which I have made, and impart not his portion, according to the law of my gospel, unto the poor and the needy, he shall, with the wicked, lift up his eyes in hell, being in torment."[627] President Young added, "The course pursued by men of business in the world has a tendency to make a few rich, and to sink the masses of the people in poverty and degradation. Too many of the Elders of Israel take this course. No matter what comes, they are for gain—for gathering around them riches; and when they get rich how are those riches used? Spent on the lusts of the flesh, wasted as a thing of nought."[628]

How, rather, should we be applying our efforts? "Take the men that can travel the earth over, preach the Gospel without purse or scrip, and then go to and lay their plans to gather the Saints. *That looks like the work of angels.*"[629]

Withholding from and Judging the Poor Harshly

Some ninety years before Alma, King Benjamin laid down constitutional laws mirroring those established by Moses. Central to King Benjamin's law was the condition of our hearts and our treatment of the unfortunate: "And also, ye yourselves will succor those that stand in need of your succor; ye will administer of your substance unto him that standeth in need; and ye will not suffer that the beggar putteth up his petition to you in vain, and turn him out to perish." Harsh judgment of the poor, he said, serves only to compound our sin against these people, and we put our inheritance in the celestial kingdom at risk: "Perhaps thou shalt say: The man has brought upon himself his misery; therefore I will stay my hand, and will not give unto him of my food, nor impart unto him of my substance that he may not suffer, for his punishments are just—but I say unto you, O man, whosoever doeth this the same hath great cause to repent; and except he repenteth of that which he hath done he perisheth forever, and hath no interest in the kingdom of God."

A terrible condemnation awaits those who judge a poor person and withhold that which does not belong to them (the withholder), but to God: "And if ye judge the man who putteth up his petition to you for your substance that he perish not, and condemn him, how much more just will be your condemnation for withholding your substance, which doth not belong to you but to God, to whom also your life belongeth; and yet ye put up no petition, nor repent of the thing which thou hast done. I say unto you, wo be unto that man, for his substance shall perish with him; and now, I say these things unto those who are rich as pertaining to the things of this world."[630]

The Evil of the Age: Life for Money

"He that oppresseth the poor to increase his riches, and he that giveth to the rich, shall surely come to want."[631] Could there be any sin more disgusting than viewing human be-

---

627   D&C 104:17–18.
628   Young, *Journal of Discourses*, 11:349.
629   Young, *Journal of Discourses*, 8:353–54; emphasis added.
630   Mosiah 4:16–18, 22–23.
631   Proverbs 22:16.

ings as property, their only value being that which they can produce for their owners or employers? At its worst, this attitude leads to slavery. To a lesser degree, this attitude de-fines the common philosophy of business: profit is more important than people—profit at all costs. Is this philosophy ethical? For Babylon, yes; for Zion, no. Often, business ethics smack of the ethics advanced by Korihor, the anti-Christ: "Every man fared in this life according to the management of the creature; therefore every man prospered according to his genius, and . . . every man conquered according to his strength; and whatsoever a man did was no crime."[632]

Hugh Nibley traced oppression of the poor back to Cain. It was Satan, he said, who taught Cain "a special course to make him prosperous in all things: the Mahan technique, the great secret of converting life into property. Later Lamech graduates with the same degree—'Master Mahan, master of that great secret' (Moses 5:49). He glories in what he has done; it becomes the normal world economy. Nearly all the posterity of Adam, we are told, entered into business, and all Adam and Eve could do about it was to mourn before the Lord (Moses 5:27). Everyone went off following the Cainites. And Cain did it all, we are told, for the sake of getting gain (Moses 5:31). He was not ashamed; he 'gloried in that which he had done.' He said, 'I am free; surely the flocks of my brother falleth into my hands' (Moses 5:33)."[633]

"Particularly reprehensible in Nibley's view is the common practice of some employ-ers who, in the spirit of the perverse 'work ethic,' withhold from laborers the necessities of life in exchange for services—'life in exchange for profits.' 'To make merchandise of another's necessity is an offense to human dignity.' 'The prevailing evil of the age' is 'that men withhold God's gifts from each other in a power game.'"[634] King Benjamin denounced such dealings: "And ye will not have a mind to injure one another, but to live peaceably, and to render to every man according to that which is his due."[635] Fair is fair. "Therefore all things whatsoever ye would that men should do to you, do ye even so to them."[636] If the tables were turned, the rich man would be the first to cry foul.

The author of Ecclesiastes speaks of accumulating wealth and withholding one's substance from the poor as vain, or, worse, the symptoms of an "evil disease" that can re-sult only in loneliness, sorrow, and misery: "There is a sore evil which I have seen under the sun, namely riches kept for the owners thereof to their hurt. . . . All his days also he eateth in darkness, and he hath much sorrow and wrath with his sickness. . . . There is an evil which I have seen under the sun, and it is common among men: A man to whom God hath given riches, wealth, and honour, so that he wanteth nothing for his soul of all that he desireth, yet God giveth him not power to eat thereof, but a stranger eateth it: this is vanity, and it is an evil disease."[637]

Clearly, beyond the sins of ignoring, withholding from, and harshly judging the poor is the sin of using a poor man's labor to enrich one's self. This sin runs contrary to the

632   Alma 30:17.
633   Nibley, *Approaching Zion*, 93–94.
634   Norton, Don, in foreword of Nibley's *Approaching Zion*, xv.
635   Mosiah 4:13.
636   Matthew 7:12.
637   Ecclesiastes 5:12–17; 6:1–2.

Lord's law of fair pay: "The laborer is worthy of his hire."[638] And as we have said, this sin is commonplace and defining for the last days.

A Curse on the Daughters of Zion

Isaiah prophesied that the Lord, along with the righteous fathers, kings, and prophets, will pronounce harsh judgment upon those who consume what rightfully belongs to the poor: "The Lord will enter into judgment with the ancients of his people and the princes thereof; for ye have eaten up the vineyard and the spoil of the poor in your houses."

Under such an indictment, we might cry, "Certainly you cannot mean us! What have we done to deserve such a denunciation?"

Then the Lord will answer, "Ye beat my people to pieces, and grind the faces of the poor."

We cannot believe that we are guilty of such a crime. After all, we are the chosen ones, the children of Zion. We would never stoop to such an abysmal level.

But, according to Isaiah, the Lord was adamant, and he pronounced a curse, which interestingly was directed in this case at his latter-day daughters, who would go about proudly, constantly wanting this and that, and who would be consumed by fashion:

> Because the daughters of Zion are haughty, and walk with stretched-forth necks and wanton eyes, walking and mincing as they go, and making a tinkling with their feet—therefore the Lord will smite with a scab the crown of the head of the daughters of Zion, and the Lord will discover their secret parts. In that day the Lord will take away the bravery of their tinkling ornaments, and cauls, and round tires like the moon; the chains and the bracelets, and the mufflers; the bonnets, and the ornaments of the legs, and the headbands, and the tablets, and the ear-rings; the rings, and nose jewels; the changeable suits of apparel, and the mantles, and the wimples, and the crisping-pins; the glasses, and the fine linen, and hoods, and the veils. And it shall come to pass, instead of sweet smell there shall be stink; and instead of a girdle, a rent; and instead of well set hair, baldness; and instead of a stomacher, a girding of sackcloth; burning instead of beauty.[639]

Clearly, our directing money toward self-indulgence and fashion rather than dedicating it to bless the poor is an affront to God.

---

638   Luke 10:7; D&C 31:5; 70:12; 84:79; 106:3.
639   2 Nephi 13:14–24.

Blessings for Those Who Rescue the Poor

From the beginning, the Lord has pled with us to step outside ourselves and help his impoverished children. The law of Moses mandated mercy and hospitality: "If there be among you a poor man of one of thy brethren within any of thy gates in thy land which the Lord thy God giveth thee, thou shalt not harden thine heart, nor shut thine hand from thy poor brother: But thou shalt open thine hand wide unto him, and shalt surely lend him sufficient for his need, in that which he wanteth."[640]

Other evidences of kindheartedness can be found in the law. For example, the Lord forbade charging interest on a loan to a poor man.[641] The temple priests were to be sensitive to the poor man, who was doing his best to comply with the law of sacrifice but who could not manage the price.[642] During the harvest, land owners were not to completely clear their fields but leave the corners and the gleanings for the poor.[643] The people's attitude toward giving was as important as their gift; they were to give because they wanted to and not begrudgingly: "Thou shalt surely give him, and thine heart shall not be grieved when thou givest unto him."[644]

The law reminded the people that the poor would ever be with them, and that their efforts to rescue the poor would not only bless the poor but the generous giver: "For this thing the Lord thy God shall bless thee in all thy works, and in all that thou puttest thine hand unto. For the poor shall never cease out of the land: therefore I command thee, saying, Thou shalt open thine hand wide unto thy brother, to thy poor, and to thy needy, in thy land."[645]

When we read these verses, we should keep in mind that the law of Moses was the lesser, or preparatory, law that required less of us than the higher law of Zion revealed by Jesus. We are under covenant to live the higher law: "Bring the poor that are cast out to thy house."[646] In our day, he told the elders that they had a special priesthood assignment to provide for the poor: "And if any man shall give unto any of you a coat, or a suit, take the old and cast it unto the poor, and go on your way rejoicing."[647] Because this particular commandment is listed in the same section as the oath and covenant of the priesthood, elders might consider this mandate as part of their priesthood responsibility. Likewise, in that same section, bishops are charged to "search after the poor to administer to their wants by humbling the rich and the proud."[648] What the prophet Micah said to the Church in his day continues to be the Lord's call to the elders of the Church today: "I will consecrate their gain unto the Lord, and their substance unto the Lord of the whole earth."[649]

---

640   Deuteronomy 15:7–8.
641   Exodus 22:25.
642   Leviticus 14:21.
643   Leviticus 19:10.
644   Deuteronomy 15:10.
645   Deuteronomy 15:11.
646   Isaiah 58:7.
647   D&C 84:105.
648   D&C 84:112.
649   Micah 4:13.

Great blessings await those who will live the higher law and bless the poor with the Lord's resources: "Blessed is he that considereth the poor."[650] The book of Proverbs promises happiness and financial security for such generosity: "He that hath mercy on the poor, happy is he."[651] Prosperity follows the man who digs deeply into his pockets to succor the poor: "He that maketh himself poor shall have great riches."[652] Security is another blessing: "He that giveth unto the poor shall not lack."[653]

The scriptures contain many evidences of righteous people who consecrated their all to save impoverished souls temporally, emotionally, or spiritually and who, in the process, experienced the Lord's security. An example is Elijah, who was fed by ravens and drank from a brook until the brook dried up. Then the Lord provided for him by sending him to a poor widow, whose food had dwindled to "an handful of meal in a barrel, and a little oil in a cruse." At that point, Elijah applied the Lord's law of abundance to save the poor widow and her son. Acting in the name of the Lord, Elijah asked the widow to make him "a little cake." She was to first "bring it unto [Elijah] and after make for [herself] and for [her] son." By faith, the widow fulfilled the law. When she consecrated what she had to the poor prophet, her security was assured. In return, Elijah, representing the Lord, gave her a blessing: "For thus saith the Lord God of Israel, The barrel of meal shall not waste, neither shall the cruse of oil fail, until the day [that] the Lord sendeth rain upon the earth." And the widow's blessings did not stop there. When her son fell ill and died, Elijah blessed him and brought him back to life.[654] We would assume that her attitude of faith and giving spirit saved her and her son. Clearly, faith in the Lord's promises and giving to bless others results in security on every front for our families.

Another example of blessings for those who aid the needy is Zacchaeus, a rich man who loved the Lord and gave generously to the poor. When Jesus drew near, "Zacchaeus stood, and said unto the Lord; Behold, Lord, the half of my goods I give to the poor; and if I have taken anything from any man by false accusation, I restore him fourfold. And Jesus said unto him, This day is salvation come to this house."[655] The same could be announced to anyone who qualifies by righteous living and strives to bless the poor: "This day is salvation come to this house."

The Poor of the Lord's People Shall Trust in Zion

The scriptures are replete with hope for the poor who are among the people of Zion. In the first place, the Lord hears the the poors' cries for relief: "I have heard your prayers, and the poor have complained before me."[656] In fact, as a response to the cries of the poor, the Lord is motivated to establish Zion, a condition that they can finally trust:

---

650   Psalm 41:1.
651   Proverbs 14:21.
652   Proverbs 13:7.
653   Proverbs 28:27.
654   1 Kings 17:1–24.
655   Luke 19:8–9.
656   D&C 38:16.

"The Lord hath founded Zion, and the poor of his people shall trust in it."[657] Now Zion becomes their place of refuge.[658] In Zion, they will never again be treated badly. Zion is their rescue, their deliverance. The Lord "raiseth up the poor out of the dust."[659]

Because of their great relief, "the poor among men shall rejoice in the Holy One of Israel."[660] There, the people of Zion will administer to their needs.[661] In Zion, the poor will find that their brothers and sisters have consecrated their properties to care for the poor.[662] Consequently, in Zion there are no poor; it is like nowhere else on earth.[663] In Zion, the rich make themselves low so that the poor might be exalted.[664] No more will the poor mourn, for in Zion they receive equally from the Lord's storehouse, which exists to protect and sustain them.[665] In every way, they will be provided for.[666] The Lord has promised, "I will satisfy the poor with bread."[667] Bread is only the beginning of their blessings. In Zion, the poor will discover that the Lord has prepared a bounteous feast for them.[668]

Finally, the poor, as equals with their brothers and sisters, will be invited to the marriage of the Lamb.[669] And after their long oppression, the poor shall inherit the earth.[670]

Consequences of Seeking Wealth and Persecuting the Poor

Ironically, on the basis of eternal salvation alone, poverty and persecution serve us better than wealth and acceptance. Brigham Young said, "When I see this people grow and spread and prosper, I feel that there is more danger than when they are in poverty. *Being driven from city to city or into the mountains is nothing compared to the danger of our becoming rich* and being hailed by outsiders as a first-class community. I am afraid of only one thing. What is that? That we will not live our religion, and that we will partially slide a little from the path of rectitude, and go part of the way to meet our friends [the people of Babylon]."[671]

Mormon, who is famous for his commentary while narrating a story, offers this scathing rebuke of the Nephites who once again were saved and prospered by the Lord only to abandon their noble intentions for the pursuit of wealth:

> And thus we can behold how false, and also the
> unsteadiness of the hearts of the children of men; yea,
> we can see that the Lord in his great infinite good-

657   Isaiah 14:32.
658   2 Nephi 14:6.
659   1 Samuel 2:7.
660   2 Nephi 27:30.
661   D&C 38:35.
662   D&C 42:30–31, 34, 39; 44:6; 51:5; 52:40; 72:12; 105:3.
663   Moses 7:18.
664   D&C 104:16.
665   D&C 78:3; 82:11–12.
666   D&C 83:6.
667   Psalm 132:15.
668   D&C 56:8–11.
669   D&C 58:11.
670   D&C 88:17.
671   Young, *Discourses of Brigham Young*, 434; emphasis added.

> ness doth bless and prosper those who put their trust
> in him. Yea, and we may see at the very time when
> he doth prosper his people, yea, in the increase of
> their fields, their flocks and their herds, and in gold,
> and in silver, and in all manner of precious things of
> every kind and art; sparing their lives, and delivering
> them out of the hands of their enemies; softening the
> hearts of their enemies that they should not declare
> wars against them; yea, and in fine, doing all things
> for the welfare and happiness of his people; *yea, then
> is the time that they do harden their hearts, and do forget
> the Lord their God, and do trample under their feet the
> Holy One—yea, and this because of their ease, and their
> exceedingly great prosperity.*[672]

The list of consequences for such actions is sobering, as detailed below.

Loss of the Providences of Heaven

Elder Joseph B. Wirthlin taught if we perceive that our prayers are not being answered, we ought to ask ourselves if we are answering the cries of the poor, the sick, the hungry, and the afflicted within our influence.[673]

Brigham Young explained the consequences when we participate in wealth-seeking: "The Latter-day Saints who turn their attention to money-making soon become cold in their feelings toward the ordinances of the house of God. They neglect their prayers, become unwilling to pay any donations; the law of tithing gets too great a task for them; and they finally forsake their God, and the providences of heaven seem to be shut from them—all in consequence of this lust after the things of this world."[674]

Loss of Priesthood Power and Exaltation

To tempt us, said Hugh Nibley, Satan would "use the strongest, the most powerful pitch he could use, the most irresistible weapon in his arsenal, the one that is tried and true"[675]—lust for riches. President Young said if a man attempts to "call around him property, be he a merchant, tradesman, or farmer, with his mind continually occupied with: 'How shall I get this or that; how rich can I get; or, how much can I get out of this brother or from that brother?' and dicker and work, and take advantage here and there—no such man ever can magnify the priesthood nor enter the celestial kingdom. Now, remember, they will not enter that kingdom."[676]

---

672   Helaman 12:1–2, emphasis added.
673   Wirthlin, "The Law of the Fast," 73.
674   Young, *Discourses of Brigham Young,* 315.
675   Nibley, *Approaching Zion,* 332.
676   Young, *Journal of Discourses,* 11:297.

Loss of the Spirit

Joseph Smith spoke of the incompatibility of simultaneously seeking wealth and the Holy Ghost. We must be careful not to "grieve the Holy Spirit," he said. Rather, we must become "properly affected one toward another, and are careful by all means to remember, those who are in bondage, and in heaviness, and in deep affliction for your sakes." Then the caution: "And if there are any among you who aspire after their own aggrandizement, and seek their own opulence, while their brethren are groaning in poverty, and are under sore trials and temptations, they cannot be benefited by the intercession of the Holy Spirit."[677]

Loss of Revelation
Amulek taught that the heavens withdraw "if ye turn away the needy, and the naked, and visit not the sick and afflicted, and impart of your substance, if ye have, to those who stand in need." Then he pronounces the curse: "I say unto you, if ye do not any of these things, behold, your prayer is vain, and availeth you nothing, and ye are as hypocrites who do deny the faith."[678]

We live beneath our privileges, declared Brigham Young. "To get . . . revelation it is necessary that the people live so that their spirits are as pure and clean as a piece of blank paper . . . ready to receive any mark the writer may make upon it. When you see the Latter-day Saints greedy, and covetous of the things of this world, do you think their minds are in a fit condition to be written upon by the pen of revelation?"[679] Joseph Smith earlier taught the same principle: "God had often sealed up the heavens because of covetousness in the Church."[680]

We recall the parable of the sower. Jesus explained that the person who "received seed among the thorns is he that heareth the word,"[681] "and the cares of this world, and the deceitfulness of riches, and the lusts of other things entering in, choke the word, and it becometh unfruitful."[682] That is, because of the deceitfulness of riches, the word of God can "bring no fruit to perfection."[683] Where there is no Spirit there is no life.

Loss of Happy Family Life and Spiritual Commitment
President Kimball added the risks of losing happy family life and spiritual decline to the dangers of pursuing wealth and withholding from the poor:

> It is hard to satisfy us. The more we have, the more we want. Why another farm, another herd of sheep, another bunch of cattle, another ranch? Why another hotel, another cafe, another store, another shop? Why another plant,

---

677   Smith, *Teachings of the Prophet Joseph Smith,* 141.
678   Alma 34:28.
679   Young, *Journal of Discourses,* 11:240–41.
680   Smith, *Teachings of the Prophet Joseph Smith,* 9.
681   Matthew 13:22.
682   Mark 4:19.
683   Luke 8:14.

another office, another service, another business? Why another of anything if one has that already which provides the necessities and reasonable luxuries? *Why continue to expand and increase holdings, especially when those increased responsibilities draw one's interests away from proper family and spiritual commitments, and from those things to which the Lord would have us give precedence in our lives?* Why must we always be expanding to the point where our interests are divided and our attentions and thoughts are upon the things of the world? Certainly when one's temporal possessions become great, it is very difficult for one to give proper attention to the spiritual things.[684]

Loss of the Lord's Help

"Whoso stoppeth his ears at the cry of the poor, he also shall cry himself, but shall not be heard."[685] Divine deafness is a terrible curse the Lord imposes on the proud, the selfish, and the insensitive. When we stop listening to the poor, the Lord stops listening to us, and when he stops listening, he stops helping.

The Nephite king Limhi knew why his people had suffered severely without the Lord's rescue. "Therefore, who wondereth that they are in bondage, and that they are smitten with sore afflictions? For behold, the Lord hath said: I will not succor my people in the day of their transgression; but I will hedge up their ways that they prosper not; and their doings shall be as a stumbling block before them."[686] When we stop our ears at the cries of the poor, we commit transgression. The Lord ceases to listen to us, and when he stops helping us, our prosperity turns to poverty. Suddenly, we find ourselves in bondage with no relief, and we wonder why.

Loss of True Worship

President Young chastised the Saints for shifting their worship from the true God to the god of mammon: "Many professing to be Saints seem to have no knowledge, no light, to see anything beyond a dollar, or a pleasant time, a comfortable house, a fine farm, &c., &c. O fools, and slow of heart to understand the purposes of God and his handiwork among the people."[687] And at another time: "Go to the child, and what does its joy consist in? Toys, we may call them, something that produces, as they think, pleasure; and so it is with our youth, our young boys and girls; they are thinking too much of this world; and the middle-aged are striving and struggling to obtain the good things of this life, and their hearts are too much upon them. So it is with the aged. Is not this the condition of the Latter-day Saints? It is. . . . *The Latter-day Saints are drifting as fast as they can into idolatry,* drifting into the spirit of the world and into pride and vanity."[688]

---

684   Kimball, *The Teachings of Spencer W. Kimball,* 354.
685   Proverbs 21:13.
686   Mosiah 7:28–29.
687   Young, *Journal of Discourses,* 8:63.
688   Young, *Journal of Discourses,* 18:239; emphasis added.

Failure in Our Mission

Our missions in life fail when we set our hearts upon riches. Again, Brigham Young said, "If the Lord ever revealed anything to me, he has shown me that the Elders of Israel must let speculation alone and attend to the duties of their calling, otherwise they will have little or no power in their missions."[689] Elder Bruce R. McConkie explained it this way:

> The children of Zion fail in their great mission for two reasons: (1) Oftentimes they set their hearts upon temporal things and are more concerned with amassing the things that moth and rust corrupt, and that thieves break through and steal, than in laying up for themselves treasures in heaven. Hence the divine direction: "But the laborer in Zion shall labor for Zion; for if they labor for money they shall perish." (2 Nephi 26:31.)(2) Others fail to live by the high standards of belief and conduct imposed by the gospel. Of them the divine word says: "Your minds in times past have been darkened because of unbelief, and because you have treated lightly the things you have received—which vanity and unbelief have brought the whole church under condemnation. And this condemnation resteth upon the children of Zion, even all. And they shall remain under this condemnation until they repent and remember the new covenant, even the Book of Mormon and the former commandments which I have given them, not only to say, but to do according to that which I have written—that they may bring forth fruit meet for their Father's kingdom; otherwise there remaineth a scourge and judgment to be poured out upon the children of Zion." (D&C 84:54–58.)[690]

Loss of Peace

Peace is forfeited when we seek wealth over the things of God and turn a deaf ear to those in need. Brigham Young did not mince words on this subject: "What is the matter with them? The god of this world has blinded their minds, they give way to selfishness, covetousness, and divers other kinds of wickedness, suffer the allurements of this world to decoy them from the paths of truth, forget their God, their religion, their covenants, and the blessings they have received, and become like beasts, made to be taken and destroyed at the will of the destroyer. This is the situation, not only of the great majority of the world, but of many of the inhabitants of these valleys; they have no correct idea of

689   Young, *Discourses of Brigham Young*, 315.
690   McConkie, *A New Witness for the Articles of Faith*, 580.

the day of destruction, the day of calamity; they have no realization of the day of sorrow and retribution. They put these things far away and do not wish to think about them, but say, 'Let us eat, drink, and lay down and sleep, and that is all we desire'; then like the brutes they are happy. *It never enters the hearts of the mass of mankind that they are preparing for the day of calamity and slaughter.*"[691]

The Doctrine and Covenants is filled with such warnings. Hugh Nibley offers the following list:

> Almost the first words spoken by the Lord himself to the boy Joseph in his first vision were, "Behold the world lieth in sin at this time and none doeth good no not one, they have turned asside [sic] from the Gospel and keep not my commandments they draw near to me with their lips while their hearts are far from me and mine anger is kindling against the inhabitants of the earth to visit them acording [sic] to this ungodliness." The preface to the Doctrine and Covenants repeats this: "They seek not the Lord, . . . but every man walketh in his own way . . . in Babylon, even Babylon the great, which shall fall" (D&C 1:16). And so on down: "Behold, the world is ripening in iniquity" (D&C 18:6). "The hour is nigh and the day soon at hand when the earth is ripe; and all the proud and they that do wickedly shall be as stubble; . . . I will take vengeance upon the wicked, for they will not repent; for the cup of mine indignation is full" (D&C 29:9, 17). "All flesh is corrupted before me; and the powers of darkness prevail upon the earth, . . . and all eternity is pained, and the angels are waiting. . . . The enemy is combined" (D&C 38:11–12). (Do such words mean nothing to us?) "Behold, the day has come, when the cup of the wrath of mine indignation is full. . . . Wherefore, labor ye; . . . for the adversary spreadeth his dominions, and darkness reigneth; and the anger of God kindleth against the inhabitants of the earth; and none doeth good, for all have gone out of the way" (D&C 43:26, 28; 82:5–6). "Darkness covereth the earth, and gross darkness the minds of the people, and all flesh has become corrupt before my face. Behold, vengeance cometh speedily . . . upon all the face of the earth. . . . And upon my house shall it begin, . . . first among . . .

---

691   Young, *Journal of Discourses*, 3:273.

you . . . who have professed to know my name and have not known me" (D&C 112:23–26).

So the word of the Lord is that Babylon is to remain in Babylon until the day of destruction. Things have not improved since Joseph Smith wrote of "the most damning hand of murder, tyranny, and oppressions, supported and urged on and upheld by the influence of that spirit which has so strongly riveted the creeds of the fathers, who have inherited lies, upon the hearts of the children, and filled the world with confusion, and has been growing stronger and stronger, and is now the very mainspring of all corruption, and the whole earth groans under the weight of its iniquity" (D&C 123:7). "Some may have cried peace," he wrote (and no man ever loved peace more than he), "but the Saints and the world will have little peace from henceforth." "*Destruction*, to the eye of the spiritual beholder, seems to be written by the finger of an invisible hand, in large capitals, upon almost every thing we behold." "There is a spirit that prompts the nations to prepare for war, desolation, and bloodshed—to waste each other away," said Brigham twenty years later. "Do they realize it? No. . . . Is it not a mystery?" "When the nations have for years turned much of their attention to manufacturing instruments of death, they have sooner or later used those instruments. . . . [They] will be used until the people are wasted away, and there is no help for it."[692]

What is the chief cause of this wickedness? As Nibley said, the Lord opened the Doctrine and Covenants with the answer: "They seek not the Lord to establish his righteousness, but every man walketh in his own way, and after the image of his own god, whose image is in the likeness of the world, and whose substance is that of an idol."[693] The Lord will tolerate this condition only for so long. Brigham Young makes the following prophetic statement: "You will see that the wisdom of the wise among the nations will perish and be taken from them. They will fall into difficulties, and they will not be able to tell the reason, nor point a way to avert them any more than they can now in this land. They can fight, quarrel, contend and destroy each other, but they do not know how to make peace. So it will be with the inhabitants of the earth."[694]

---

692   Nibley, *Approaching Zion*, 44–45, quoting Smith, *Teachings of the Prophet Joseph Smith*, 160, 15; Young, *Journal of Discourses*, 8:174–75, 157.
693   D&C 1:16.
694   Young, *Journal of Discourses*, 10:315.

Loss of National Security

Commenting on the global implications of wealth-seeking, Joseph Fielding McConkie and Robert Millet offer this insight: "A civilization that wastes its strength in the pursuit of either wealth or glory will not stand. A nation that fosters or encourages selfishness, that allows greed and lust to go unchecked, will sink under its own weight. Babylon will fall because its citizenry will come in time to shun and hate and destroy all that oppose them. Zion will arise and shine forth as an ensign to the nations because its municipals seek the interest of their neighbors and do all things with an eye single to the glory of God (D&C 82:19)."[695]

The poor are the victims of individual and national selfishness. Hugh Nibley writes: "A community which can at tolerable expense eliminate human distress but refrains from doing so either must believe that it benefits from unemployment or poverty, or that the poor and unemployed are bad people, or that other more important values will be impaired by attempts to help the lower orders—or all of these statements." Quoting a well-known economist Daniel Yergin, Nibley points out the poverty of the 1970s "could have been eliminated at a modest shift of $10–15 billion to the poor from the rest of the community. 15 billion is less than 1.5% of the GNP, about the size of one of the cheaper weapons systems."[696]

Imagine, now, the law of consecration as a solution for the world's woes. How would life appear if love motivated the actions of governments and citizenry? We need not look beyond The Church of Jesus Christ of Latter-day Saints for an answer. Perhaps better than any other organization, the Saints voluntarily take care of each other by their consecrations, which are motivated by pure love. No wonder, then, that President George Q. Cannon called for a change of heart and putting first things first: "We must serve God with all our hearts, our love and affections reaching after Him, and the things of this world must be looked upon by us as secondary considerations. They are good enough in their place; right enough to be attended to; but subordinate always to the love of God."[697]

Who Shall Enter?

The Savior's parable of the sheep and goats lays out the criteria for "everlasting punishment" or "eternal life." First, to the sheep, who represent the righteous, he says, "Then shall the King say unto them on his right hand, Come, ye blessed of my Father, inherit the kingdom prepared for you from the foundation of the world: For I was an hungered, and ye gave me meat: I was thirsty, and ye gave me drink: I was a stranger, and ye took me in: Naked, and ye clothed me: I was sick, and ye visited me: I was in prison, and ye came unto me."

Then to the goats, who represent the unrighteous: "Then shall he say also unto them on the left hand, Depart from me, ye cursed, into everlasting fire, prepared for the devil and his angels: For I was an hungered, and ye gave me no meat: I was thirsty, and

695   McConkie and Millet, *Doctrinal Commentary on the Book of Mormon,* 3:5.
696   Nibley, *Approaching Zion,* 515.
697   Cannon, *Journal of Discourses,* 22:288–89.

ye gave me no drink: I was a stranger, and ye took me not in: naked, and ye clothed me not: sick, and in prison, and ye visited me not."[698]

Gospel writer Matthew B. Brown asks:

> How should Latter-day Saints prepare themselves to be counted among the sheep instead of the goats during the Final Judgment? The way is pointed out in simplicity within the text of the parable itself. According to the Son of God, true Saints who are prepared will (1) give food to the hungry and water to the thirsty, (2) provide shelter and clothing to the needy, and (3) minister to the sick and imprisoned.
>
> The Lord considers such charitable service for the benefit of His brethren as if it were being done for Him. As aptly stated in the Book of Mormon, those who are in the service of their fellow beings are considered to be in the service of God (see Mosiah 2:17). And the reward for engaging in freewill service is to be "blessed" by the Creator of heaven and earth with a blessing with eternal ramifications. Those who fail to act in mortality with a benevolent heart will also receive recompense for which they qualify. . . . To be counted among the sheep when the Lord comes and plumbs the depths of mortal souls will require a sincere effort to bless the lives of others.[699]

What Doth It Profit?

Jesus' brother James had much to say about the attitude of the rich concerning their wealth and their treatment of the poor. He peppered his epistle with prophetic counsel that should give us cause to reflect. As an example, he wrote, "For the sun is no sooner risen with a burning heat, but it withereth the grass, and the flower thereof falleth, and the grace of the fashion of it perisheth: so also shall the rich man fade away in his ways."[700] That is, the rich man might prosper for a season, but his status is fleeting. As sure as the grass will wither in the heat of the sun or petals will one day fall from a flower, so will a rich man's affluence also fade.

James continued by stating that we often hold to an attitude that the Lord finds totally abhorrent, favoring the rich while oppressing the poor: "For if there come unto your assembly a man with a gold ring, in goodly apparel, and there come in also a poor man in vile raiment; and ye have respect to him that weareth the gay clothing, and say unto him, Sit thou here in a good place; and say to the poor, Stand thou there, or sit here

698   Matthew 25:31–46.
699   Brown, *Prophecies—Signs of the Times*, 129–30.
700   James 1:11.

under my footstool, Are ye not then partial in yourselves, and are become judges of evil thoughts?" This is an ugly practice: "If ye have respect to persons, ye commit sin."[701]

"What doth it profit?" James asked. "If a brother or sister be naked, and destitute of daily food, and one of you say unto them, Depart in peace, be ye warmed and filled; notwithstanding ye give them not those things which are needful to the body; what doth it profit?"[702] That is, when we see someone in need, do we pat them on the head, and send them away only with hollow words of comfort that will neither warm nor fill? When a coat is needed, words will not provide warmth; when food is needed, sympathy will not fill an empty belly.

James was indignant with those who pray and ask God to add to their prosperity. Is there not hypocrisy in a prayer that solicits personal needs when the underlying intent is to gain more for ourselves? Are we justified in asking God whether or not we should purchase things that accrue to our lusts? God will not answer such prayers: "Ye ask, and receive not, because ye ask amiss, that ye may consume it upon your lusts."[703] This brand of hypocrisy incensed Brigham Young: "I have seen [men] who, when they had a chance to buy a widow's cow for ten cents on the dollar of her real value in cash, would make the purchase, and then thank the Lord that he has so blessed them."[704] James called such people enemies of God: "Know ye not that the friendship of the world is enmity with God? whosoever therefore will be a friend of the world is the enemy of God."

Are we really willing to act this way? This is not the gospel of Jesus Christ. James gave us a definition: "Pure religion and undefiled before God and the Father is this, To visit the fatherless and widows in their affliction, and to keep himself unspotted from the world."[705] The essence of the gospel is to help the helpless and to remain separate from Babylon and her ways.

James pronounced woes upon the selfish rich: "Go to now, ye rich men, weep and howl for your miseries that shall come upon you. Your riches are corrupted, and your garments are moth-eaten. Your gold and silver is cankered; and the rust of them shall be a witness against you, and shall eat your flesh as it were fire. Ye have heaped treasure together for the last days." He condemned the businessman who oppresses the hirelings and enriches himself on their labor: "Behold, the hire of the labourers who have reaped down your fields, which is of you kept back by fraud, crieth: and the cries of them which have reaped are entered into the ears of the Lord of Sabaoth. Ye have lived in pleasure on the earth, and been wanton; ye have nourished your hearts, as in a day of slaughter."[706]

Throughout James's epistle, his question haunts us: "What doth it profit?" Jesus posed the same question to his disciples: "For what doth it profit a man if he gain the whole world . . . and he lose his own soul, and he himself be a castaway?"[707] And yet we persist.

---

701   James 2:2–4, 9.
702   James 2:15–16.
703   James 4:4.
704   Young, *Journal of Discourses*, 17:362.
705   James 1:27.
706   James 5:1–5.
707   JST, Luke 9:25.

The Voice of Seven Thunders

Brigham Young could not stand the ever-growing tendency toward covetousness, and he continually taught against it. In the last speech he ever gave, he cried: "Now those that can see the spiritual atmosphere can see that many of the Saints are still glued to this earth and lusting and longing after the things of this world, in which there is no profit. . . . According to the present feelings of many of our brethren, they would arrogate to themselves this world and all that pertains to it. . . . Where are the eyes and the hearts of this people? . . . All the angels in heaven are looking at this little handful of people, and stimulating them to the salvation of the human family. So also are the devils in hell looking at this people, too, and trying to overthrow us, *and the people are still shaking hands with the servants of the devil, instead of sanctifying themselves.*"

He appealed to us to imagine what wisdom our forefathers would impart to us: "What do you suppose the fathers would say if they could speak from the dead? . . . What would they whisper in our ears? Why, if they had the power the very thunders of heaven would be in our ears, if we could but realize the importance of the work we are engaged in. . . . *When I think upon this subject, I want the tongues of seven thunders to wake up the people.*"[708]

Choosing God over Mammon

As we have said, the Lord gave us the law of consecration, in part, for our safety, security, and salvation. This law provides the *only* way to pass the mortal test of money and arrive in the celestial kingdom. That lofty goal requires that we be willing to choose consecration as a way of life over the way of Babylon. We must consider everything we are and have as belonging to God; we must view ourselves as stewards rather than owners; we must agree to be accountable to God and his servants for the things God places in our safekeeping; and we must labor for the cause of Zion and not for selfish reasons or for the sake of making and accumulating money. In other words, the law of consecration requires that we give God our hearts, our all, and that we dedicate ourselves to his work and his children.

Our eventual placement in a kingdom of glory depends upon our adherence to the law of consecration and our living its principles out of love. According to John Tvedtnes, this law is illustrated in Doctrine and Covenants 76, the revelation that describes the various resurrections. He concludes, "Only those who obey the Lord's commandments out of love and a simple desire to do good will inherit the celestial kingdom. Those who obey out of fear of punishment or hope of reward, while good people, will inherit the terrestrial kingdom."[709] And we would add that telestial people are those who must be constrained to obey. These people have lived with scant desire to do good. They have rejected and despised God, and a worse group still, the sons of Perdition, have hated him.

How, then, might we choose God over mammon, cease compromising, and stop trying to marry the two? We return to Jacob's formula for the answer: "Think of your

---

708   Young, *Journal of Discourses*, 18:305, emphasis added.
709   Tvedtnes, "They Have Their Reward," Feb. 21, 2007.

brethren like unto yourselves, and be familiar with all and free with your substance, that they may be rich like unto you."[710] We must start with love—love for God and his children. "Therefore all things whatsoever ye would that men should do to you, do ye even so to them."[711] If we truly love, we cannot stand to see suffering or lack of any kind. We attack these situations and smother conditions of lack with kindness and charity until they cease to exist among us. Then, because charity is the "pure love of Christ,"[712] this love expands with each charitable act until our love approaches the Savior's love, which is infinite and "broad as eternity."[713] When we encounter more suffering, we feel more empathy, which causes our capacity to love to grow. When that happens, we yearn for more resources so that we might alleviate more misery. That yearning conveys us to God, who is the source of all good things. To him we make our request, for that is the eternal law; we must ask to receive: "And whatsoever ye shall ask the Father in my name, which is right, believing that ye shall receive, behold it shall be given unto you."[714]

At this point, we make an interjection based on the words of Jacob: "But before ye seek for riches, seek ye for the kingdom of God."[715] The kingdom of God is defined by the new and everlasting covenant, which includes the covenant of baptism and the oath and covenant of the priesthood. Hence, Jesus ordained and commissioned the Seventy, saying in part, "And heal the sick that are therein, and say unto them, The kingdom of God is come nigh unto you."[716] That is, "We, the ordained servants of God who are preaching the gospel and administering its covenants and ordinances have come to you." When we have received the new and everlasting covenant by baptism (men and women), then the ordination of the priesthood (men), followed by the temple blessings associated with the priesthood (men and women), we, by covenant, are clearly of the kingdom of God. We have the right to ask the Lord for his help and for resources in another's behalf.

Obtaining a Hope in Christ

We enhance our ability to ask by taking the next step as stated by Jacob: "Obtain a hope in Christ."[717] It is one thing to believe that Christ exists, but it is quite another to believe *who* he is. Therein lies hope. When we understand that he, like his Father, knows our past, present, and future in detail, has all power in heaven and on earth, is perfectly consistent, and loves us completely, we have obtained a hope in him. In *Lectures on Faith*, the Prophet Joseph Smith stated that our faith pivots on our hope and belief that God possesses certain attributes and characteristics in absolute perfection. In times of urgency, we *hope* that he has the power to help, we *hope* that he is aware of us, and we *hope* that he loves us enough to rush to our rescue. Because of our hope in him, we are willing

---

710   Jacob 2:18.
711   Matthew 7:12.
712   Moroni 7:47.
713   Moses 7:53.
714   3 Nephi 18:20.
715   Jacob 2:18.
716   Luke 10:9.
717   Jacob 2:19.

to reach out to him and plead for his help. We make this effort because we hope that he has both the ability and the disposition to grant our request. Therefore, when we search our faith and find it lacking, we might ask, "Which of these characteristics do I believe that God does not possess?" Our hope in Christ provides the answer: The Savior lacks neither the perfection of godlike attributes nor divine characteristics.

Personalized, the *Lectures on Faith* might read as follows:

> *POWERFUL.* God is all-powerful. Otherwise, how could we believe that he could help us if we imagined that something was beyond his ability? Nothing is too hard for him. He can do anything, in any situation, at anytime, in our behalf.
>
> *KNOWLEDGEABLE.* God possesses all knowledge about everything, including past, present, and future events. Otherwise, how could we believe that he can anticipate and solve our problems if there were something he didn't know, or if his attention were momentarily diverted away from us, or if we thought he had forgotten us? He intimately knows and "foreknows" us and is constantly aware of our thoughts and our circumstances.
>
> *LOVING.* We are God's children. We have all of his attention all of the time. He loves us completely. He is merciful, compassionate, kind, comforting, patient, gracious, and abundant in goodness. Otherwise, how could we seek his help to face unbearable situations or to take the difficult steps of change if anything we were going through or had done could distance us from his love? His love for us is unconditional and continual and is the consistent motivating force in his interactions with us.
>
> *CONSISTENT.* God is perfectly unchangeable. What he did yesterday he will be doing today and tomorrow. Otherwise, how could we anticipate the whims or circumstances that could change his attitude toward us from mercy to reproach or from love to hatred?
>
> *JUST.* God is perfectly equitable and no respecter of persons. Otherwise, how could we believe in him if we thought that he played favorites? If God's laws specify blessings and consequences, we can count on his justice prevailing and his judgment to be correct.
>
> *TRUTHFUL.* God cannot lie. He does not make promises casually. Otherwise, how could we believe

that our future with him is secure if we thought that
he didn't mean what he said, or might seek an out, or
might change his mind? He will keep his word, even if
in his own way and in his own time.[718]

Ultimately, our faith in the Father and the Son is strengthened or injured according to our trusting in their divine attributes of character. *Faith* and *trust* are synonyms. There are only three reasons for not trusting someone: (1) I don't know you well enough; (2) My past experience with you was disappointing or inconsistent; (3) I don't think you can help me. We might ask ourselves which of these reasons retards our trusting Christ as we should. Clearly, the deficit is ours alone.

Jacob said that if we can attain a hope in Christ, "ye shall obtain riches, if ye seek them; and ye will seek them for the intent to do good—to clothe the naked, and to feed the hungry, and to liberate the captive, and administer relief to the sick and the afflicted."[719] The act of administering to the needy is the testimony that we have received a hope in Christ.

Freely Ye Have Received, Freely Give

And administer we must.

Jesus admonished the Seventy, "Freely ye have received, freely give."[720] By baptism and ordination, the Seventy had embarked on a new path leading to eternal life. Along the way, they would freely receive covenants and ordinances, *gifts*, "without price."[721] Because the *only* way to arrive in the celestial kingdom is to "freely give" of what we have received to alleviate misery, the Seventy went forth distributing their gifts freely so as to bring people to Christ, who could heal them. From this point forward, the Seventy were called the "salt of the earth," the "light of the world,"[722] and "saviors on Mount Zion,"[723] representing the Savior in every way and doing things as he would do them. Jesus commanded them: "Heal the sick, cleanse the lepers, raise the dead, cast out devils."[724]

Representing Jesus is a weighty responsibility. In a remarkable manner, we become to Jesus what he is to his Father: "As my Father hath sent me, even so send I you."[725] Given these truths, can we justify ourselves in dividing our affections from the One who has entrusted and endowed us? Can we receive the Lord's goods then hoard them and ignore his children—the very ones whom he has sent us into the world to save? The Seventy knew better. They fulfilled their commission and returned rejoic-

---

718   This list is a partial adaptation from *Lectures on Faith.*
719   Jacob 2:19.
720   Matthew 10:8.
721   2 Nephi 9:50; 26:25; Alma 1:20; Isaiah 55:1.
722   Matthew 5:13–14.
723   Obadiah 1:21.
724   Matthew 10:8.
725   John 20:21.

ing, absolutely astonished at the power of the gifts the Lord had given them: "And the seventy returned again with joy, saying, Lord, even the devils are subject unto us through thy name."[726]

Feeding the Lord's Lambs

To become Zion people and represent the Savior, we must become like him. That is the burden of baptism, according to Alma.[727] In the New Testament, those who desired to enter into the new and everlasting covenant and make such a transformation asked John the Baptist, "What shall we do then? He answereth and saith unto them, He that hath two coats, let him impart to him that hath none; and he that hath meat, let him do likewise."[728] Change begins with that simple formula: We must being selfish; step outside of ourselves, and help someone.

Peter took seriously his giving freely of what he had been given. When a lame man begged alms of him, he replied, "Silver and gold have I none; but such as I have give I thee: In the name of Jesus Christ of Nazareth rise up and walk."[729] Peter had previously given away all his silver and gold in the service of the Savior, but that did not stop him from continuing to minister. Such as he had, he gave freely. He had evidently learned this lesson on two special occasions when he had participated in feeding the five thousand and later the four thousand.[730] In each giving experience, Jesus commanded Peter and the Apostles to gather up the fragments, which, to their amazement, filled their baskets. Peter must have learned at least two lessons on these occasions: (1) My job is to feed the Lord's sheep; Jesus' job is to bless my meager offering so that it becomes enough to feed many. He is my perfect partner. (2) When it is my turn to eat, I will always have enough; in fact, I will have more than I started with.

By giving away our goods will we end up with less? No. As Peter learned, we are not really giving away our goods or money; we are planting them with the hope of an abundant harvest. Our offering is an act of faith in the Lord of the Harvest—faith that he will keep his promise and that we will reap untold blessings. This is Zion's celestial law of prosperity, the law that guarantees incredible returns, even "an hundredfold."[731] Our covenant relationship with the Lord ensures our safety while we are giving. This is also called the "manna principle," which supplies our daily bread,[732]—that which is sufficient for our needs. But to obtain these blessings requires that we put first things first: "Seek ye first the kingdom of God, and his righteousness; and all these things shall be added unto you."[733] Then we can be assured that while we are feeding the Lord's lambs, he will take care of us. That is the promise of security enjoyed by Zion people.

---

726   Luke 10:17.
727   Mosiah 18:8–10.
728   Luke 3:10–11.
729   Acts 3:6.
730   Mark 6:35–44; 8:1–9.
731   Luke 8:8; Matthew 19:29.
732   Matthew 6:11.
733   Matthew 6:33.

Choosing God's Marvelous Work over Babylon's Charms

To live this way calls for a new way of thinking. While Babylon shouts, "Gather about you property for your security," Zion counters with "Man shall not live by bread alone, but by every word that proceedeth out of the mouth of God."[734] Our choice should be clear. When we took upon us the new and everlasting covenant and thereafter received the blessings of the priesthood, we agreed to come out of Babylon and choose God over mammon forevermore.

Choosing God over mammon also suggests that we also choose to do his marvelous work, as stated in Doctrine and Covenants 4: "Now behold, a marvelous work is about to come forth among the children of men. Therefore, O ye that embark in the service of God, see that ye serve him with all your heart, might, mind and strength, that ye may stand blameless before God at the last day." By taking upon us the new and everlasting covenant and receiving the priesthood, we signal our desire to choose and serve God over mammon, therefore we are "called to the work."

The work we have to do is as daunting as Peter's feeding of the five thousand with five loaves and two fishes: "For behold the field is white already to harvest." Only the Lord of the Harvest can increase our meager efforts to reap such a harvest. Nevertheless, if we will courageously thrust in our sickle with our might, the Lord assures us success and salvation to our soul.

While Babylon would qualify her servants with gold, silver, intellect, and flattering words, Zion would qualify her servants with "faith, hope, charity and love, with an eye single to the glory of God and, additionally, "faith, virtue, knowledge, temperance, patience, brotherly kindness, godliness, charity, humility, diligence." Admittedly, Zion is a far cry from Babylon. But if we will embrace such a Zion-like lifestyle, the Lord promises us the key to his abundance: "Ask, and ye shall receive; knock, and it shall be opened unto you."[735]

It is interesting to note that the humble servants of Zion are often referred to as the "weak things"[736] whom the Lord makes strong through his grace.[737]

Invoking the Law of Asking to Receive

Feeding the Lord's lambs with scanty resource is a monumental act of faith. Only with love and driven by a determined desire to serve and trust in the Lord can we accomplish such a feat. This act of donating the widow's mite to help another person is a clear indication that we have chosen God over mammon. The Lord helps us by giving us the Law of Asking.

The law of asking provides that we may draw upon the Lord's vast resources to feed his sheep with the promise that as we do, we will always have enough to feed ourselves. Asking is an act of faith: We recognize the sovereignty of God; we acknowledge that he has infinite resources that he is willing to give us; and we concede that he has the power

---

734   Matthew 4:4.
735   D&C 4:1–7.
736   D&C 1:19; 35:13; 124:1; 133:59.
737   Ether 12:27.

to make and keep promises, and to do anything for or give anything to us. By asking, we acknowledge that we share with him a child-to-parent relationship—a covenant bond that makes us *partners* in his work.

Asking is an eternal principle; our eternal progression depends upon the law of asking. Throughout eternity, we will surely go to God countless times to ask permission to draw resources from his higher kingdom so that we might grow and manage the affairs of our emerging kingdoms.

In this life, by invoking the law of asking, we *receive* the Holy Ghost;[738] husbands and wives *receive* each other as gifts from God; worthy men *receive* the priesthood and thus *receive* the Lord;[739] and ultimately, by continuing to ask to receive, we obtain the promise: "he that *receiveth* my Father *receiveth* my Father's kingdom; therefore all that my Father hath shall be given unto him."[740] To receive any good thing from God, we must first ask.

This is the doctrine of Zion that provides for the abundant life Jesus promises.[741] This is a reward for those who choose God over mammon.

Summary and Conclusion

Among the tests of life, one test stands supreme: the choice between God and mammon. Because we cannot serve both, we are forced to choose. The test of wealth determines if we can we be trusted with God's resources. Therefore, in part, the Lord gave us the law of consecration to keep us safely on his side and free from the destructive nature of mammon-seeking. We are to manage our stewardship according to God's desires and use the surplus for its intended use: to take care of God's children and build up the kingdom of God for the establishment of Zion. Because the choice between God and mammon is difficult and the stakes are high, only the pure in heart can pass the test. Without divine intervention, we could not have the power to choose God over mammon.

To give us sufficient faith to make this choice, the Lord makes us an offer to be tested on the principles of consecration. That is, as we choose him over mammon, he gives us evidence that he will take care of us and even prosper us. The law God offers to be tested upon is the law of tithes and offerings. Because this law is a celestial law, the math never makes sense in a telestial setting, so we are forced to live it on faith alone. That we always end up with more than we donate is a truism, but we are hard-pressed to explain how that can be. As we live this manifestation of consecration, we discover that tithing *prepares* us to become Zion-like, and that offerings are the *opportunity* to become Zion-like. While tithing is a defined amount, offerings are not; offerings, therefore, are more a condition of the heart than tithing, and thus offerings require more faith. In the end, consecration is about love—the proving of the heart. Consecration is about relationship: either we love God or we love mammon. If we give God our heart, giving him our money is easy.

---

738   John 20:22.
739   D&C 84:35.
740   D&C 84:38; emphasis added.
741   John 10:10.

The Restoration of the gospel marked the beginning of a change of orders in the world. The order of Babylon, which has oppressed God's people for millennia, will collapse and a new order—Zion—will burst upon the stage of human history. Zion's advent will be an act of mercy for the salvation of all mankind.[742] Until then, we are to choose God over mammon while living among the people of Babylon, calling as many of them as possible out of Babylon and into Zion.

In one phrase, the Apostle James identifies the origin of all sin: "the love of money." President Anthon H. Lund said, "There is hardly a commandment but is violated through this seeking for riches."[743] The love of money violates the last of the Ten Commandments, which directs us to not covet. This broken law results in the loss of the "fulness of the law" of the priesthood, which enables men to become kings and priests after the order of Melchizedek with the promise of endless life. The same could be said of women, who would become queens and priestesses. We cannot break this last law, covetousness, and expect to receive the fulness of the priesthood, along with its attendant blessings.

As covetousness was the last law given in the lesser law, the law of consecration is the last law given in the higher law. Consecration protects us from covetousness and idolatry by defining the usage of our surpluses. If we keep this last law, we will prosper and experience abundance beyond any telestial effort we might make to enrich ourselves.

Choosing between God and mammon is a "weighty matter." Our success in arriving in Zion depends upon our attitude toward money: "Let them repent of all their sins, and of all their covetous desires, before me, saith the Lord; for what is property unto me? saith the Lord." The things of the world are but a drop in an ocean of blessings. Therefore, why would we choose to "covet that which is but the drop, and neglect the more weighty matters?"[744] The Zoramites chose the drop over the weighty matters and lost their blessings. To rationalize their choice, they defined gain as godliness.[745] They tried to make mammon holy. They saw themselves as good and thus reasoned that their wealth-seeking must be good. When the original premise is wrong, all points that stem from the premise are wrong. Joseph Smith observed that the Saints, like the Zoramites, were trying to mix mammon with Zion and were rationalizing their actions with supposed pious purposes. The Prophet cried, "Now I want to tell you that Zion cannot be built up in any such way."[746]

We have been warned repeatedly against compromise. Despite our imaginations, we simply cannot embrace Zion and mammon simultaneously. "Zion cannot be built up unless it is by the principles of the law of the celestial kingdom." Nevertheless, the Latter-day Saints still try to compromise: "We will not go up unto Zion, and will keep our moneys."[747] But it is not possible.

---

742   D&C 1.
743   Lund, Conference Report, Apr. 1903, 97.
744   D&C 117:4, 8.
745   1 Timothy 6:5.
746   Stevenson, *Life and History of Elder Edward Stevenson*, 40–41; emphasis added.
747   D&C 105:5, 8.

Whereas mammon is unholy, consecrated wealth is holy as it is acquired for the purposes and in the order the Lord prescribed. Jacob said, "But before ye seek for riches, seek ye for the kingdom of God." First things first. "And *after* ye have obtained a hope in Christ, ye shall obtain riches, if ye seek them; and ye will seek them for the intent to do good— to clothe the naked, and to feed the hungry, and to liberate the captive, and administer relief to the sick and the afflicted."[748] We are not justified in seeking riches *before* we seek the kingdom of God; but *after* we obtain a hope in Christ, we may ask for riches with the intent to level people up. "Think of your brethren like unto yourselves, and be familiar with all and free with your substance, that they may be rich like unto you."[749] It is this attitude toward money that brings us to a hope in Christ, and it is this attitude that places us in a position to make a request for more resources to bless more people.

Moroni foresaw the condition of the last days and condemned mammon choosers. He said, "Behold, I speak unto you as if ye were present. . . . Ye do love money, and your substance, and your fine apparel, and the adorning of your churches, more than ye love the poor and the needy, the sick and the afflicted."[750]

From the outset of the dispensation of the fulness of times, the Lord commanded us against mammon-seeking. The first two commandments were: (1) "Seek to bring forth and establish the cause of Zion," and (2) "Seek not for riches but for wisdom." The promised blessings distinguished Zion from Babylon: "And behold, the mysteries of God shall be unfolded unto you, and then shall you be made rich. Behold, he that hath eternal life is rich."[751]

There is no security in mammon. Conversely, the quest for riches is a powerful opiate and Satan's most "deadly and effective" weapon.[752] Seeking security in mammon was defined by Nephi as a latter-day Satanic strategy to destroy the Latter-day Saints: "And others will he pacify, and lull them away into carnal security, that they will say: All is well in Zion; yea, Zion prospereth, all is well—and thus the devil cheateth their souls, and leadeth them away carefully down to hell."[753] There is a curse placed on mammon: It becomes "slippery treasure" when we "hide" those treasures unto ourselves instead on "hiding" them unto God, or in other words, consecrating them to God. But if we insist on hiding our treasures unto ourselves, we, as Jesus explained, will suffer an abrupt change of status in the spirit world, where the righteous poor are exalted and the selfish rich are made low. Then the formerly selfish rich will look up and cry out to the poor for relief as the poor once cried out to the rich.[754]

Nothing compares to the danger of choosing mammon over God. Brigham Young said, "I am more afraid of covetousness in our Elders than I am of the hordes of hell."[755] The scriptures are filled with lessons concerning wealth-seeking. In each case, the Lord forbids such a focus: "Seek not after riches nor the vain things of this world; for behold, you cannot

---

748   Jacob 2:18–19; emphasis added.
749   Jacob 2:17.
750   Mormon 8:35–37; emphasis added.
751   D&C 6:6–7.
752   Nibley, *Approaching Zion,* 39, 332.
753   2 Nephi 28:21.
754   Luke 16:19–31.
755   Young, *Discourses of Brigham Young,* 306.

carry them with you."[756] Choosing mammon over God is the equivalent of idolatry, and it leads to forgetting God, inequality, and divisiveness. Mormon described the perils of mammon-seeking. Before long, peace devolves into to prideful disputation. The further pursuit of riches leads to more pride, boasting, and persecution of those less fortunate. Merchandising becomes prominent as a distinguishing element of a society where riches define rank and opportunity. The resulting oppression of the poor shackles them to their low station.

Because we are not ignorant of the law, we do not sin ignorantly, "for," as Mormon explained of the Nephites, "they knew the will of God concerning them, for it had been taught unto them; therefore they did wilfully rebel against God."[757] Every prophet since Adam has warned against this dangerous practice, and yet people still insist on trying to serve both God and mammon. But, as Jesus predicted, they only succeed in hating God.[758]

The Lord despises selfishness; when those consumed by selfishness knock, "he will not open unto them."[759] Selfish mammon-seekers persecute the poor—temporally, emotionally, and spiritually. "They rob the poor because of their fine sanctuaries; they rob the poor because of their fine clothing; and they persecute the meek and the poor in heart, because in their pride they are puffed up."[760] In this sense, sanctuaries are places that we build to ourselves to hold our treasures, that which we worship most. But if we claim or hoard the resources of our stewardship, pamper ourselves with the Lord's goods, and withhold these things from the poor, whom the goods could help, we are thieves.

Mammon-seeking is a sin that hinders and destroys the Church. It promotes the ugliness of inequality, keeps the masses in poverty, and lavishes the rich with lusts of the flesh. Brigham Young said, "The course pursued by men of business in the world has a tendency to make a few rich, and to sink the masses of the people in poverty and degradation. Too many of the Elders of Israel take this course. No matter what comes they are for gain—for gathering around them riches; and when they get rich how are those riches used? Spent on the lusts of the flesh, wasted as a thing of nought."[761] Rather, choosing God over mammon applies a different set of criteria: "Take the men that can travel the earth over, preach the Gospel without purse or scrip, and then go to and lay their plans to gather the Saints. *That looks like the work of angels.*"[762]

The sin of withholding from poor is often coupled with the sin of harshly judging or looking down on the poor for the circumstances of their condition. Such a despicable treatment puts at stake our inheritance in the celestial kingdom. A terrible condemnation awaits those who judge a poor person and withhold that which does not belong to them, that which is God's. This attitude lends to the evil of the age: exchanging life for money. Few sins are more disgusting than viewing human beings as property, their only value being that which they can produce for their owners or employers. This attitude defines the common philosophy of business: profit is more important than people, profit at all costs. Hugh Nibley traced oppression of the poor back to Cain. It was Satan, he said, who taught Cain "a special course

756   Alma 39:14.
757   3 Nephi 6:9–18.
758   Matthew 6:24.
759   2 Nephi 9:42.
760   2 Nephi 28:13.
761   Young, *Journal of Discourses*, 11:349.
762   Young, *Journal of Discourses*, 8:353–54; emphasis added.

to make him prosperous in all things: the Mahan technique, the great secret of converting life into property. Later Lamech graduates with the same degree   'Master Mahan, master of that great secret.'" Beyond the sins of ignoring, withholding from, and harshly judging the poor is the sin of using a poor man's labor to enrich one's self: "converting life into property."[763] This sin runs contrary to the Lord's law of fair pay: "The laborer is worthy of his hire."[764]

Perhaps because self-indulgence and fashion-seeking run contrary to the true nature of covenantal womanhood, a curse is placed upon the daughters of Zion when they engage in these offenses. Too many women fall into this trap, and because they are so self-absorbed, they look down on or neglect the poor rather than using their money, talents, and time to selflessly bless the poor and serve the purposes of God. On the other hand, the Lord promises an abundance of blessings for those who rescue the poor.

From the beginning, the Lord has pled with us to step outside ourselves and help his impoverished children. Two hallmarks of the law of Moses were mercy and hospitality. Just so, the higher law of Zion promises great blessings to those who bless the poor with the Lord's resources: "Blessed is he that considereth the poor."[765] Therefore, Zion becomes the consummate hope for the Lord's poor. Because the poor have complained before [the Lord],"[766] the Lord is motivated to establish Zion, a condition they can finally trust.

The Lord has decreed stiff consequences for seeking wealth and persecuting the poor. Some of these consequences include:
- Loss of the providences of heaven
- Loss of priesthood power and exaltation
- Loss of the Spirit
- Loss of revelation
- Loss of happy family life and spiritual commitment
- Loss of the Lord's help
- Loss of true worship
- Failure in our mission
- Loss of peace
- Loss of national security

The Savior's parable of the sheep and goats outlines the criteria for "everlasting punishment" or "eternal life." First, to the sheep, who represent the righteous: "Then shall the King say unto them on his right hand, Come, ye blessed of my Father, inherit the kingdom prepared for you from the foundation of the world: For I was an hungered, and ye gave me meat: I was thirsty, and ye gave me drink: I was a stranger, and ye took me in: Naked, and ye clothed me: I was sick, and ye visited me: I was in prison, and ye came unto me." Then, to the goats, who represent the unrighteous: "Then shall he say also unto them on the left hand, Depart from me, ye cursed, into everlasting fire, prepared for the devil and his angels: For I was an hungered, and ye gave me no meat: I was thirsty,

---

763   Nibley, *Approaching Zion*, xv.
764   Luke 10:7; D&C 31:5; 70:12; 84:79; 106:3.
765   Psalm 41:1.
766   D&C 38:16.

and ye gave me no drink: I was a stranger, and ye took me not in: naked, and ye clothed me not: sick, and in prison, and ye visited me not."[767]

Jesus asked the question, "For what doth it profit a man if he gain the whole world . . . and he lose his own soul, and he himself be a castaway?"[768] James, the Lord's brother, asked the same question, "What doth it profit?" Expounding, he said, "If a brother or sister be naked, and destitute of daily food, and one of you say unto them, Depart in peace, be ye warmed and filled; notwithstanding ye give them not those things which are needful to the body; what doth it profit?"[769] Brigham Young wanted to cry against choosing mammon with "the voice of seven thunders." Seeing the ever-growing tendency toward covetousness, he continually taught against it, and in the last speech he ever made, he said, "The people are still shaking hands with the servants of the devil instead of sanctifying themselves." He appealed to the Saints to imagine what words of wisdom their forefathers would impart to them: "What do you suppose the fathers would say if they could speak from the dead? . . . What would they whisper in our ears? Why, if they had the power the very thunders of heaven would be in our ears, if we could but realize the importance of the work we are engaged in. . . . *When I think upon this subject, I want the tongues of seven thunders to wake up the people.*"[770]

The Lord gave us the law of consecration, in part, for our safety, security, and salvation. This law provides the *only* way to pass the mortal test of money and arrive in the celestial kingdom. That lofty goal requires that we must be willing to choose consecration as a way of life over the way of Babylon. We must consider everything we are and have as belonging to God; we must view ourselves as stewards rather than owners; we must agree to be accountable to God and his servants for the things that God places in our safekeeping; and we must labor for the cause of Zion and not for selfish reasons or for the sake of making and accumulating money. In other words, the law of consecration requires that we give God our hearts, our all, and that we dedicate ourselves to his work and his children. Our eventual placement in a kingdom of glory depends upon our adherence to the law of consecration and our living its principles out of love.

How do we choose God over mammon, cease compromising, and stop trying to marry the two? Jacob's answer was this: "Think of your brethren like unto yourselves, and be familiar with all and free with your substance, that they may be rich like unto you."[771] Love for God and his children is the answer. "Therefore all things whatsoever ye would that men should do to you, do ye even so to them."[772] If we truly love, we cannot stand to see suffering or lack of any kind, and our covenants give us the power to attack lack. If we truly love, we have the right to ask the Lord for his help and for resources in another's behalf. Our ability to ask for the Lord's help is dependent upon "obtain[ing] a hope in Christ."[773] Jacob said if we can persevere and obtain a hope in Christ, "ye shall obtain riches, if ye seek them; and ye will seek them for the intent to do good—to clothe

767   Matthew 25:31–46.
768   JST, Luke 9:25.
769   James 2:15–16.
770   Young, *Journal of Discourses*, 18:305.
771   Jacob 2:18.
772   Matthew 7:12.
773   Jacob 2:19.

the naked, and to feed the hungry, and to liberate the captive, and administer relief to the sick and the afflicted."[774] The act of administering to the needy is the testimony that we have received a hope in Christ.

Because we have received freely, we must freely give. In the process of feeding the Lord's lambs, we learn that we are in partnership with the Lord: (1) We bring to the Lord the extent of our consecrated resource, he blesses it, and the resource becomes enough to feed many. (2) When it is our turn to eat, we will always have enough; in fact, we will have more than we started with. This is Zion's celestial law of prosperity, the law that guarantees incredible returns of "an hundredfold."[775] Our covenant relationship with the Lord ensures our safety while we are giving. This is also called the manna principle, which supplies our daily bread,[776] that which is sufficient for our needs. But to obtain these blessings requires that we put first things first: "Seek ye first the kingdom of God, and his righteousness; and all these things shall be added unto you."[777] Then we can be assured that while we are feeding the Lord's lambs, he will take care of us. That is the promise of the security enjoyed by Zion people.

To live this way calls for a new way of thinking. While Babylon shouts, "Gather about you property for your security," Zion counters with "Man shall not live by bread alone, but by every word that proceedeth out of the mouth of God."[778] Zion is the polar opposite of Babylon. But if we will embrace such a Zion-like lifestyle, the Lord promises us the key to his abundance: "Ask, and ye shall receive; knock, and it shall be opened unto you."[779]

Feeding the Lord's lambs with scanty resources requires monumental faith. Only with love and driven by a determined desire to serve and trust in the Lord can we accomplish such a feat. This act of donating the widow's mite to help another person is a clear indication that we have chosen God over mammon. The Lord helps us by giving us the law of asking. The law of asking provides that we may draw upon the Lord's vast resources to feed his sheep, with the promise that as we do, we will always have enough to feed ourselves. Asking is an act of faith wherein we recognize the sovereignty of God; we acknowledge that he has infinite resources that he is willing to give us; and we concede that he has the power to make and keep promises, to do anything for us or give anything to us. By asking, we acknowledge that we share with him a child-to-parent relationship—a covenant bond that makes us partners in his work. Asking is an eternal principle; our eternal progression depends upon the law of asking. Throughout eternity, we surely will go to God countless times to ask permission to draw resources from his higher kingdom so that we might grow and manage the affairs of our emerging kingdoms. To receive any good thing from God, we must first ask.

This doctrine of Zion provides safety, security, and abundance for both the giver and the receiver.[780] This is the essence of the law of consecration, and these blessings are given as a reward to those who choose God over mammon.

---

774   Jacob 2:19.
775   Luke 8:8; Matthew 19:29.
776   Matthew 6:11.
777   Matthew 6:33.
778   Matthew 4:4.
779   D&C 4:1–7.
780   John 10:10.

Section 5
The Royal Law

Beyond all other considerations, the law, or covenant, of consecration is a law of love. James called it the royal law:[781] "Thou shalt love the Lord thy God with all thy heart, and with all thy soul, and with all thy mind. This is the first and great commandment. And the second is like unto it, Thou shalt love thy neighbour as thyself." The royal law is "the first and great commandment," according to Jesus, and upon it "hang all the law and the prophets."[782] When all is said and done, we consecrate ourselves and all that we have and are because we love God and we love his children.

As we have mentioned throughout this series, the covenant of consecration is very much like the covenant of marriage. In Hebrew culture, a bridegroom and bride consecrate themselves to each other in symbolic rituals. First, the groom offers the bride's father a bride price—she is "bought with a price."[783] Then the bridegroom offers his bride a written covenant of marriage, which, when she agrees to the terms, he and his bride sign. In the betrothal ceremony, he gives his bride a "gift of value," or a "token" of his promise, and an "emblem" of his love, whereupon he recites a pledge to irrevocably bind and consecrate himself to her forever. Then, in the presence of two witnesses, the bride drinks a cup of wine to ratify, or seal, the marriage covenant. By this action, she indicates her willingness to take upon herself her husband's name. At that point, the couple, along with their guests, shares a covenantal meal.

Thus, by these elaborate rituals the bridegroom and bride consecrate themselves to each other with rites rich in symbolism, all of which represent giving their hearts to each other. When the ceremony is complete, the only question that remains is will the ritual of consecration translate into lifelong acts of consecration? That is, will the covenant of consecration become *royal* by the couple's subsequent loyalty, patience, sacrifice, and love? Or will the covenant remain a set of symbols and a piece of paper upon which promises were made but never enacted?

---

781 James 2:8.
782 Matthew 22:36–40.
783 1 Corinthians 6:20.

The Royal Law Explains the Principles of Consecration

When we view consecration through the lens of an eternal marriage built on love, the principles of this law begin to become clear. President James E. Faust reminded us that in order for a temple marriage to be sealed by the Holy Spirit of Promise and thus transcend its initial provisional promises and become more sure, the couple must faithfully abide the marriage covenant they made with God and keep the promises they made with each other.[784] When God joins a man and a woman, the two embark on a new, consecrated life in which they are no more separate but one, pursuing in tandem a single life with a singular purpose that is greater than the sum of their individual parts. To accomplish such unity, the husband and wife make covenants of obedience to live the laws, rites, and ordinances pertaining this new and everlasting covenant of marriage.[785] They agree to sacrifice anything and everything to sustain and defend their new kingdom, even to the sacrifice of their lives, placing their marriage above any personal concern or agenda. They agree to live the totality of the gospel, which defines their new life, protects them as they journey toward their promised land, and ensures their safe arrival. They agree to live a celestial lifestyle called chastity, in which they agree to never divide their affections or be disloyal in any way. They agree to give themselves totally to their beloved—that is, they unrestrictedly give the fulness of their hearts: all that they have and are. They promise to withhold nothing from their spouse—neither their time nor their abilities nor anything that they possess. These are evidences of true, consecrated, eternal love.

From the time of their sealing and throughout the remainder of their lives and forever, the husband and wife are equals. Although they have different personalities and fill diverse roles in the marriage, they are, nevertheless, one. Their equality becomes evident when we see them sacrificing for and serving each other without thought for themselves. They possess things jointly and enjoy equal and common access to the marriage's resources. One spouse is not poor while the other is rich; one does not go without while the other enjoys luxuries—they are equal, and there are "no poor among them."[786] To maintain their unity and equality, they order their lives so that they love God first. They know that their eternal destiny lies with him, and they show their love for God by keeping their covenants and loving each other.

Their marriage is marked by agency, stewardship, accountability, and labor. By the exercise of agency, they chose to enter into the marriage covenant, and thereafter by the exercise of agency, they continue to choose to live it. At the marriage altar, they abandon their claims to individual ownership of assets; now they abide in the covenant by pooling their resources, fairly dividing familial responsibilities, and jointly managing their resources. They agree to discuss with and account to each other for the discharge of their responsibilities. They agree to work hard for the marriage and not for selfish interests. Such an ordered and structured marriage will one day be sealed by the Holy Spirit of

---

784   Faust, "The Gift of the Holy Ghost—A Sure Compass," 2; emphasis added.
785   D&C 131:2.
786   Moses 7:18.

Promise and receive the unconditional guarantee of eternal duration. This marriage will become royal, "inheriting thrones, kingdoms, principalities, and powers, dominions, all heights and depths."[787] Such a marriage is welded together by the highest manifestation of love—consecrated love.

Royal love perpetuates itself. When a husband and wife love God, they can better love each other; when a husband and wife truly love each other, they desire to love children into existence and rear those children in love. Because love begets love, love will increase with each act of love. Soon the couple discovers that they have love to spare. Now their love wants an outlet and looks beyond the marriage and family. When love sees someone who is impoverished, love spills over and becomes the act of serving a child of God; then love multiplies and suddenly is "not content with blessing his family alone, but ranges through the whole world, anxious to bless the whole human race."[788]

Each time a couple gives love to a child of God, they apply the same loving principles of consecration that apply to love in their marriage. For example, they first choose to exercise their agency and choose to extend loving service; they consider all people as equals and draw them by love into a unifying bond; knowing that they are stewards of the Lord's resources, they ask for and receive the Lord's resources so that they are better equipped to serve his children; they are willing to work hard at loving other people, and they accept the responsibility to account to God for their service. When we see the law of consecration through the lens of a loving marriage, we begin to understand both the purpose and the power of this law. We see meaning behind the symbols, tokens, and the contractual language. We discover that the single, driving principle of consecration is love—the royal law.

Doctrine and Covenants 42—The Cornerstones of the Law of Consecration

At the beginning of 1831, "the Lord revealed to the Prophet Joseph Smith in Fayette, New York, that anciently he had taken the Zion of Enoch to himself and then commanded him to go to Ohio to receive the law [of Zion]."[789] A month later, on February 9, 1831, the Lord revealed to the Prophet "the law," or the law of Zion, which the Prophet specified as "embracing the law of the Church."[790] This law became known as section 42 of the Doctrine and Covenants. The revelation listed a variety of commandments—teach by the Spirit; preach the gospel as contained in the New Testament and the Book of Mormon; do not kill, steal, lie, commit adultery or lust, or speak evil of others; beware of pride; and avoid idleness.[791] Moreover, the revelation defined the four cornerstones of the law of consecration:

1. *Mutual assistance*—the Lord expects his disciples to sustain and help one another.
2. *Proper use of priesthood*—the priesthood is to be used to benefit those who are physically and spiritually ill or needy.

787 D&C 132:19.
788 Smith, *History of the Church,* 4:227.
789 *Encyclopedia of Mormonism,* 312.
790 D&C 42, section heading.
791 D&C 42:4–5, 7–8, 12, 18–29, 41–42, 74–93.

3. *The need for faith*—according to God's will, a person can be healed [physically, emotionally and spiritually] by the power of the priesthood, if that individual has faith in Jesus Christ and if he is "not appointed unto death." This revelatory information is provided through the priesthood to give a person hope that the Lord is with him and that the Lord will give him time to work out his exaltation.

4. *Reciprocal love*—the Lord expects his disciples to love one another and to become one.[792]

Mutual Assistance

The cornerstone of mutual assistance is something we immediately identify with Zion. Because we love God and our neighbor, we do not send away any who are naked, hungry, athirst, sick, or who have not been nourished. We do not set our hearts upon riches; rather, we are "liberal to all, both old and young, both bond and free, both male and female, whether out of the church or in the church, having no respect to persons as to those who [stand] in need."[793] To assist another person, we appeal to God for a stewardship or an increase in our stewardship. We do this because we recognize that everything we have and are belongs to God, and we are stewards.[794] We recognize that the underlying purpose of any stewardship is to assist God in his work to bring to pass the immortality and eternal life of man.[795] Therefore, we assist God and his children with the resources of our stewardship, and we receive assistance from the stewardships of others.

Faith and the Proper Use of the Priesthood

At first glance, the next two cornerstones of the law of Zion—proper use of the priesthood and the need for faith—might seem misplaced in a revelation describing consecration. But when we remember that we cannot achieve exaltation without serving others,[796] which is a stipulation of the priesthood covenant,[797] the message begins to come clear. Consecration demands that by faith we give all that we are and have to God. This action increases faith. Faith vitalizes the priesthood and transforms priesthood authority into priesthood power. By faith, we consecrate all that we have received from God for the purpose of ministering to God's children, bringing them the announcement of the proximity of the kingdom of heaven, and blessing them so that they might come to Christ, take upon them his name, and achieve salvation. This is the proper use of the priesthood, and central to the priesthood's proper use is the authority to administer to the sick and afflicted—the poor.

792   Johnson, "The Law of Consecration," 99.
793   Alma 1:30.
794   D&C 38:17; 104:11–14.
795   Moses 1:39.
796   Holland and Holland, "However Long and Hard the Road," n.p.
797   D&C 84:33, 48.

The first latter-day mention of an actual priesthood ordinance to heal the sick is sandwiched in the language of the law of the Church—the law of Zion. It is in this amazing section (D&C 42) that the Lord fulfills his promise to give the Saints information that will endow them with power from on high.[798] It is in this section that the law of consecration is revealed, and embedded in that law is the ordinance of healing the sick. Two previous revelations had alluded to the miracle of healing[799] and to the need for faith on both the elders' and the recipients' parts, but apparently the actual ordinance was not revealed until this revelation was received on February 9, 1831.

Why would it be so important that the law of consecration reference healing the sick? The answer may be found in the fact that consecration is a lifestyle that defines the kingdom of heaven with its attendant powers and miracles. We recall that after Jesus ordained the Seventy in his day, he sent them on missions, saying, "Heal the sick therein, and say unto them, The kingdom of heaven is come nigh unto you."[800] Notice that Jesus connected evidence that the kingdom of heaven had come with the healing of distressed souls. Apparently, the Seventy, as authorized representatives of the kingdom of heaven, were to go out to the people, announce that the kingdom of heaven had come, and provide undeniable proof that the kingdom had the power to save. Thus, the ordinance of healing the sick became evidence that the kingdom of heaven had come.

The priesthood is the authority to use the name of Jesus Christ; more pointedly, the priesthood is the name of Jesus Christ,[801] for its name is "the Holy Priesthood, after the Order of the Son of God."[802] Keep in mind that the name *Jesus Christ* is both the name of the Savior and the *key word* that makes the priesthood operative: "Behold, *Jesus Christ is the name* which is given of the Father, and there is none other *name* given whereby man can be saved [both temporally or spiritually]."[803] Thus, the Lord told Abraham, "Behold, I will lead thee by my hand, and I will take thee, to put upon thee *my name, even the Priesthood.*"[804]

The name and authority of Jesus Christ allow his servants to duplicate his works, which is one of the great miracles of the kingdom of heaven. To duplicate the works of Jesus, the Seventy needed both the Lord's authority *and* his name. Now they could authoritatively represent the kingdom of God and provide evidence to the people that the kingdom was indeed upon the earth. In a great way, the proof in their duplicating the signature miracles of the Savior lay in their healing the sick and casting out devils by the power and in the name of Jesus Christ. "And the seventy returned again with joy, saying, Lord, even the devils are subject unto us *through thy name.*"[805]

Likewise, we exercise proper use of the priesthood by using Jesus' name and authority to duplicate his works and by representing and announcing the kingdom of heaven.

---

798   D&C 38:32.
799   D&C 24:13–14; 35:9.
800   Luke 10:9.
801   John 10:41.
802   D&C 107:3.
803   D&C 18:21, 23; emphasis added.
804   Abraham 1:18; emphasis added.
805   Luke 10:17; emphasis added.

Announcing the Kingdom of Heaven through Administrations

Previous to Jesus' commissioning the Seventy, he gave the Twelve a similar charge on the occasion of their missions: "And as ye go, preach, saying, The kingdom of heaven is at hand. Heal the sick, cleanse the lepers, raise the dead, cast out devils: freely ye have received, freely give."[806] We observe here the abundance that the Lord wishes his servants to bestow on the people: freely give of the gift of power you have been given. Remarkably, the closer we come to the ideal of Zion, the more healings we will experience among us. To ancient Israel the Lord offered the promises of cessation of illness and eternal increase if they would apply to the ideal of Zion: "Thou shalt be blessed above all people: there shall not be male or female barren among you, or among your cattle. And the Lord will take away from thee all sickness."[807]

Imagine! In the ideal of Zion there is simply no sickness! "No poor among them!"[808] No lack of any kind!

Significantly, we prepare for the establishment of Zion in the same way the kingdom of heaven is announced: by first experiencing the miracle of healing through the priesthood. A model is found in the Savior's visit to the Nephites. Before Jesus instituted Zion among the people, he called them to him and healed each sick person. He said, "I see that your faith is sufficient that I should heal you. And it came to pass that when he had thus spoken, all the multitude, with one accord, did go forth with their sick and their afflicted, and their lame, and with their blind, and with their dumb, and with all them that were afflicted in any manner; and he did heal them every one as they were brought forth unto him. And they did all, both they who had been healed and they who were whole, bow down at his feet, and did worship him; and as many as could come for the multitude did kiss his feet, insomuch that they did bathe his feet with their tears."[809]

Evidently, the essential step of healing precedes the establishment of the ideal of Zion. Until that ideal is realized, the administration ordinance announces that the kingdom of heaven is at hand and that its purpose for being is to prepare the people for the establishment of Zion.

Consecrating a Sickness and a Life to the Lord

The concept of consecration permeates gospel principles. Healing the sick is one example. The administration ordinance effectively consecrates or *reconsecrates* a life to the Lord. To consecrate is to set something apart as holy. Thus, the administration ordinance consecrates, or sets apart, the illness for a holy purpose, and that purpose is always the welfare of the afflicted person's soul—whether the expression of that purpose is spoken or unspoken in the ordinance.[810] The ordinance also consecrates the person's

---

806   Matthew 10:7–8.
807   Deuteronomy 7:14–15.
808   Moses 7:18.
809   3 Nephi 17:10.
810   2 Nephi 32:9.

healed and saved life to the Lord. When considered in this light, every affliction is an opportunity to bring a person to Christ, who will heal the afflicted both spirit and body. Therefore, our being saved from sickness and affliction by the power of the priesthood might be viewed as symbolic of Christ's power to deliver us from all our enemies,[811] including spiritual and physical death. Joseph Fielding McConkie and Robert L. Millet wrote: "It may be that all of the miraculous healings performed by Jesus were but tangible symbols of the greatest healing that he alone could perform—the healing of sick spirits and the cleansing of sin-stained souls."[812]

A sickness or affliction reminds a person of his fallen state, and it drives him to recognize his helplessness and his need for the Lord's intervention.[813] That is, because of the Fall, a sick person finds himself in a weakened situation, but he knows that Christ has overcome the Fall and can help him. In the context of Zion, that person finds himself afflicted by the world and desperately seeks deliverance into the health and safety of Zion. When a person is sick or afflicted, he places his hope in the Savior and in the Lord's saving power. Then the sick and afflicted person humbly beseeches the Lord for help, which motivates him to call for the Lord's authorized priesthood representatives. The person recognizes the Lord's servants as having the authority of Jesus Christ to use his name and answer the person's request.[814] The elders come in response to that request. Preceding the administration ordinance, the sick person (or a friend, loved one, or the elders[815]) should offer a sincere prayer of faith in which the person humbly declares his testimony of the Lord. In the prayer of faith, he expresses his belief that the Lord, through His servants, can heal him from the specific effects he is suffering because of the Fall, and he asks the Lord to heal him.[816] At that point, the elders authoritatively perform the ordinance of administration through the power and in the name of Jesus Christ.[817] Because the administration is *sealed*, it is recognized in heaven and on earth,[818] and the Lord promises to confirm or validate it.[819]

By means of the administration ordinance, certain powers on earth and in heaven are set in motion, and now the Lord begins to direct the process of healing, both spiritually and physically. When the healing process is completed, the Fall symbolically has been overcome, and the once-afflicted person is now in a position to bear heightened testimony of the reality of the Savior, the Lord's power to deliver, and of the certainty of the Restoration of the gospel and priesthood. Throughout the process of healing, the person has rededicated and reconsecrated his life to the Lord. No wonder then that the person, through his illness and healing, is brought closer to the Lord and the ideal of Zion. Such a person becomes a witness—someone who can bear testimony of the power resident in Zion and of the quality of salvation that can be found there.

---

811   Mosiah 29:22; D&C 49:6; 58:22.
812   McConkie and Millet, *Doctrinal Commentary on the Book of Mormon,* 4:41.
813   Alma 26:12; Moses 1:9–10.
814   Alma 15:5–11.
815   James 1:14.
816   Alma 15:5–11.
817   McConkie, *Mormon Doctrine,* 21–22.
818   D&C 128:8, 10.
819   Mormon 9:24–25; D&C 132:59.

Administration and Forgiveness of Sins

Consecrating a life to the Lord by means of healing is borne out in James's instruction: "Is any sick among you? let him call for the elders of the church; and let them pray over him, anointing him with oil in the name of the Lord: And the prayer of faith shall save the sick, and the Lord shall raise him up; *and if he have committed sins, they shall be forgiven him.*"[820] Whether a person is healed immediately by the administration or subsequent to the administration, the resulting healing carries with it the promise of both physical and spiritual renewal. The healed person's body becomes a sanctified receptacle where the Holy Ghost can reside. Therefore, because Zion people are those who are purified and sanctified, the ordinance of administration is essential to their salvation and their spiritual progress.

Perhaps for the purposes of purification and consecration, we anoint a sick person with consecrated olive oil before we seal the anointing and before the blessing is pronounced. Elder Gerald N. Lund said, "Olive oil is a symbol of the Holy Ghost and its power to provide peace and to purify."[821] Apparently, the anointing literally infuses the sick person with the power of the Holy Ghost, who, according to President James E. Faust, is the Great Physician's agent of healing.[822] Elder Lund wrote, "'The olive tree from the earliest times has been the emblem of peace and purity.' (*Doctrines of Salvation*, 3:180) Also, in the Parable of the Ten Virgins, the wise were prepared with oil. (See Matt. 25:1–13.) Modern revelation equates that preparation (having olive oil) with taking 'the Holy Spirit for their guide.' (D&C 45:55–57.) To touch with oil suggests the effect of the Spirit on the same organs of living and acting that had previously been cleansed by the blood of Christ. Thus, every aspect of the candidate's life was purified and sanctified by both the Atonement and the Holy Ghost."[823]

Remarkably, during the healing process, the Lord restores the person both spirit and body: "and the Lord shall raise him up; and if he have committed sins, they shall be forgiven him."[824] The Lord's healing brings remission of sins; the entire soul is healed, both body and spirit. Symbolically, the rescued person is snatched from the grasp of Babylon and delivered into Zion.

Consecration Requires Faith

Whether we are consecrating our property or our lives to the Lord, we need to immerse ourselves in faith. The Lord requires faith for receiving, performing, or participating in a miracle. As we have discussed, the miracle of being delivered from Babylon and being placed in the safety of Zion is represented in the administration ordinance. When we are delivered from illness or affliction, we are cognizant that deliverance has come as an act of faith. And as much as healings come by faith, just so, no one can truly live the law of consecration without faith.

---

820   James 5:14–15.
821   Lund, "Old Testament Types and Symbols," 184–86; emphasis added.
822   Faust, "He Healeth the Broken Heart," 2–7.
823   Lund, *Jesus Christ, Key to the Plan of Salvation*, 61.
824   James 5:14–15.

Embedded in the law of the Church (D&C 42) are the Lord's instructions concerning the administration ordinance: "And the elders of the church, two or more, shall be called, and shall pray for and lay their hands upon them in my name; and if they die they shall die unto me, and if they live they shall live unto me . . . And again, it shall come to pass that he that hath faith in me to be healed, and is not appointed unto death, shall be healed. He who hath *faith* to see shall see. He who hath *faith* to hear shall hear. The lame who hath *faith* to leap shall leap."[825] Again, we note the need for faith, and we also note the sweeping language that describes the result. Of course, we are aware that not every administration is followed by a healing miracle[826]—the phrase, "Thy will be done," is either said or implied in every administration—but in the vast number of cases a customized healing is prescribed and directed by the Lord.

Clearly, the administration ordinance exemplifies the healing power of the priesthood resident in the kingdom of heaven (Zion) and in the law of consecration. For example, an afflicted person who is sick as a result of the Fall cries out to the Lord for deliverance from the effects of this telestial condition. In response, the Lord sends his authorized servants to use his name and power to answer the afflicted's prayer. The elders come as angels, clothed with authority, representing the kingdom of God. That which these angels (elders) have received from the Lord, they consecrate and now give freely to lift up and save the *impoverished* person. The elders stand in proxy for Jesus Christ, authorized to *consecrate* both the sick person's life and his affliction to the Lord. To that end, the elders anoint the sick person with consecrated oil, which anointing is thereafter sealed so that it is recognized and validated both on earth and in heaven. By this means, a process of healing begins that will restore the person both spirit and body. During that process, the administration ordinance cleanses the afflicted person from sin and attempts to draw him out of the world, making him separate and sanctifying him for a holy purpose. Now his consecrated life belongs to the Lord, who saved him, and the person's faith is such that he can bear witness of the saving power of Jesus Christ. As the healed person brings other people to the Lord for healing, he becomes to them a savior in the similitude of the Savior, and the cycle of Zion is repeated—each saved person consecrating his healing to the Lord so that others might likewise be saved. Freely they have received, and freely they must give.

Reciprocal Love

To truly live the law of consecration and thus be endowed with power from on high,[827] we must enjoin mutual assistance, employ the priesthood for its intended purposes, and exercise great faith in the Lord and his promises. Only then are we fully able to love one another and become one. The law of the Church (D&C 42) simply states: "Thou shalt live together in love."[828] That is, we must be willing to give and receive love—true love

---

825   D&C 42:43, 48–51; emphasis added.
826   Oaks, "He Heals the Heavy Laden," 6–9.
827   D&C 38:32.
828   D&C 42:45.

is reciprocal. We must love both God and his children, and in turn we must receive love from them. This is the "the first and great commandment,"[829] the royal law.[830]

If we were limited to use only one word to define Zion, that word would be *love*; likewise, if we were limited to use only one word to describe the power of Zion, it would be *love*. Significantly, of all the words John could have used to portray God, he chose *love*.[831] *President Gordon B. Hinckley wrote: "This principle of love is the basic essence of the gospel of Jesus Christ. Without love of God and love of neighbor there is little else to commend the gospel to us as a way of life."*[832] *Therefore, for the pure purpose of love we live the law of Zion by caring for the poor and the sick "with all tenderness."*[833] *Elder John A. Widtsoe taught:*

> The full and essential nature of love we may not
> understand. But there are tests by which it may be
> recognized. Love is always founded in truth. . . . Lies
> and deceit, or any other violation of the moral law, are
> proofs of love's absence. Love perishes in the midst of
> untruth. Thus . . . [he] who falsifies to his loved one,
> or offers her any act contrary to truth, does not really
> love her. Further, love does not offend or hurt or injure
> the loved one. . . . Cruelty is as absent from love . . .
> as truth is from untruth. . . . Love is a positive active
> force. It helps the loved one. If there is need, love tries
> to supply it. If there is weakness, love supplants it with
> strength. . . . Love that does not help is a faked or
> transient love. Good as these tests are, there is a greater
> one. True love sacrifices for the loved one. . . . That is
> the final test. Christ gave of Himself, gave His life, for
> us, and thereby proclaimed the reality of his love for his
> mortal brethren and sisters.[834]

Reciprocal love is the grand key of happiness and glory, wrote Elder Joseph B. Wirth-lin. Jesus taught his disciples this "new commandment," to "love one another; as I have loved you."[835] His quality of love is the model, and we are to love likewise. Reciprocal love—freely giving and freely receiving love—should be our primary focus if we desire to be disciples of Jesus Christ. Improvement comes more readily to the soul filled with love than any other.[836] Neither can the law of consecration be lived nor Zion be established in our lives upon any other principle.

---

829   Matthew 22:36–40.
830   James 2:8.
831   1 John 4:8.
832   Hinckley, *Faith: The Essence of True Religion*, 49.
833   D&C 42:43.
834   Widtsoe, *An Understandable Religion*, 72.
835   John 13:34.
836   Wirthlin, "The Great Commandment," 28–31.

Charity—The Pure Love of Christ

True love—unconditional love—is called charity. This quality of love encompasses the two laws upon which hang all the law and the prophets—(1) "Thou shalt love the Lord thy God with all thy heart, with all thy might, mind, and strength; and in the name of Jesus Christ thou shalt serve him," and (2) "Thou shalt love thy neighbor as thyself."[837] Charity, then, not the outward rites of the law of Moses, is the driving force of Jesus' higher gospel law. Charity is the "new commandment"[838] Jesus attached to the higher law—new because it replaced the gospel motivation linked to the old law of rites and performances with the gospel motivation centered on the condition of the heart. Charity is saving love; charity lifts and rescues; charity forgives from enormous distances. As we experience the giving and receiving of charity, we eventually discover that we cannot escape its loving embrace: "charity endureth forever."[839]

We have two witnesses—Paul and Mormon—whose testimonies anchor the principles of Zion-like charity in our souls:

- Charity suffers long (endures hardship in faith or endures in faith with someone during his/her hardship)
- Charity is kind
- Charity does not envy
- Charity is not vaunted up (does not boast)
- Charity is not puffed up (is not proud)
- Charity does not behave unseemly (act inappropriately)
- Charity seeks not her own (is not selfish)
- Charity is not easily provoked (keeps anger under control)
- Charity thinks no evil (tries to focus on the good)
- Charity does not rejoice in iniquity but rejoices in the truth (does not enjoy the evil things of the fallen world but rather the true things of God)
- Charity bears all things (bears up under the weight of problems)
- Charity believes all things (recognizes and follows truth)
- Charity hopes all things (knows that God is ultimately in charge)
- Charity endures all things (is willing to make the necessary sacrifices in order to win the prize).[840]

Without charity, Paul says, we are nothing. Although we might accomplish many good works, speak with the tongue of angels, enjoy incredible spiritual gifts, bestow all our goods to feed the poor, and give our lives as martyrs, if we have not charity our good deeds profit us nothing.[841] In other words, as mentioned above, we might go through the motions of Christian living, but without charity our actions are hollow, and Zion will remain a distant ideal.

---

837   Matthew 22:40.
838   John 13:34.
839   Moroni 7:47.
840   1 Corinthians 13:4–8; commentary added; see also Moroni 7:45.
841   1 Corinthians 13:1–3.

The lesser law of Moses was constructed on the bedrock of rites and performances, but the higher law of Jesus Christ is built on the condition of the heart. Consequently, Mormon notes, "charity never faileth." This "pure love of Christ" endures forever and transcends a world in which everything is programmed to fail. Therefore, charity stands above every other virtue and "is the greatest of all."[842] We could never live the highest of gospel laws—consecration—without having cultivated the highest of gospel virtues—charity.

Charity Strengthened by Faith and Hope

Having listed the characteristics of charity, Paul submits a roadmap on to achieve this quality of love: "And now abideth faith, hope, charity, these three; but the greatest of these is charity."[843] Faith, hope, charity—Christianity's quintessential virtues. Mormon expands our understanding by adding hope to the front of the list: Hope, faith, hope, charity. "And again, my beloved brethren, I would speak unto you concerning hope. How is it that ye can attain unto faith, save ye shall have hope? . . . Wherefore, if a man have faith he must needs have hope."[844] The fact that hope is repeated is significant. Hoping that a principle is true leads us to experiment, or act, upon the principle. When we notice a desirable result from our action, hope increases. This cycle of faith and hope increases our charity, because the action of faith inevitably and by design leads to reconciliation with God as well as service to him and his children.

Alma takes the formula one step further by adding *desire* to the process of developing charity. He says that hearing the word of God starts us down this path. When we hear the word of God, we desire to know more; we desire to see if the principle will work in our lives; we begin to hunger and thirst for righteousness. Alma informs us that the word of God, which leads us to charity, is delivered to us by angels: "And now, [God] imparteth his word by angels unto men."[845] Nephi informs us that angels are both mortal and immortal beings who "speak the words of Christ" "by the power of the Holy Ghost."[846] Somewhere along the path, we begin to understand that charity is dissimilar to the substitute forms of love produced by the world; charity's uniqueness lies in the fact that it is a spiritual gift.

Alma continues by explaining that the word of God delivered by angels under the direction of the Holy Ghost is structured so that once it is planted in the soul, it will stir desire and hope: "And now my beloved brethren, as ye have *desired* to know of me what ye shall do . . ."[847] That is, upon hearing the word, we begin to experience hunger pangs for light and truth—we are filled with desire. At some point, desire and hope motivate us to experiment with charity. *If we extend charity, will charity rciprocate and grow?* Therefore, on faith alone, we summon courage to test to see if the desired result will actually happen. The action of experimenting is not only an act of faith but a manifestation of our agency and an action that flows from our hope. The moment that action is applied to

---

842   Moroni 7:46–47.
843   1 Corinthians 13:13.
844   Moroni 7:40, 42.
845   Alma 32:23.
846   2 Nephi 32:3.
847   Alma 32:24; emphasis added.

hope, hope becomes faith. Borrowing Alma's analogy of comparing faith with a seed, the prophet explained that even a "particle"   the smallest of actions—enables the seed of charity to take root in our souls.

Alma explained that something marvelous begins to happen at this point. Beyond our consciousness, stirring occurs beneath the surface; roots start to extend from the hull of the seed, and an independent life has begun. If we will hang on and tend the spot of ground where the seed of charity has been planted, a new life will soon burst into open view. One day a tender plant will erupt through the soil; it will have changed from a seed of charity to a seedling of charity, like a caterpillar transforming into a butterfly. As the seedling matures with measurable "swelling motions,"[848] we start to recognize that our experiment with the seed of charity is "good." As Alma said, "It beginneth to enlarge my soul."

The evidence of growth leads us to hope more—hope is confirmable expectation. That is, as we experience and receive charity, we allow ourselves to imagine the harvest that the seed of charity will yield; more importantly, we *expect* an abundant harvest. Charity is always a product of hope and faith.

Alma explained that the trueness of the seed is confirmed by four tests:

1. We feel something positive stirring within us.
2. We feel invigorated, and we are motivated to become a better person.
3. The idea corresponds with, builds upon, and clarifies other ideas we have had, and now it sparks new ideas.
4. The idea feels so good that we want to keep seeking after it to follow it to its perfect conclusion.

The seed, or the word of God, is expansive, enlightening, and delicious. It increases faith; it is discernible; it is clearly good. If we do not neglect or reject it, the seed will grow into a tree that bears the beautiful fruit of charity, the love of God,[849] "which is most precious, which is sweet above all that is sweet, and which it white, yea, and pure above all that is pure."[850]

Charity Transforms the Heart

What is said of faith could be said of charity. Like faith, charity originates and emerges from the word of God. If nurtured, the seed of charity, which carries the genotype of divinity, will transform its host into the image of God. With every swelling motion toward maturity, the seed will change our heart until it resembles the heart of Jesus Christ. The more the seed of faith grows, the more we talk, act, serve, and love like the Savior. Eventually, we are filled with charity; we become the personification of it. We become the "pure love of Christ."[851] As much as "God is love,"[852] so we become "this love."[853] Fully blossomed, we can fully consecrate; now we can fully become Zion people.

---

848   Alma 32:28.
849   1 Nephi 11:22.
850   Alma 32:26–43.
851   Moroni 7:47.
852   1 John 4:8.
853   Moroni 7:48.

We commence on the road to becoming charity by first receiving charity from God: "Herein is love, not that we loved God, but that he loved us."[854] When charity is presented to us, it tastes "delicious," as the scripture states; we desire more charity and we hope that what we have heard and encountered is true. Desire and hope motivate us to exercise our agency and try an experiment. On faith alone, we nurture the seed of charity that was planted in our souls by the God's charity toward us. As we care for the seed, it takes root. Our experiment of faith is rewarded when the seed sprouts, whereupon we recognize that the seed of charity was "good." This causes us to hope for a bountiful harvest. Now our hope is strengthened, helping us to become determined to endure in faith until end: the time of harvest.

The glory of Zion is first to obtain charity and then to duplicate the process in others. Now we become the angels who plant the word of God; now we become God's servants,who help another hope-filled experimenter nourish his tender plant; now we become saviors in Zion who encourage, strengthen, and hold up the grower when the hot sun scorches his plant and when all seems lost; now we become God's friends who finally share in his harvest. We *are* charity! We are those whose countenances reflect that of the Lord of the Harvest;[855] we are the ones who have loved with the pure love of Christ until we have brought our fellow beings into the full image of Christ.

This process never falls short or breaks down: "Charity *never* faileth." If charity can never fail, Zion can never fail, because Zion is built upon charity, "the greatest of all," the celestial quality of love that "endureth forever."[856] Clearly, charity is the quintessential virtue, "the end of the commandment,"[857] the power that invigorates and propels the law of consecration and the establishment of Zion.

Charity Defines Discipleship

Zion people order their lives exactly opposite the people of Babylon. Zion people "seek . . . first the kingdom of God and his righteousness"[858] and exemplify the defining characteristic of Deity that comprehends all righteousness: *charity.*[859] *They do this by consecrating themselves to the Lord and extending loving service to God and his children. In every way, they are disciples of Jesus Christ who do his works.*

Beyond every other virtue, charity defines discipleship. The measure of our belief is how, and how much we love. Therefore, the Lord lists charity as being a central qualification for the ministers of Jesus Christ.[860] We simply cannot assist the Lord in his work without charity;[861] therefore, as Elder McConkie reminded us, "The saints of God are

854   1 John 4:10.
855   Alma 5:14.
856   Moroni 7:46–47.
857   1 Timothy 1:5.
858   Matthew 6:33; 3 Nephi 13:33.
859   Matthew 22:36–40.
860   D&C 4:5.
861   D&C 12:8; 18:19.

commanded to seek and attain it."[862] Why? Because we cannot give something we do not have. We must first receive love from God, who is the source of love,[863] and then we must give that love to God's children. Otherwise, all that has been given to us will be lost.

Charity not only defines the pathway of discipleship, it marks every point along the way. Charity transforms a natural man into a sanctified Saint, someone who by nature seeks to comfort the downtrodden; charity counsels the oppressed in faith, heals the sick and afflicted, and consoles the brokenhearted. Charity is the light that guides us through valleys of darkness, and ultimately charity leads us to the magnificence of eternal life.[864]

If charity is the defining characteristic of Jesus Christ, it is also the defining characteristic of his servants. A number of people have wondered how Joseph Smith was able to attract and retain so many followers. His answer epitomizes the connection between charity and consecration: "It is because I possess the principle of love. All I can offer the world is a good heart and a good hand."[865] The Prophet gave all that he had and was to help others. He did not do these things to fulfill a commandment; rather he did what he did because he was filled with love. When he encountered need, he confronted it; he would not allow lack and suffering to exist in his presence.

Keeping and Feeding—The Two Tests of Charity

Jesus gave us two tests of charity:
1. "If ye love me, *keep* my commandments."[866]
2. "If ye love me *feed* my sheep."[867]

Clearly, charity—*Christlike love*—is defined by action. A declaration of love is meaningless unless it is demonstrated by remaining faithful and proffering service: *keeping* and *feeding*. The person who professes love but is disloyal is a liar; the person who proclaims love but who is selfish and nonsacrificing is a hypocrite.

Conversely, charity keeps its vows and goes out to find and nourish others; charity heals on every front, physically, mentally, morally, and spiritually. Elder Marvin J. Ashton taught that the *keeping* element of charity centers on keeping the commandments, most specifically the first and great commandment,[868] the royal law.[869] We show our love for the Lord by obeying the second great commandment, to "love [our] neighbor as [ourselves]—to go out to find and feed his sheep. Keeping this commandment motivates us to care for, share with, uplift, extend sympathy and kindness, and provide for the comfort of God's children. Keeping and feeding are to stand proxy for the Savior and do as he would do if he were present. Therefore, to the extent that we *keep* the Lord's command-

862   McConkie, *Mormon Doctrine,* 121–22; see also 1 Corinthians 16:14; 1 Timothy 4:12; 2 Timothy 2:22; Titus 2:2; 2 Peter 1:7; 2 Nephi 33:7–9; Alma 7:24; D&C 121:45; 124:116.
863   1 John 4:19.
864   Wirthlin, "The Great Commandment," 28–31.
865   Smith, *Teachings of the Prophet Joseph Smith,* 313.
866   John 14:15; emphasis added.
867   Paraphrased from John 21:16; emphasis added.
868   Ashton, "Love Takes Time," 108.
869   Matthew 22:36–40.

ments, we show our love for him; and to the proportion that we *feed* the Lord's sheep, we *keep* the second great commandmen and, consequently, the first.

Feeding and keeping are embedded in King Benjamin's teachings concerning charity. Blaine Yorgason points out: "Benjamin then instructed his people to (1) live peaceably and kindly with each other; (2) give diligent attention to the spiritual and temporal needs of their children; (3) teach their children the peaceable way of Christ; (4) impart freely of their substance to any who stood in need of it, 'every man according to that which he hath, such as feeding the hungry, clothing the naked, visiting the sick and administering to their relief, both spiritually and temporally, according to their wants'; (5) never take advantage of another by borrowing and not returning; (6) always watch their thoughts, words, and deeds, observing the commandments of God, and 'continue in the faith of what ye have heard concerning . . . our Lord, even unto the end of your lives' (Mosiah 4:13–30)."[870]

Charity—The Lifeblood of Zion

Most certainly, charity is love in action, and that action always involves sacrifice. Without the action of charitable sacrifice, Zion could not be established in the life of an individual, or in a marriage, a family, a ward, or a society. It is by consecrated sacrifice that we *keep* the commandments and hold true to our covenants.[871] It is by sacrifice that we *feed* the Lord's sheep. It is by sacrifice that we love God. President Gordon B. Hinckley wrote: "Without sacrifice there is no true worship of God. 'The Father gave his Son, and the Son gave his life,' and we do not worship unless we give—give of our substance, . . . our time, . . . strength, . . . talent, . . . faith, . . . [and] testimonies."[872]

Helping, giving, and loving always require selfless sacrifice. It is sacrifice, we sing, that "brings forth the blessings of heaven."[873] As we have mentioned, charitable service creates a positive imbalance that demands correcting. This is the "hundredfold" law,[874] which President Thomas S. Monson described this way: "It is an immutable law that the more you give away, the more you receive." Then, referencing a quote attributed to Winston Churchill, he said, "'You make a living by what you get, but you make a life by what you give.'"[875] This "immutable law"—the hundredfold law—drives Zion's cycle of abundance and makes Zion people exceedingly prosperous.[876] In accordance with this law, we give what we have and are, and the Lord rewards us beyond our sacrifice. As long as we do not stop the cycle by keeping what we receive, we will become a *vessel of help*; the Lord will pour down blessings through us to his needy children, and in the process our prosperity will increase until it approaches the infinite abundance of the kingdom of heaven. Thus, charity is the lifeblood of Zion, and consecrated sacrifice is the principle that propels Zion's prosperity.

870   Yorgason, *I Need Thee Every Hour,* 213.
871   D&C 97:8.
872   Hinckley, *The Teachings of Gordon B. Hinckley,* 565.
873   Phelps, "Praise to the Man," *Hymns,* no. 27.
874   Genesis 26:12; 2 Samuel 24:3; Matthew 13:8–23; 19:29; Mark 10:30; Luke 8:8; D&C 98:25; 132:55.
875   Monson, "In Quest of the Abundant Life," 2.
876   4 Nephi 1:7.

Charity is the principle upon which Zion people achieve equality and unity: "And above all things, clothe yourselves with the bond of charity, as with a mantle, which is the bond of perfectness and peace."[877] When Zion people give and receive charity, they cease to be afraid: "perfect love casteth out all fear."[878] Therefore, in the life of a Zion person *all* things are to be done in charity. According to Peter, we are to array ourselves in "fervent charity." Over time, this "pure love of Christ" becomes an integral part of our natures.[879] Elder McConkie taught: "Charity is more than love, far more; it is everlasting love, perfect love, the pure love of Christ which endureth forever. It is love so centered in righteousness that the possessor has no aim or desire except for the eternal welfare of his own soul and for the souls of those around him."[880]

When charity, the love exemplified by Zion people, is planted in the hearts of a few people, it acts as leaven "until the whole [of humanity is] leavened."[881] Again we recall the words of Joseph Smith: "A man filled with the love of God is not content with blessing his family alone, but ranges through the whole world, anxious to bless the whole human race."[882] It is charity that infuses Zion people with power. According to Elder Ashton, charity is the crowning principle that makes possible eternal joy and progression.[883]

Charity Is Defined by Service

President Hinckley called love "the lodestar of life." Citing the Savior's reference to the Final Judgment, President Hinckley reminded us that Jesus will say to those on his right hand that they shall inherit his kingdom because they effectively "fed, clothed, and visited Him" by blessing his children. President Hinckley wrote: "One of the greatest challenges we face in our hurried, self-centered lives is to follow this counsel of the Master, to take the time and make the effort to care for others, to develop and exercise the one quality that would enable us to change the lives of others—what the scriptures call charity. . . . Best defined, charity is that pure love exemplified by Jesus Christ. It embraces kindness, a reaching out to lift and help, the sharing of one's bread, if need be."[884]

We become angels to the poor and afflicted. We are taught that there are "angels round about [us], to bear [us] up."[885] As much as angels are instruments in the Lord's hands to sustain us and help to carry our heavy burdens, so we, by our charitable service, are angels to God's children and instruments in the Lord's hands to steady the weak and to heft their weighty loads.[886] Often in our lives, angels are the charitable people around us, people who love us, people who yield their hearts to God that they might be

877   D&C 88:125; see also Colossians 3:14.
878   Moroni 8:16.
879   1 Peter 4:8.
880   McConkie, *Mormon Doctrine,* 121, quoting 2 Nephi 26:30; Moroni 7:47; 8:25–26.
881   Matthew 13:33; Luke 13:21.
882   Smith, *History of the Church,* 4:227.
883   Ashton, "Be a Quality Person," 64.
884   Hinckley, *Standing for Something,* 6.
885   D&C 84:88.
886   Tanner, "All Things Shall Work Together for Your Good," 104.

instruments in his hands. President Spencer W. Kimball said, "God does notice us, and he watches over us. But it is usually through another person that he meets our needs. Therefore, it is vital that we serve each other in the kingdom."[887]

President Kimball gave other essential counsel concerning charitable service:

- *Sharing Our Abundant life.* "One has hardly proved his life abundant until he has built up a crumbling wall, paid off a heavy debt, enticed a disbeliever to his knees, filled an empty stomach, influenced a soul to wash in the blood of the lamb, turned fear and frustration into peace and sureness, led one to be 'born again.' One is measuring up to his opportunity potential when he has saved a crumbling marriage, transformed the weak into the strong, changed a civil to a proper temple marriage, brought enemies from the cesspool of hate to the garden of love, made a child trust and love him, changed a scoffer into a worshiper, melted a stony heart into one of flesh and muscle."[888]

- *To become like Christ, "give yourselves away."* "Christ's life is the epitome of service. *Give yourselves away.* That's the life of the Savior of this world. He gave himself away when he personally went to the house of Peter and blessed his mother-in-law 'who was sick of a fever.' He gave himself away when he stood on the mount and preached for hours 'the way of salvation' to the multitude. He gave himself away when he walked long, dusty, tortuous miles to Bethany to bring comfort and even life back to Lazarus, and to Mary and Martha, the sisters who were grieving. He gave himself away when he healed the sick and opened the blind eyes and cleared the stopped hearing and gave strength to the sick. He gave much of himself in every blessing. When the woman reached forth to touch the hem of his garment, he felt that power had gone out of him. He gave that power and part of himself willingly, and after three years of spectacular ministry, he voluntarily walked back into the trap set for him, announced his approaching fate, walked out of Gethsemane into the hands of mobsters and to the courts of politicians and to the cross and gave himself for all mankind."[889]

- *Perfect service by practicing service.* "A striking personality and good character is achieved by practice, not merely by thinking it. Just as a pianist masters the intricacies of music through hours and weeks of practice, so mastery of life is achieved by the ceaseless practice of mechanics which make up the art of living. *Daily unselfish service to others is one of the rudimentary mechanics of the successful life.* 'For whosoever will save his life,' the Galilean said, 'shall lose it, and whosoever will lose his life for my sake shall find it.' (Matthew 16:25.) What a strange paradox this! And yet one needs only to analyze it to be convinced of its truth."[890]

887   Kimball, *The Teachings of Spencer W. Kimball,* 252.
888   Kimball, *The Teachings of Spencer W. Kimball,* 249.
889   Kimball, *The Teachings of Spencer W. Kimball,* 250.
890   Kimball, *The Teachings of Spencer W. Kimball,* 250.

- *The "divine paradox" of service.* "Only when you lift a burden, God will lift your burden. Divine paradox this! The man who staggers and falls because his burden is too great can lighten that burden by taking on the weight of another's burden. *You get by giving, but your part of giving must be given first.*"[891]

- *Glorious rewards from small charitable acts.* "So often, our acts of service consist of simple encouragement or of giving mundane help with mundane tasks—*but what glorious consequences can flow from mundane acts and from small but deliberate deeds!*"[892]

- *"Most essential" quality.* "[This is] perhaps the most essential godlike quality: *compassion and love*—compassion shown forth in service to others, unselfishness, that ultimate expression of concern for others we call love."[893]

- *Service is the next step in spiritual growth.* "Let us not shrink from the next steps in our spiritual growth, brothers and sisters, by holding back, or sidestepping our *fresh opportunities for service* to our families and our fellowmen."[894]

- *"Difficulties are opportunities for service."* "Let us trust the Lord and take the next steps in our individual lives. . . . Sometimes the solution is not to change our circumstance, but to change our attitude about that circumstance; *difficulties are often opportunities for service.*"[895]

- *Service is a testimony.* "The most vital thing we can do is to *express our testimonies through service*, which will, in turn, produce spiritual growth, greater commitment, and a greater capacity to keep the commandments."[896]

- *Service puts problems in perspective.* "When we are engaged in the service of our fellowmen, not only do our deeds assist them, but we put our own problems in a fresher perspective. When we concern ourselves more with others, there is less time to be concerned with ourselves. In the midst of the miracle of serving, there is the promise of Jesus, that by losing ourselves, we find ourselves. Not only do we 'find' ourselves in terms of acknowledging guidance in our lives, but *the more we serve our fellowmen in appropriate ways, the more substance there is to our souls.*"[897]

- *Antidote for loneliness.* "Perhaps you could take a loaf of bread or a covered dish to someone in need. Uncompensated service is one answer, one good answer to overcome loneliness."[898]

---

891 Kimball, *The Teachings of Spencer W. Kimball,* 251.
892 Kimball, *The Teachings of Spencer W. Kimball,* 252.
893 Kimball, *The Teachings of Spencer W. Kimball,* 253.
894 Kimball, *The Teachings of Spencer W. Kimball,* 253.
895 Kimball, *The Teachings of Spencer W. Kimball,* 254.
896 Kimball, *The Teachings of Spencer W. Kimball,* 254.
897 Kimball, *The Teachings of Spencer W. Kimball,* 254.
898 Kimball, *The Teachings of Spencer W. Kimball,* 256; emphasis added.

Charitable Service Saves and Exalts

It is a gospel verity that charity saves the lives of both the giver and the receiver. What the Lord has said of missionaries could be said of anyone who is willing to enter the field of need and thrust in his sickle: "For behold the field is white already to harvest; and lo, he that thrusteth in his sickle with his might, the same layeth up in store that he perisheth not, *but bringeth salvation to his soul.*"[899] *Clearly, there is so much need, and the Lord has placed within our reach the spiritual power to supply that need. A joyful and bounteous harvest awaits those who give charitable service to the Lord's poor: "And if it so be that you should labor all your days in crying repentance unto this people, and bring, save it be one soul unto me, how great shall be your joy with him in the kingdom of my Father! And now, if your joy will be great with one soul that you have brought unto me into the kingdom of my Father, how great will be your joy if you should bring many souls unto me!"*[900]

Charity is sometimes a handout, but it is always a hand up. Salvation comes to our souls when we lift another and give of ourselves and our means in the purest and highest of motivations—*love.* President Joseph F. Smith said, "I would advise that we learn to love each other, and then friendship will be true and sweet. It has been said by one, that 'we may give without loving, but we cannot love without giving.'"[901] We note with interest that it was only when the people of Limhi repented, became unified, and began to practice a form of consecration—caring for the widows and orphans—that deliverance from bondage came.[902] Likewise, it was the Mormon Battalion whose men consecrated their earnings and service, thereby saving the Church from financial ruin and providing the necessary capital to equip the impoverished Saints for their westward trek.

Moroni's Prayer for Latter-day Charity

Salvation, or the forfeiture of it, swings on the hinge of charity. Moroni looked into the future with the eyes of a seer and saw the woeful latter-day deficit of charitable service. He mourned that our salvation would be at risk: "If the Gentiles have not charity, because of our weakness, . . . thou wilt prove them, and take away their talent, yea, even that which they have received, and give unto them who shall have more abundantly." At this point, Moroni offered a prayer that we might receive the gift of charity for our own salvation. At least to a degree, we might trace the level of charity that we presently enjoy back to Moroni's prayer: "And it came to pass that I prayed unto the Lord that he would give unto the Gentiles grace, that they might have charity."[903]

During Moroni's prayer, Jesus promised this prophet that he would provide us "Gentiles" of the last days with his grace so that we might receive and exhibit charity, which virtue would open the door to our salvation: "I will show unto them that

---

899   D&C 4:4; emphasis added.
900   D&C 18:15–16.
901   Smith, *Teachings of Presidents of the Church: Joseph F. Smith,* 192.
902   Mosiah 21:16–18.
903   Ether 12:35–36.

faith, hope and charity bringeth [souls] unto me." Moroni understood the foundation and importance of charity, and he bore his testimony concerning it: "I remember that thou hast said that thou hast loved the world, even unto the laying down of thy life for the world, that thou mightest take it again to prepare a place for the children of men. And now I know that this love which thou hast had for the children of men is charity; wherefore, except men shall have charity they cannot inherit that place which thou hast prepared in the mansions of thy Father."[904] Salvation is simply not possible without charity. This virtue is the prerequisite for our entering into the kingdom of heaven. Moroni concludes with these words: "Except ye have charity ye can in nowise be saved in the kingdom of God."[905]

When the Lord comes in his glory, he will divide out the sheep from the goats. To the sheep on his right hand he will say, "Come, ye blessed of my Father, inherit the kingdom prepared for you from the foundation of the world." The criteria for their salvation will be three-fold: (1) They gave food and drink to those in need; (2) They used their time, talents, and resources for the poor; and (3) They ministered to the sick and the imprisoned. In all their ministrations, they saw in each impoverished soul the image of Jesus Christ, the Savior of the impoverished, sick, or captive person.[906] For what they did and who they became, and through the grace of Christ, they earned their exaltation.

Charitable Service Protects the Giver

Cain first stated the motto of Babylon in the form of a question: "Am I my brother's keeper?"[907] That self-centered statement became the foundation of the anti-Christ doctrine advanced by Korihor:

1. Hope and faith in Christ are foolish and vain.
2. Those who believe in Christ and his coming are not free but in bondage.
3. There is no such thing as prophecy and revelation.
4. The words of the prophets are foolish traditions.
5. Seeing is believing; reality is only measurable by applying scientific methods.
6. The concept of sin against God's laws and remission of sin based on repentance are evidences of a frenzied, deranged mind that is held captive by false traditions.
7. An atonement for sin is unnecessary and impossible.
8. In this dog-eat-dog world, men get by according to their individual management; they prosper according to their genius, and they conquer according to their strength. Everything depends on me; everything revolves around me.
9. Men legislate the standards of morality. Because God does not exist, men are not accountable to him, and whatever they do is not a crime against God.
10. Wickedness brings happiness.

---

904 Ether 12:28–34.
905 Moroni 10:21.
906 Matthew 25:34–40.
907 Genesis 4:9.

11. Live for today, because when we die, it is the end.
12. The servants of God operate by intrigue. They pretend to receive visions and revelations to keep their people in ignorance. They do this so that they might usurp power and authority over the people, keep them in bondage, and profiteer on the labor and offerings of the people.
13. Lest the people should offend their leaders and forfeit their place in the Church, the people are coerced into consecrating their goods.[908]

None of these statements is Zion-like. The entire anti-Christ philosophy is faithless, immoral, destructive, and selfish. In no way does it draw us to Christ, encourage us to depend on him, shelter us from the consequences of sin, provide for the poor, or make us our brother's keeper. To Cain's selfish motto—"Am I my brother's keeper?"—the Lord countered with the doctrine of Zion that carries several promises: "Blessed is he that considereth the poor: the Lord will deliver him in time of trouble. The Lord will preserve him, and keep him alive; and he shall be blessed upon the earth: and thou wilt not deliver him unto the will of his enemies. The Lord will strengthen him."[909]

The mantra of Zion is a way of life. President Heber J. Grant said, "Make a motto in life: always try and assist someone else to carry his burden."[910] The prophet of Ecclesiastes stated that when we plant seeds of service to bless God's children, we save our own souls, "for thou knowest not what evil shall be upon the earth." Our safety is on the line. When evil attempts to overwhelm us, when terrifying storms gather above us, when temptations encompass us, charity will protect us—"there [our safety] shall be." The prophet said we do not understand how God transforms our charitable acts into cloaks of safety; we only know that it happens. Therefore, we are to go about liberally planting the seeds of charitable service: "In the morning sow thy seed, and in the evening withhold not thine hand." We do not know which seeds of charity will take root and how they will prosper.[911] We only know that by sowing and nourishing charitable acts, many people are blessed by our actions and we will be kept safe.

Charitable Service Prospers the Giver

The promise of charitable service is that of an abundant return. President Marion G. Romney taught the following truth: "You cannot give yourself poor in this work; you can only give yourself rich."[912] His statement is a confirmation of the ancient prophet's teaching: "Cast thy bread upon the waters: for thou shalt find it after many days."[913] This suggests both a boomerang effect and a germination period. Bread that is cast upon the water will most certainly float back to land on the tide or a current; that is,

---

908   Alma 30:12–28.
909   Psalm 41:1–2.
910   Grant, *Teachings of Presidents of the Church: Heber J. Grant,* 139.
911   Ecclesiastes 11:2–6.
912   Romney, Welfare Services: The Savior's Program," 92.
913   Ecclesiastes 11:1.

our charitable actions will always return to bless us. Moreover, the seed will eventually find land, set down roots, sprout, and grow; that is, charitable acts carry the potential of life within them; charitable acts might take time to find ground and take root, but in time, those acts will become a beautiful and fruitful tree. We cannot be impoverished by casting the seeds of our charity upon the water. We cannot consecrate ourselves poor.

We recall our discussion about abundance flowing to us as we manifest charity: We grow from grace *to* grace by giving grace *for* grace. We also have learned that it is upon the principle of service that we progress toward perfection. Therefore, by receiving grace (the Lord's help) *for* grace (our service), we grow *from* grace (light, truth, power, and perfection) *to* grace (more light, truth, power, and perfection). According to John the Baptist's testimony, Jesus grew in grace (light, truth, power, and perfection) by giving grace (service): "And I, John, saw that he received not of the fulness at the first, but received grace *for* grace. And he received not of the fulness at first, but continued from grace *to* grace, until he received a fulness."[914] Likewise, we progress incrementally from grace *to* grace to a fulness of glory by keeping the commandments and giving service, whereupon the Lord blesses us by granting us grace for our having given grace to another: "For if you keep my commandments you shall receive of his fulness, and be glorified in me as I am in the Father; therefore, I say unto you, you shall receive grace *for* grace."[915]

The hundredfold principle applies here.[916] When we receive the seed of *grace* from God or a charitable person, we should plant that seed by giving charity to another person rather than hoard that seed of charity . The replanting of the seed will urge a stalk containing many seeds to grow. If we will plant again, this time with a great number of seeds that will cover an expansive swath of ground, we will realize a marvelous harvest. Thus, ever repeating the cycle of planting and harvesting constitutes the mystery of Zion's prosperity. It is the Zion principle of giving and receiving a return with increase.[917]

Therefore, should we be concerned about keeping the commandment to consecrate? Do we really believe that we will end up with less? President Kimball refuted the idea and challenged our faith: "What are we to fear when the Lord is with us? Can we not take the Lord at his word and exercise a particle of faith in him? Our assignment is affirmative: to forsake the things of the world as ends in themselves; to leave off idolatry and press forward in faith; to carry the gospel to our enemies, that they might no longer be our enemies. We must leave off the worship of modern-day idols and a reliance on the 'arm of flesh,' for the Lord has said to all the world in our day, 'I will not spare any that remain in Babylon.'"[918] Clearly, our ultimate safety is found only in extending charity and consecrating our lives, property, time, and talents for the building up of God's kingdom and for the establishment of Zion.

---

914   D&C 93:12–13; emphasis added.
915   D&C 93:20; emphasis added.
916   Matthew 19:29; Mark 10:30.
917   Packer, "The Candle of the Lord," 54–55.
918   Kimball, *The Teachings of Spencer W. Kimball,* 417, quoting D&C 64:24.

Patience and Charity

President Heber J. Grant explained that charity is often characterized by patience: "The gospel of Christ is a gospel of love and peace, of patience and long suffering, of forbearance and forgiveness, of kindness and good deeds, of charity and brotherly love. Greed, avarice, base ambition, thirst for power, and unrighteous dominion over our fellow men, can have no place in the hearts of Latter-day Saints nor of God-fearing men everywhere."[919] Our leaders have offered insight into the relationship between patience and charity. Of the thirteen elements of charity listed by Mormon, four of them relate to patience:

1. charity suffereth long
2. is not easily provoked
3. beareth all things
4. endureth all things

We can no more achieve a Christlike character without patience than we can achieve personal value without charity, for if we "have not charity, [we] are nothing."[920]

Patience means to wait:

"I will wait *for* you."

"I will wait *with* you."

"I will wait *upon* you." In other words, "I will serve you."

It is the virtue of charity that perfects the virtue of patience, and it is patience that perfects all other virtues. Patience finishes the process of perfection and moves us toward completion and abundance: "But let patience have her perfect work, that ye may be perfect and entire, wanting nothing."[921] It is by means of patience that we both manifest and receive charity. Moreover, it is by means of patience that we consecrate ourselves in faith, because we cannot see the end of our consecration from our present vantage point. In patience we suffer, or *allow*, adversity to be our companion for a long time while waiting in faith for the Lord's deliverance. In patience we restrain from giving offense. In patience we forgive multiple times. In patience we show kindness when kindness is not returned. In patience we offer brotherly love over an extended period. Clearly, in patience we wait *for*, *with*, and *upon* the Lord and his children.

Charity and Virtue—Essential Elements of Priesthood Power

We have learned that we demonstrate our love for God by keeping his commandments and feeding his sheep. We have also have learned that showing love to others is requisite for the doctrine of the priesthood to distill upon our souls as the dews from heaven.[922] With confidence, then, we might point to charity as the preeminent virtue that trans-

---

919   Grant, *Teachings of Presidents of the Church: Heber J. Grant*, 139.
920   Oaks, "The Power of Patience," 15–17, quoting Moroni 7:44–46.
921   James 1:4.
922   D&C 121:45.

forms priesthood authority into priesthood power. Without charity, priesthood fails, and if priesthood fails, so does Zion.

In addition to all other considerations, charity transforms those who are *called* into those who are *chosen*. Such people are the products of a new and purified heart. They operate "by persuasion, by long-suffering, by gentleness and meekness, and by love unfeigned . . . by kindness, and pure knowledge." Such people are filled with "charity towards all men, and to the household of faith," and virtue garnishes their thoughts unceasingly. Their charitable service and virtue summon the greatest of priesthood blessings: "Then shall thy confidence wax strong in the presence of God; and the doctrine of the priesthood shall distil upon thy soul as the dews from heaven. The Holy Ghost shall be thy constant companion, and thy scepter an unchanging scepter of righteousness and truth; and thy dominion shall be an everlasting dominion, and without compulsory means it shall flow unto thee forever and ever."[923] Clearly, priesthood power depends on a consecrated heart, virtue, and charitable service. Then when priesthood power is in place, it prepares the way for the establishment of Zion.

Charity Draws the Lord Near

Things that are alike attract each other: "For intelligence cleaveth unto intelligence; wisdom receiveth wisdom; truth embraceth truth; virtue loveth virtue; light cleaveth unto light; mercy hath compassion on mercy and claimeth her own; justice continueth its course and claimeth its own; judgment goeth before the face of him who sitteth upon the throne and governeth and executeth all things."[924] The Charitable One draws near when we manifest charity.

Conversely, when we fail to exhibit charity, we create distance between the Lord and ourselves. President Marion G. Romney suggested that we can close the gap by extending charity. To demonstrate this point, he used the example of the law of the fast as explained in Isaiah 58:3–12. Sometimes we wonder why it is that our fast seems to go unnoticed by the Lord. "Wherefore have we fasted . . . and thou seest not?" Isaiah gave the Lord's answer. It is because we do not understand and keep the true law of the fast. We accomplish only two of the three criteria of that law (prayer and humility), but we neglect the third criterion: dealing our bread to the hungry, providing for the poor, and covering the naked. According to Isaiah, a fast without extending charity yields no more blessings than shedding a few extra pounds.

On the other hand, a fast that would "loose the bands of wickedness," "undo the heavy burdens," "let the oppressed go free," and "break every yoke" requires that we extend charity to the needy, including the hurting members of our family; and from our lives we must eliminate strife, debate, anger, and contention: "Is not this the fast that I have chosen? . . . Is it not to deal thy bread to the hungry, and that thou bring the poor that are cast out to thy house? when thou seest the naked, that thou cover him; and that thou hide not thyself from thine own flesh [family]?"

---

923 D&C 121:40–46.
924 D&C 88:40.

The law of the fast serves as model for other laws of God. The principle of charity is woven into the fabric of each of them. If we would obtain the promised blessing for any law, we must extend charitable service to our family and to others of the children of God; we must not allow strife, debate, anger, or contention to invade our lives in any degree. Otherwise, the desired blessings for living any law will be forfeited, and the distance between the Lord and us will remain unaltered.

But if we will live the laws of God, eliminate strife, debate, anger, and contention from our lives, and give generous charitable service, then the Lord will draw near: "Then shalt thou call, and the Lord shall answer; thou shalt cry, and he shall say, Here I am." The Lord always draws near to those who follow such a course, and when he comes, he always brings blessings with him:

> Then shall thy light break forth as the morning, and thine health shall spring forth speedily: and thy righteousness shall go before thee; the glory of the Lord shall be thy rereward [protector]. . . . And if thou draw out thy soul to the hungry, and satisfy the afflicted soul; then shall thy light rise in obscurity, and thy darkness be as the noonday: and the Lord shall guide thee continually, and satisfy thy soul in drought, and make fat thy bones: and thou shalt be like a watered garden, and like a spring of water, whose waters fail not. And they that shall be of thee [your posterity] shall build the old waste places: thou shalt raise up the foundations of many generations; and thou shalt be called, The repairer of the breach, The restorer of paths to dwell in.[925]

Consider the blessings of combining charity with obedience! Answers to prayers; light bursting upon the soul, dispelling darkness; restoration of health; increase of righteousness and righteous influence; divine protection and guidance; relief and deliverance; sustenance; abundance; a constant flow of blessings; power; redemption; exaltation; a healing of our generations; multiplication of righteous posterity; and, finally, a savior to our family and to others.

President Romney stated that extending charitable service to the needy is the primary purpose and a fixed requirement of the royal law. For example, Amulek taught the people that the law of prayer, like the law of the fast, requires charitable giving to be effective: "After ye have done all these things, if ye turn away the needy, and the naked, and visit not the sick and afflicted, and impart of your substance, if ye have, to those who stand in need—I say unto you, if ye do not any of these things, *behold, your prayer is*

---

925   Isaiah 58:8–12.

vain, and availeth you nothing, and ye are as hypocrites who do deny the faith."[926] This is the proper way to pray. If we pray and do not extend charitable service, we have not fulfilled the law that governs prayer, and, therefore, we cannot expect our prayers to be answered.

Neither fasting nor prayer nor any other law of God becomes valid as a principle of power without charity. Neither can our testimony be a declaration of the truth unless our lives are filled with charity. Mormon said, "If a man be meek and lowly in heart, and confesses by the power of the Holy Ghost that Jesus is the Christ, he must needs have charity; for if he have not charity he is nothing; wherefore he must needs have charity."[927] Clearly, without charity, we are nothing.

Charity Is an Absolute

Few scriptural absolutes are as stunning as those describing charity:
- "If ye have not charity, ye are nothing."
- "Charity never faileth."
- "Charity . . . is the greatest of all."
- "Charity . . . endureth forever.[928]

In a world where everything fails, only those things that are built upon the foundation of charity will not fail. When we seek charity first, as exemplified by our seeking the kingdom of God and his righteousness first, we are promised that all else will fall into place and be added unto us.[929] Because of charity, the blessings of the priesthood will flow to us forever without compulsory means.[930]

Charity Is a Gift—The Greatest Gift

Despite our best efforts, we never will obtain charity or know its power in our lives unless the Holy Ghost delivers it to us. Charity is a spiritual gift that must be sought. Like the principle that states that we are saved by grace only after all we can do,[931] we receive charity as a gift only after we do all we can to obtain it. Therefore, because salvation is impossible without charity and because charity is delivered to us as a gift of the Spirit, Mormon pleads with us to "pray unto the Father with all the energy of heart, that ye may be filled with this love, which he hath bestowed upon all who are true followers of his Son, Jesus Christ."

When charity finally enters our souls, Mormon continues, this love becomes the vehicle to make of us "sons of God." Charity has the power to make us "like him." Ultimately, upon the principle of charity, we will become "as he is." This is our "hope; that

---

926   Romney, "The Royal Law of Love," 95, quoting Alma 34:28; emphasis added.
927   Moroni 7:44.
928   Moroni 7:46–47.
929   3 Nephi 13:33.
930   D&C 121:46.
931   2 Nephi 25:23.

we [through our charity] may be purified even as he is pure."[932] This is the principal aim and the ultimate destination of the royal law, the celestial law of love. It is this quality of love that propels the law of consecration and fulfills the first and second commandments: "Thou shalt love the Lord thy God with all thy heart, and with all thy soul, and with all thy mind. This is the first and great commandment. And the second is like unto it, Thou shalt love thy neighbour as thyself." Upon these commandments, said Jesus, "hang all the law and the prophets."[933] We consecrate because we love.

Summary and Conclusion

The law of consecration is the last and most difficult law to live. Only by our agreeing to obey this law and abide its precepts can we qualify for celestial glory and become like God. Consecration cannot be lived without charity; consecration is the natural outgrowth of charity.

This quality of love—"the pure love of Christ"—has the capacity to lift and to save others; therefore, it is unlike any other type of love, and it is completely foreign to the natural man. Only a fervent effort on our part can summon the Holy Ghost to infuse us with this spiritual gift. Once we have it, charity will provide us with the motivation and power to live a consecrated life. The evidence of charity and consecration is our yielding our hearts to God and our giving him the totality of who we are and what we have.

When we make the decision to yield our hearts to God and to consecrate our lives to him, we signal our desire that the Holy Ghost will come and perform in our lives the miracles of purification and sanctification.[934] We understand that only by our submitting to this process can we obtain the highest degree of salvation, which is exaltation. We also understand that only the virtue of charity can convey us there. It is charity that saturates us with the necessary courage to consecrate our lives and to change the nature of our hearts.

Our leaders have taught us that the Final Judgment will be more an accounting of what we have become than a tally of our good and bad actions. Unfortunately, many of us go through the motions of gospel living as if we were making deposits into a heavenly account we hope will save us. But going through the motions of keeping the commandments, ordinances, and covenants does not have power to save us. *Becoming* is the key to obtaining eternal life; the more we become as God is, the more we embrace his lifestyle; and fundamental to his lifestyle is the law of consecration.

Therefore, we must allow the Holy Ghost to purify and change our hearts, or we will come up short.[935] Our actions must be motivated not by regulations, rites, and performances, but by a purified and consecrated heart that holds nothing back from God and his children, a heart that wants to be transformed into the similitude of the heart of its Maker, who is describes as love.[936] As much as God is love, God is also a consecrated being.

---

932   Moroni 7:48.
933   Matthew 22:36–40.
934   Helaman 3:35.
935   Oaks, "The Challenge to Become," 32–34.
936   1 John 4:8.

Consecration flows from "the first and great commandment," upon which hangs "all the law and the prophets."[937] James calls this law the royal law, which is the law of saving, Christlike love.[938] Jesus stated it thus: "Thou shalt love the Lord thy God with all thy heart, and with all thy soul, and with all thy mind. This is the first and great commandment. And the second is like unto it, Thou shalt love thy neighbour as thyself."[939] Because we love God and his children, we consecrate ourselves: our time, abilities, all that we have, and all that we are. We do this for the purpose of building up the kingdom of God, which prepares the way for the establishment of Zion.

Zion and consecration are as inseparable as consecration and charity, or charity and unity and equality. Because we love, we unite and esteem all people as equals. We gather with them and insist that they receive equal treatment and equal access to the blessings of the Lord. This is consecration; this is the love of Zion.

Consecration is also characterized by agency, stewardship, accountability, and labor.

By our agency, we choose to love, and we also choose to give of ourselves and the goods in our stewardship to help others. Because we choose to live the order of consecration, we abandon our claims of ownership, and we consider all that we have and are as belonging to the Lord. Forevermore, we are stewards, not owners, of the Lord's resources, and, as stewards, we use the resources under our management for the Owner's intended purpose: to facilitate the highest possible quality of immortality for God's children with the goal of their achieving eternal life.[940] The law of stewardship provides us with the highest level of safety and security. God becomes our paymaster. As we faithfully manage the stewardship he has given us, laboring honestly and diligently for him, God allows us to receive sufficient for our needs *and* wants. We agree to be accountable to God and his servant, the bishop, for the management of our stewardship. Presently, we account to the bishop during tithing settlement and when we seek a temple recommend. We also account whenever he or we feel the need. Beyond those occasions of accounting, our leaders have instructed us that we should account to God daily in our evening prayers.[941]

The law of consecration is further characterized by the four cornerstones listed in the law of the Church (D&C 42). These cornerstones are: (1) Mutual assistance, (2) proper use of the priesthood, (3) the need for faith, and (4) reciprocal love.[942]

Concerning reciprocal love—true love, unconditional Christlike love—we learn that this love, which is charity, defines and drives the higher law of the gospel, including the highest law of that higher law, which is the law of consecration. Charity is the only love that can save both the giver and the receiver. This saving love has the ability to lift, forgive, and rescue from enormous distances. This saving love "never faileth."[943] Charity emerges from desire, faith, and hope. As we have said, all gospel actions are profitless

---

937 Matthew 22:38–40.
938 James 2:8.
939 Matthew 22:37–40.
940 Moses 1:39.
941 Bednar, "Pray Always," 41–44.
942 Johnson, "The Law of Consecration," 99.
943 Moroni 7:47.

without charity, and Paul reminds us that we are nothing if we have not cultivated this God-defining .[944] Charity is the very definition of discipleship. Charity is the primary motivating factor that inspires true disciples of Jesus Christ to live obediently, to sacrifice, to hold to the law of the gospel, to embrace the celestial lifestyle called chastity, and to consecrate all that they are and have to God. Clearly, charity vitalizes consecration and is the lifeblood of Zion.

By means of charitable consecration, the immutable law of abundance is set in motion: that which we give returns to us with increase—even an hundredfold. When the principles of charity and consecration are anchored on the earth, they act as leaven "until the whole [of humanity is] leavened."[945] Then we who give charitable service become angels to the poor and the afflicted; we go about attacking poverty of every kind with the sword of charity. We seek to eliminate suffering by consecrating our time, talents, and means. Wherever we encounter lack, we apply the remedy of love. We, the saviors on Mount Zion, do as the Savior would do: we lift, heal, console, save, and exalt. And we doggedly keep at it until there are no poor among us.[946] While we go about extending charitable, consecrated service, the Lord protects us in our labors. Our motto is that of Zion: "Always try and assist someone else to carry his burden."[947]

By giving charitable, consecrated service, we prosper. We grow from one grace to another by giving grace—grace *to* grace by grace *for* grace. By seeking for the kingdom of God first, we become a conduit through which God can funnel blessings to the poor. Instructing us in the celestial law of obtaining wealth, Jacob said: "But before ye seek for riches, seek ye for the kingdom of God. And after ye have obtained a hope in Christ ye shall obtain riches, if ye seek them; and ye will seek them for the intent to do good—to clothe the naked, and to feed the hungry, and to liberate the captive, and administer relief to the sick and the afflicted."[948]

Charity is inseparably connected to the virtue of patience, which perfects charity, consecration, and every other gospel principle; patience perfects our lives.[949] By applying patience, we learn to trust in God's timing. We are willing to wait *with* God and his children; we also wait *for* them; and we wait *upon* them—that is to say, we serve them. We cannot live the law of consecration, exhibit charity, or become perfected without patience.

Patience is also essential to obtaining power in the priesthood. By patience and charity we minister among God's children, dispensing the gifts he has given us through consecrated service. Priesthood power depends upon charity, which we manifest by keeping his commandments—the greatest commandment being loving God and our neighbor, which includes feeding the Lord's sheep. When we do that, the doctrine of the priesthood will distill upon our souls as the dews from heaven,[950] and we who were once

---

944   1 Corinthians 13:1–3.
945   Matthew 13:33; Luke 13:21.
946   Moses 7:18.
947   Grant, *Teachings of Presidents of the Church: Heber J. Grant,* 139.
948   Jacob 2:18–19.
949   James 1:4.
950   D&C 121:45.

called to eternal life will become those who are chosen for eternal life.[951] There, in that glorious setting, we will finally experience the perfection of consecration: In love, we will give all that we are and have to God, and, in return, we will receive "all that the Father hath."[952] Then, forevermore, we will receive and increase our stewardships in his kingdom according to this law, and eternally we will never lack. By means of consecration and charity, we will become one with our Father, and he will give us liberal and equal access to the resources of his infinite kingdom. We will labor in his kingdom forever as we build our kingdoms, and we will offer accountings to him.

In the meantime, we struggle with celestial laws in a telestial setting. By faith alone, we must accept eternal laws and try to live them, but usually we do so without a full understanding of their eternal import. Therefore, in our weakness, we cry unto the Lord for strength and for the spiritual gift of charity so that we can be obedient, willing to sacrifice, devoted to the law of the gospel, loyal, and faithful, and so that we can have the courage to consecrate. As we extend ourselves and provide charitable service to others, God will hear our prayers and respond to them. Our sincere effort to give service draws him near, and when he comes, he answers our cries and brings blessings of light, health, righteousness, glory, protection, sustenance, relief, deliverance, guidance, abundance, power, redemption, and exaltation.[953]

Such are the blessings of charity; such are the blessings of consecration; such are the blessings of Zion.

Postlude

The third pillar of Zion is the law of consecration. This law emerges from the new and everlasting covenant and is introduced to us in a temple setting as an outgrowth of the oath and covenant of the priesthood. Now the three pillars of Zion are complete. They stand on the foundation of the Atonement, and according to the law of the Church (D&C 42), they are sufficient to establish us as Zion people.

The law of consecration is the foundational law of the celestial kingdom[954] and consequently is the foundational law of Zion. Although it is often associated with Church programs from earlier times, consecration is a template, the guiding principles of which can be used (and have been used) in any number of situations. Nevertheless, in the final analysis, consecration describes a celestial lifestyle and a condition of the heart.

Any individual or group of individuals who live this law will achieve the celestial condition of equality and unity. Nevertheless, these characteristics, along with other benefits of Zion, are wholly foreign to the world we live in. In Babylon, competition and selfishness rule and ruin lives. Therefore, when we are introduced to the law of consecration or any other celestial law, we will not be able to make much sense of it in a telestial environment. Ultimately, celestial laws must be lived by faith, but their rewards are astounding.

---

951   D&C 121:40.
952   D&C 84:38.
953   Isaiah 58:3–9.
954   D&C 105:5.

Finally, we learn that the law of consecration is an outgrowth of the royal law,[955] which is love: "Thou shalt love the Lord thy God with all thy heart, and with all thy soul, and with all thy mind. This is the first and great commandment. And the second is like unto it, Thou shalt love thy neighbour as thyself."[956] Clearly, love is the greatest power and motivator in the universe. Ultimately, we consecrate ourselves and all that we have and are because we love God and we love his children.

955   James 2:8.
956   Matthew 22:36–40.

Bibliography

American Heritage Dictionary. Boston, MA: Houghton Mifflin, 2000.

Anderson, Dawn Hall, Susette Fletcher Green, and Dlora Hall Dalton, eds. *Clothed with Charity: Talks from the 1996 Women's Conference.* Salt Lake City, UT: Deseret Book, 1997.

Asay, Carlos E. "The Oath and Covenant of the Priesthood," *Ensign,* November 1985.

—*Family Pecan Trees: Planting a Legacy of Faith at Home.* Salt Lake City, UT: Deseret Book, 1992.

—*The Seven M's of Missionary Service: Proclaiming the Gospel as a Member or Full-time Missionary.* Salt Lake City, UT: Bookcraft, 1996.

Ashton, Marvin J. "Be a Quality Person," *Ensign,* February 1993.

—"Love Takes Time," *Ensign,* November 1975.

Bednar, David A. "Pray Always," *Ensign,* November 2008.

Benson, Ezra Taft. "A Vision and a Hope for the Youth of Zion," *Devotional Speeches of the Year.* Provo, UT: Brigham Young University Press, 1978.

—*A Witness and a Warning: A Modern-Day Prophet Testifies of the Book of Mormon.* Salt Lake City, UT: Deseret Book, 1988.

—"Beware of Pride," *Ensign,* May 1989.

—*Devotional Speeches of the Year.* Provo, UT: Brigham Young University Press, 1978.

—*God, Family, Country: Our Three Great Loyalties.* Salt Lake City, UT: Deseret Book, 1975.

—"In His Steps," *Ensign,* September 1988.

—"Jesus Christ—Gifts and Expectations," *New Era,* May 1975.

—*The Teachings of Ezra Taft Benson. Salt Lake City, UT: Deseret Book, 1988.*

—"What I Hope You Will Teach Your Children about the Temple," *Ensign,* August 1985;

Bible Dictionary. Salt Lake City, UT: The Church of Jesus Christ of Latter-day Saints, 1989;

Black , Susan Easton, et al. Doctrines for Exaltation: The 1989 Sperry Symposium on the Doctrine and Covenants. Salt Lake City, UT: Deseret Book, 1989.

—*The Iowa Mormon Trail: Legacy of Faith and Courage.* Orem, UT: Helix Publishing, 1997.

Bowen, Albert E. *The Church Welfare Plan.* Salt Lake City, UT: The Church of Jesus Christ of Latter-day Saints, 1946.

Brewster, Hoyt W. Jr. *Doctrine and Covenants Encyclopedia.* Salt Lake City, UT: Bookcraft, 1988.

Brown, Hugh B. *Continuing the Quest.* Salt Lake City, UT: Bookcraft, 1961.

Brown, Matthew B. *Prophecies: The Gate of Heaven.* American Fork, UT: Covenant Communications, 1999.

—*Signs of the Times, Second Coming, Millenium.* American Fork, UT: Covenant Communications, 2006.

Budge, Ernest A. Wallis. *Coptic Martyrdoms Discourse on Abbaton. London: British Museum,* 1914.

Burton, Alma P., ed. *Discourses of the Prophet Joseph Smith. Salt Lake City, UT: Deseret Book, 1956.*

Cannon, Donald Q. *Teachings of the Latter-day Prophets.* Salt Lake City, UT: Bookcraft, 1998.

Cannon, Elaine. "Agency and Accountability." Salt Lake City, *Ensign,* November 1983.

Cannon, George Q. "Beware Lest Ye Fall." Discourse delivered at the Morgan Utah Stake Conference, Sunday, February 16, 1896.

—*Gospel Truth: Discourses and Writings of President George Q. Cannon.* Salt Lake City, UT: Deseret Book, 1974.

Cannon, Joseph A. "Sanctification," *Mormon Times,* June 12, 2008, http://www.mormontimes.com.

Clark, E. Douglas. *The Blessings of Abraham—Becoming a Zion People.* American Fork, UT: Covenant Communications, 2005.

Clark, J. Reuben. *Church Welfare Plan: A Discussion. Salt Lake, City, UT* General Church Welfare Committee, 1939.

Clark, James R., comp., *Messages of the First Presidency of The Church of Jesus Christ of Latter-day Saints.* Salt Lake City: Bookcraft, 1965–75.

Clarke, Adam. *Clarke's Commentary on the Bible.* Grand Rapids, MI: Baker Book House, 1967.

Clarke, J. Richard. "Successful Welfare Stewardship," *Ensign,* November 1978.

Conference Report, 1897–2009, Salt Lake City, UT: The Church of Jesus Christ of Latter-day Saints.

Cook, Gene R. "Home and Family: A Divine Eternal Pattern," *Ensign,* May 1984.

—"The Seat Next to You," *New Era,* October 1983.

Cook, Lyndon. *Joseph Smith and the Law of Consecration.* Provo, UT: Keepsake Books, 1991.

Cowley, Matthew. *Matthew Cowley Speaks: Discourses of Elder Matthew Cowley of the Quorum of the Twelve of the Church of Jesus Christ of Latter-day Saints.* Salt Lake City, UT: Deseret Book Company, 1954.

Dalrymple, G. Brent. *The Age of the Earth.* Stanford, CA: Stanford University Press, 1991.

Dellenbach, Robert K. "Hour of Conversion," *New Era,* June 2002.

DeMille, Cecil B. *BYU Speeches of the Year.* Provo, UT: Brigham Young University Press, May 1957.

Durham, G. Homer, ed. *The Gospel Kingdom: Selections from the Writings and Discourses of John Taylor, Third President of The Church of Jesus Christ of Latter-day Saints.* Salt Lake City, UT: Bookcraft, 1943.

—*Gospel Ideals: Selections from the Discourses of David O. McKay.* Salt Lake City, UT: Improvement Era, 1953.

Dibble, Philo. "Recollections of the Prophet Joseph Smith," *Juvenile Instructor,* June 1892.

Duffin, James G. "A Character Test," *Improvement Era,* February 1911.

Easton, M. G. *Illustrated Bible Dictionary.* Nashville: TN: Thomas Nelson, 1897.

"The Bondage of Sin," *Improvement Era,* February 1923.

Ehat, Andrew F. and Lyndon W. Cook. *The Words of Joseph Smith: The Contemporary Accounts of the Nauvoo Discourses of the Prophet Joseph.* Provo, UT: Religious Studies Center Brigham Young University, 1980.

Encarta World English Dictionary. New York, NY: St. Martins Press, 1999.

Eyring, Henry B. "Faith and the Oath and Covenant of the Priesthood," *Ensign,* May 2008.

Farley, S. Brent. "The Oath and Covenant of the Priesthood." *Sperry Symposium on the Doctrine and Covenants.* Salt Lake City: Desert Book, 1989.

First Presidency, "What is the Doctrine of the Priesthood?" Salt Lake City, UT: *Improvement Era*, February 1961.

Faust, James E. "A Royal Priesthood," *Ensign*, May 2006.

—*In the Strength of the Lord: The Life and Teachings of James E. Faust.* Salt Lake City, UT: Deseret Book, 1999.

—"He Healeth the Broken Heart," *Ensign* July 2005.

—"Our Search for Happiness, *Ensign*, Oct. 2000.

—"Standing in Holy Places," *Ensign*, May 2005.

—"The Devil's Throat," *Ensign*, May 2003.

—"The Gift of the Holy Ghost—A Sure Compass," *Ensign*, April 1996.

—"The Shield of Faith," *Ensign*, May 2000.

"Galaxy Map." Washington D.C.: The National Geographic Society, June 1983.

Galbraith, David B., D. Kelly Ogden, and Andrew C. Skinner. *Jerusalem—The Eternal City.* Salt Lake City, UT: Deseret Book, 1996.

Gardner, R. Quinn. "Becoming a Zion Society," *Ensign*, February 1979.

—"I Have a Question," *Ensign*, March 1978.

Gibbons, Ted L. *Be Not Afraid*, Springville, UT: Cedar Fort, Inc., 2009.

Goddard, Wallace H. "Blessed by Angels." *MeridianMagazine.com*, July 27, 2009.

—*Drawing Heaven into Your Marriage.* Fairfax, VA: Meridian Publishing, 2007.

Grant, Heber J. *Teachings of Presidents of the Church. Salt Lake City, UT: The Church of Jesus Christ of Latter-day Saints*, 2002.

Guralnik, David B., ed. *Webster's New World Dictionary, 2nd College Edition.* New York City, NY: The New World Publishing Company, 1970.

Hafen, Bruce C. *The Broken Heart: Applying the Atonement to Life's Experiences.* Salt Lake City, UT: Deseret Book, 1989.

Haight, David B. "The Sacrament and the Sacrifice," *Ensign*, November 1989.

Hamilton, Edith. *Spokesman for God. New York, NY: Norton and Company, 1977.*

Hinckley, Gordon B. "Blessed Are the Merciful," *Ensign*, May 1990.

—*Faith: The Essence of True Religion. Salt Lake City, UT: Deseret Book, 1989.*

—"Our Mission of Saving," *Ensign*, November 1991.

—"Priesthood: The Power of Godliness," *Improvement Era*, December 1970.

—*Stand a Little Taller.* Salt Lake City, UT: Eagle Gate, 2000.

—*Standing for Something.* New York, NY: Three Rivers Press, 2000.

—*Teachings of Gordon B. Hinckley.* Salt Lake City, UT: Deseret Book, 2002.

—"The Dawning of a Brighter Day," *Ensign*, May 2004.

—"The Stone Cut Out of the Mountain," *Ensign*, 2007.

—"Till We Meet Again," *Ensign*, November 2001.

—"We Thank Thee for This Sacred Structure," *Church News*, 8 November 1997.

— "Your Greatest Challenge, Mother," *Ensign*, November 2000.

Holland, Jeffrey R. "Broken Things to Mend," *Ensign*, May 2006.

—"However Long and Hard the Road," *Ensign*, September 2002.

—*On Earth As It Is in Heaven.* Salt Lake City, UT: Deseret Book, 1989.

Holzapfel, Richard Neitzel and Thomas A. Wayment, eds., *The Life and Teachings of Jesus Christ: From the Transfiguration through the Triumphant Entry.* Salt Lake City, UT: Deseret Book, 2006.

Horton, George A. "Abraham's Act of Faith Reflects 'a Soul Like Unto Our Savior,'" *LDS Church News,* April 2, 1994.

"'Hymn of the Pearl': an Ancient Counterpart To 'O My Father.'" *BYU Studies,* vol. 36, 1996–97.

Hymns of the Church of Jesus Christ of Latter-day Saints. Salt Lake City, UT: The Church of Jesus Christ of Latter-day Saints, 1985.

Jackson, Kent P. and Robert L. Millet. eds. *Studies in Scripture.* Salt Lake City, UT: Deseret Book 1989.

Jensen, Marlin K. "Living after the Manner of Happiness," *Ensign,* December 2002.

Jenson, Andrew, *Historical Record: A Monthly Periodical.* Salt Lake City, UT: Deseret News, 1886—1890.

Jessee, Dean. "Joseph Knight's Recollection of Early Mormon History." Provo, UT: *BYU Studies,* vol. 17, no. 1, 1976.

Johnson, Clark V. *Doctrines for Exaltation: The 1989 Sperry Symposium on the Doctrine and Covenants. Salt Lake City, UT: Deseret Book, 1989.*

Josephus. *Complete Works.* William Whiston, trans., Grand Rapids, MI: Kregal Publications, 1960.

Kimball, Spencer W. "A Gift of Gratitude," *Tambuli,* December 1977.

—"Becoming the Pure in Heart," *Ensign,* May 1978.

—*Faith Precedes the Miracle: Based on Discourses of Spencer W. Kimball.* Salt Lake City, UT: Deseret Book, 1972.

—"The Fruit of Our Welfare Services Labors," *Ensign,* November 1978.

—"The Role of Righteous Women," *Ensign,* November 1979.

—*The Teachings of Spencer W. Kimball.* Salt Lake City, UT: Bookcraft, 1982.

—"Welfare Services: The Gospel in Action," *Ensign,* November 1977.

—"Young Women Fireside 1981—In Love and Power and without Fear," *New Era,* July 1981.

Kirchhoff, Frederick. "Reconstruction of Self in Wordsworth's 'Ode on Intimations of Immortality from Recollections of Early Childhood.'" *Narcissism and the Text.* New York, NY: New York University Press, 1986.

Kirtland Council Minute Book, eds. Fred Collier and William S. Hartwell, Salt Lake City, UT: Collier's Publishing, 1996.

Largey, Dennis L. *Book of Mormon Reference Companion.* Salt Lake City, UT: Deseret Book, 2003.

Larsen, Dean L. "A Royal Generation," *Ensign,* May 1983.

Larson, Stan "The King Follett Discourse: a Newly Amalgamated Text." Provo, UT: *BYU Studies,* Vol. 18, 1977–1978.

Layton, Lynne and Schapiro, Barbara A. *Narcissism and the Text: Studies in Literature and the Psychology of Self.* New York, NY: New York University Press, 1986.

Lee, Harold B. *Decisions for Successful Living.* Salt Lake City, UT: Deseret Book, 1973.

—"Stand Ye in Holy Places," *Ensign*, July 1973.

—*The Teachings of Harold B. Lee*. Salt Lake City, UT: Deseret Book, 1974.

Lightner, Mary. Address to Brigham Young University. *BYU Archives and Manuscripts, Writings of Early Latter-day Saints*, 1905.

Ludlow, Daniel H. *A Companion to Your Study of the Book of Mormon*. Salt Lake City, UT: Deseret Book, 1976.

—*Encyclopedia of Mormonism*. New York City, NY: Macmillan Publishing, 1992.

Lund, Gerald N. *Jesus Christ, Key to the Plan of Salvation*. Salt Lake City, UT: Deseret Book, 1991.

—"Old Testament Types and Symbols," *A Witness of Jesus Christ: The 1989 Sperry Symposium on the Old Testament*. ed. Richard D. Draper, Salt Lake City, UT: Deseret Book, 1990.

Lundquist, John M. and Stephen D. Ricks, eds. *By Study and Also by Faith: Essays in Honor of Hugh W. Nibley on the Occasion of His Eightieth Birthday*. Provo, UT: Maxwell Institute, 1992.

Lundwall, N. B. *Temples of the Most High*. Salt Lake City, UT: Bookcraft, 1965.

"Map: Old Testament Stories: Part Two," *Deseret News*. Jan. 8, 1994.

Maxwell, Cory H., ed. *The Neal A. Maxwell Quote Book*. Salt Lake City, UT: Bookcraft, 1997.

Maxwell, Neal A. *A Wonderful Flood of Light*. Salt Lake City, UT: Deseret Book, 1991.

—*But for a Small Moment*. Salt Lake City, UT: Bookcraft, 1987.

—"Consecrate Thy Performance." *Ensign*, May 2002.

—*Disposition of a Disciple*. Salt Lake City, UT: Deseret Book, 1976.

—"Enduring Well," *Ensign*, April 1997.

—*Even As I Am*. Salt Lake City, UT: Deseret Book, 1991.

—*If Thou Endure It Well*. Salt Lake City, UT: Bookcraft, 2002.

—*Lord, Increase Our Faith*. Salt Lake City, UT: Bookcraft, 1994.

—*Men and Women of Christ*. Salt Lake City, UT: Deseret Book, 1991.

—*Notwithstanding My Weakness*. Salt Lake City, UT: Deseret Book, 1981.

—*One More Strain of Praise*. Salt Lake City, UT: Deseret Book, 2003.

—"Patience," *Ensign*, October 1980.

—*That Ye May Believe*. Salt Lake City, UT: Bookcraft, 1994.

—*The Promise of Discipleship*. Salt Lake City, UT: Deseret Book, 2001.

—"These Are Your Days," *New Era*, January 1985.

McConkie, Bruce R. *A New Witness for the Articles of Faith*. Salt Lake City, UT: Deseret Book, 1985.

—*Doctrinal New Testament Commentary*. Salt Lake City, UT: Deseret Book, 1972.

—*Doctrines of Salvation: Sermons and Writings of Joseph Fielding Smith*, Salt Lake City, UT: Bookcraft, 1954–1956.

—*Mormon Doctrine*. Salt Lake City, UT: Bookcraft: 1966.

—"Obedience, Consecration, and Sacrifice," *Ensign*, May 1975.

—"The Doctrine of the Priesthood," *Ensign*, May 1982.

—*The Mortal Messiah: From Bethlehem to Calvary*. Salt Lake City, UT: Deseret Book, 1981.

—"*The Probationary Test of Mortality.*" Address delivered at the University of Utah Institute, January 10, 1982.

—*The Promised Messiah: The First Coming of Christ.* Salt Lake City, UT: Deseret Book, 1981.

—"The Ten Blessings of the Priesthood," *Ensign*, November 1977.

McConkie, Joseph Fielding and Robert L. Millet. *Doctrinal Commentary on the Book of Mormon.* Salt Lake City, UT: Deseret Book, 1987–1993.

—*Joseph Smith: The Choice Seer.* Salt Lake City, UT: Bookcraft, 1996.

—*Revelations of the Restoration.* Salt Lake City, UT: Deseret Book, 2000.

McKay, David O. *Gospel Ideals: Selections from the Discourses of David O. McKay.* Salt Lake City, UT: Deseret Book, 1993.

----*Pathways to Happiness.* Salt Lake City, UT: Bookcraft, 1957.

McMullin, Keith B. "Come to Zion! Come to Zion!" Salt Lake City, UT: *Ensign*, November 2002.

Merriam Webster's New World Dictionary, Third Edition. New York, NY: Simon and Schuster, 1998

Middlemiss, Clare. *Man May Know for Himself: Teachings of President David O. McKay.* Salt Lake City, UT: Deseret Book, 1967.

Millet, Robert L. "Quest for the City of God: The Doctrine Of Zion In Modern Revelation," *1989 Sperry Symposium on the Doctrine and Covenants.* Salt Lake City, UT: Desert Book, 1989.

—*The Capstone of Our Religion: Insights into the Doctrine and Covenants.* Salt Lake City, UT: Deseret Book, 1989.

—*The Life Beyond.* Salt Lake City, UT: Deseret Book, 1986.

—*The Power of the Word: Saving Doctrines from the Book of Mormon. Salt Lake City, UT: Deseret Book,* 2000.

Monson, Thomas S. "In Quest of the Abundant Life." *Ensign*, March 1988.

Nelson, Russell M. "Personal Priesthood Responsibility," *Ensign*, October 2005.

—*The Power within Us. Salt Lake City, UT: Deseret Book, 1989.*

Nelson, William O. "Enoch and His Message for Latter Days," *Deseret News*, Feb. 5, 1994.

Neuenschwander, Dennis. "Ordinances and Covenants," *Ensign*, August 2001.

Nibley, Hugh. *Abraham in Egypt.* Salt Lake City, UT and Provo, UT: Deseret Book and FARMS, 2000.

—*An Approach to the Book of Mormon.* Salt Lake City, UT: Deseret Book, 1988.

—*Approaching Zion.* Salt Lake City, UT: Deseret Book, 1989.

—"Educating the Saints—A Brigham Young Mosaic." Provo, UT: *BYU Studies*, Vol. 11, Autumn 1970.

—*Nibley on the Timely and the Timeless. Provo, UT: Religious Studies Center, Brigham Young University, 2004.*

—*Teachings of the Book of Mormon.* Provo, UT: Covenant Communications, 2004.

—*Temple and Cosmos: Beyond This Ignorant Present.* Salt Lake City, UT: Deseret Book, 1992.

Nibley, Preston. *Brigham Young: The Man and His Work,* 4th ed. Salt Lake City, UT: Deseret Book, 1960.

Nielsen, Donna B. *Beloved Bridegroom*. Salt Lake City, UT: Onyx Press, 1999.

Nyman, Monte S. and Charles D. Tate, Jr., eds. *Fourth Nephi through Moroni: From Zion to Destruction*. Salt Lake City, UT: Bookcraft, 1992.

—*The Capstone of Our Religion: Insights into the Doctrine and Covenants*. Salt Lake City, UT: Bookcraft, 1989.

Oaks, Dallin H. "Good, Better, Best," *Ensign*, November 2007.

—"He Heals the Heavy Laden," *Ensign*, November 2006

—"Preparation for the Second Coming," *Ensign*, November 2004.

—"Taking Upon Us the Name of Jesus Christ," *Ensign*, May 1985.

—"The Challenge to Become," *Ensign*, November 2000.

—"Timing," *Ensign*, October 2003.

Oaks, Robert C. "The Power of Patience," *Ensign*, November 2006.

Otten, L. G. and C. M. Caldwell. *Sacred Truths of the Doctrine and Covenants*. Salt Lake City, UT: Deseret Book, 1982–1983.

Pack, Frederick J. "Was the Earth Created in Six Days of Twenty-Four Hours Each?" *Improvement Era*, October 1930.

Packer, Boyd K. "Personal Revelation: The Gift, the Test, and the Promise," *Ensign*, November 1994.

—"Restoration," *First Worldwide Leadership Training Meeting*. Salt Lake City, UT: The Church of Jesus Christ of Latter-day Saints, January 2003.

—*That All May Be Edified*. Salt Lake City, UT: Bookcraft, 1982.

—"The Candle of the Lord," *Ensign*, January 1983.

—"The One Pure Defense (An Evening with President Boyd K. Packer)," Intellectual Reserve, 2004. Address to CES Religious Educators, 6 February 2004, Salt Lake Tabernacle.

Parry, Donald W., ed. *Temples of the Ancient World: Ritual and Symbolism*. Salt Lake City, UT and Provo, UT: Deseret and FARMS, 1994.

—*Understanding the Book of Revelation*. Salt Lake City, UT: Deseret Book, 1998.

Peterson, H. Burke. "Your Special Purpose," *New Era*, October 2001.

Pratt, Orson. *Times and Seasons*, vol. 6. no. 10, 1 June 1845.

Riddle, Chauncey C. "The New and Everlasting Covenant," 1989 *Sperry Symposium on the Doctrine and Covenants*. Salt Lake City: Desert Book, 1989.

Roberts, B.H. *Comprehensive History of the Church of Jesus Christ of Latter-day Saints*. Salt Lake City, UT: Church of Jesus Christ of Latter-day Saints, 1930.

—*Seventy's Course of Theology*. Salt Lake City, UT: Deseret Book, 1931.

Romney, Marion G. "Church Welfare Services' Basic Principles," *Ensign*, May 1976.

—"Church Welfare—Temporal Service in a Spiritual Setting," *Ensign*, May 1980

—"Priesthood," *Ensign*, May 1982.

—"'In Mine Own Way,'" *Ensign*, November 1976.

—"The Celestial Nature of Self-reliance," *Ensign*, November 1982.

—"The Oath and Covenant Which Belongeth to the Priesthood," *Ensign*, November 1980.

—"The Purpose of Church Welfare Services," *Ensign*, May 1977.

—"The Royal Law of Love," *Ensign*, May 1978.

  "Unity," *Ensign*, May 1983.

—"Welfare Services: The Savior's Program," *Ensign*, October 1980.

Salt Lake School of the Prophets Minutes. Salt Lake City, UT: The Church of Jesus Christ of Latter-day Saints, 1899.

"Sermon Given to Different People," *LDS Church News*, Feb. 18, 1995.

Skidmore, Rex A. "What Part Should a Teenager Play in a Family?" *Improvement Era*, 1952.

Skinner, Andrew C. *Temple Worship: 20 Truths That Will Bless Your Life*. Salt Lake City, UT: Deseret Book, 2008.

—*The Old Testament and the Latter-Day Saints*. Salt Lake City, UT: Deseret Book, 2005.

Smith, Hyrum M. and Janne M. Sjodahl. *Doctrine and Covenants Commentary*. Salt Lake City, UT: Deseret Book, 1960.

Smith, Joseph. *Evening and Morning Star*, July, 1833.

—*History of The Church of Jesus Christ of Latter-day Saints*. Salt Lake City, UT: Deseret Book, 1980.

—*Lectures on Faith*. Salt Lake City, UT: Deseret Book, 1993.

Smith, Joseph F. *Gospel Doctrine: Selections from the Sermons and Writings of Joseph F. Smith. Deseret News Press, 1919.*

—*Teachings of Presidents of the Church*. Salt Lake City, UT: The Church of Jesus Christ of Latter-day Saints, 1998.

Smith, Joseph Fielding. *Church History and Modern Revelation*. Salt Lake City, UT: The Church of Jesus Christ of Latter-day Saints, 1946.

—"Our responsibility as Priesthood Holders," *Ensign*, June 1971.

—*Teachings of the Prophet Joseph Smith*. Salt Lake City, UT: Deseret Book, 1938.

—"The Duties of the Priesthood in Temple Work," *The Utah Genealogical and Historical Magazine*, vol. 30, no. 1, January 1939.

—*The Restoration of All Things*. Salt Lake City, UT: Deseret News Press, 1945.

Snow, Lorenzo. *The Teachings of Lorenzo Snow*, Salt Lake City, UT: Bookcraft, 1984.

Sorensen, A. D. "No Respector of Persons: Equality in the Kingdom," ed. Mary E. Stoval, *.As Women of Faith: Talks Selected from the BYU Women's Conferences*. Salt Lake City, UT: Deseret Book, 1989, 55.

Stevenson, Edward. "Life and History of Elder Edward Stevenson." Provo, UT: Special Collections, Harold B. Lee Library, Brigham Young University, n.d.

Stuy, Brian H., comp., *Collected Discourses*. Burbank, CA: B.H.S. Publishing, 1988.

Summerhays, James T. "The Stripling Elect." *MeridianMagazine.com*, February 20, 2009.

Talmage, James E. *Articles of Faith*. Salt Lake City, UT: Deseret Book, 1984.

—*Jesus the Christ*. Salt Lake City: Deseret News Press, 1915.

—"The Eternity of Sex," *Young Woman's Journal*, October 1914.

—*The House of the Lord*. Salt Lake City, UT: Bookcraft, 1962.

Tanakh: A New Translation of the Holy Scriptures According to the Traditional Hebrew Text. Philadelphia, PA: Jewish Publication Society of America, November 1985.

Tanner, N. Eldon. "Constancy Amid Change," Ensign, November 1979.

Tanner, Susan W. "All Things Shall Work Together for Your Good," *Ensign*, May 2004.

—"My Soul Delighteth in the Things of the Lord," *Ensign*, 2008.

Taylor, John. *Teachings of the Latter-day Prophets*. Salt Lake City, UT: Bookcraft, 1998.

Times and Seasons, vol. 6. no. 10, 1 June 1845.

Thomas, M. Catherine. "Alma the Younger, Part 1," Provo, UT: Neal A. Maxwell Institute for Religious Scholarship, 1996.

—"Alma the Younger, Part 2," Provo, UT: Neal A. Maxwell Institute for Religious Scholarship, 1996.

—"Benjamin and the Mysteries of God," *King Benjamin's Speech*. Provo, UT: Foundation for Ancient Research and Mormon Studies, 1998.

Turner, Rodney. *Woman and the Priesthood*. Salt Lake City, UT: Deseret Book, 1972.

Tvedtnes, John A. *The Church of the Old Testament*. Salt Lake City, UT: Deseret Book, 1967.

—"They Have Their Reward," *MeridianMagazine.com*, February 21, 2007.

Van Orden, Bruce A. and Brent L. Top. *Doctrines of the Book of Mormon: The 1991 Sperry Symposium*, Provo, UT: Maxwell Institute, 1993.

Watt, George D., ed. *Journal of Discourses*. Liverpool, England: F.D. Richards, et al., 1854–1886.

Whitney, Newell K. in *Messenger and Advocate*, 3 September 1837.

Whitney, Orson F. *Gospel Themes*. Salt Lake City, UT: n.p., 1914.

—*Life of Heber C. Kimball*. Salt Lake City, UT: Bookcraft, 1975.

—*Saturday Night Thoughts*. Salt Lake City, UT: Deseret News, 1927.

Wickman, Lance B. "Today," *Ensign*, May 2008.

Widtsoe, John A. *An Understandable Religion*. Salt Lake City, UT: The Church of Jesus Christ of Latter-day Saints, 1944.

—*Priesthood and Church Government*. Salt Lake City, UT: Deseret Book, 1939.

—*Utah Genealogical and Historical Magazine*. Salt Lake City, UT: October 1934.

Williams, Clyde J. *The Teachings of Lorenzo Snow, Fifth President of the Church of Jesus Christ of Latter-day Saints*. Salt Lake City, UT: Bookcraft, 1984.

Wilson, Marvin. *Our Father Abraham*, Grand Rapids, MI: Eerdmans Publishing Co., 1989.

Winder, Barbara W. "Finding Joy in Life," *Ensign*, November 1987.

Wirthlin, Joseph B. "The Great Commandment," *Ensign*, November 2007.

—"The Law of the Fast," *Ensign*, May 2001.

Woodruff, Wilford. *The Discourses of Wilford Woodruff*. Salt Lake City, UT: Bookcraft, 1946.

Yarn, David H. *The Gospel: God, Man, and Truth*. Salt Lake City, UT: Deseret Book, 1965.

Yorgason, Blaine M. *I Need Thee Every Hour*. Salt Lake City, UT: Deseret Book, 2003.

—*Spiritual Progression in the Last Days*. Salt Lake City, UT: Deseret Book, 1994.

Young, Brigham in *Deseret News*, 10 October 1866.

—*Discourses of Brigham Young*. Salt Lake City, UT: Deseret Book, 1926.

—*Journal History*. 28 September 1846.

—*Millennial Star, Vol. 16*. Salt Lake City, UT: The Church of Jesus Christ of Latter-day Saints, 1840–1970.

Index and Concordance

This is a master index of the book series. The page number is specific to the book in which it is located. For example: 101:3 means page 101 in book 3. Marker "P" refers to Portrait of a Zion Person.

Aaronic Priesthood. *See* **Oath and Covenant of the Priesthood;** *See* **Patriarchal Order of the Priesthood;** *See* **Priesthood**
> 40:2, 41:2, 12:3, 22:3, 23:3, 36:3, 39:3, 42:3, 59:3, 60:3, 76:3, 92:3, 93:3, 103:3, 104:3, 202:3, 204:3, 50:4, 131:5

abundance
> 5:6, 8:6, 10:6, 13:6, 17:6, 18:6, 31:6, 41:6, 44:6, 46:6, 52:6, 70:6, 82:6, 87:6, 96:6, 101:6, 103:6, 106:6, 107:6, 110:6, 111:6, 112:6, 114:6, 115:6

Adam
> empowered to become a savior to his family
>> 11:1

adultery. *See also* **immoral**
> Babylon distinguished by
>> 50:2

adversary. *See also* **devil;** *See also* **hell;** *See also* **Lucifer;** *See also* **Satan**
> attacks Saints more viciously than others
>> 44:1

adversity. *See also* **opposition;** *See also* **trial(s)**
> 33:2, 51:2, 54:2, 56:2, 58:2, 61:2, 34:3, 66:3, 117:3, 132:3, 186:3, 178:4, 10:5, 27:5, 30:5, 76:5, 50:6, 101:6

affluence. *See also* **mammon;** *See also* **riches;** *See also* **wealth**
> 85:1, 139:4, 103:5, 64:6, 71:6

agency
> a discussion of
>> 62–68:4

Amulek
> 52:1, 80:1, 51:2, 52:2, 55:3, 42:4, 59:4, 133:4, 180:4, 36:5, 71:5, 56:6, 104:6

angels
> involved in crucible experiences
>> 26:5

anger. *See also* **contention**
> 19:1, 57:1, 64:1, 75:1, 86:1, 87:1, 93:1, 96:1, 97:1, 98:1, 55:2, 23:3, 152:3, 169:3, 176:3, 5:4, 29:4, 34:4, 101:4, 111:4, 116:4, 121:4, 136:4, 165:4, 179:4, 180:4, 4:5, 15:5, 22:5, 41:5, 46:5, 79:5, 104:5, 107:5, 124:5, 17:6, 28:6, 34:6, 39:6, 60:6, 94:6, 116:6

anti-Christ
> 17:P, 21:1, 49:1, 50:1, 51:1, 61:1, 79:1, 84:1, 85:1, 101:1, 54:2, 67:3, 87:4, 127:4, 175:4, 176:4, 33:5, 48:5, 7:6, 47:6, 88:6

apostasy
> 27:1, 33:1, 34:1, 60:1, 68:1, 84:4, 108:5

apostle
> 59:1, 17:2

Atonement

   6:P, 14:P, 15:P, 24:P, 42:P, 11:1, 12:1, 22:1, 23:1, 42:1, 45:1, 47:1, 66:1, 70:1, 1:2, 3:2, 6:2, 7:2, 9:2, 10:2, 16:2, 17:2, 18:2, 19:2, 20:2, 23:2, 24:2, 25:2, 26:2, 27:2, 28:2, 29:2, 30:2, 31:2, 32:2, 34:2, 35:2, 36:2, 37:2, 38:2, 39:2, 45:2, 55:2, 57:2, 66:2, 67:2, 72:2, 93:2, 98:2, 1:3, 10:3, 17:3, 20:3, 21:3, 35:3, 63:3, 70:3, 73:3, 76:3, 158:3, 180:3, 196:3, 211:3, 214:3, 1:4, 16:4, 18:4, 19:4, 20:4, 31:4, 41:4, 42:4, 56:4, 57:4, 59:4, 64:4, 99:4, 122:4, 162:4, 185:4, 1:5, 4:5, 29:5, 64:5, 84:5, 87:5, 91:5, 106:5, 107:5, 111:5, 113:5, 117:5, 129:5, 133:5, 137:5, 15:6, 42:6, 67:6, 75:6

Babel

   a counterfeit gate of God

       54:1

   Nimrod established kingdom in

       53:1

Babylon. *See also* **world**

   a discussion of

       49–105:1

   state of mind defined by excess, self-indulgence

       54:1

baptism

   2:P, 18:P, 21:P, 25:P, 11:1, 19:1, 23:1, 9:2, 18:2, 19:2, 21:2, 28:2, 31:2, 33:2, 34:2, 35:2, 36:2, 37:2, 38:2, 40:2, 41:2, 44:2, 45:2, 49:2, 53:2, 60:2, 63:2, 64:2, 67:2, 68:2, 70:2, 73:2, 75:2, 81:2, 82:2, 91:2, 93:2, 98:2, 1:3, 2:3, 4:3, 5:3, 9:3, 10:3, 11:3, 17:3, 21:3, 23:3, 27:3, 39:3, 42:3, 66:3, 70:3, 71:3, 76:3, 80:3, 93:3, 99:3, 117:3, 143:3, 144:3, 153:3, 179:3, 187:3, 193:3, 200:3, 210:3, 214:3, 1:4, 14:4, 26:4, 39:4, 51:4, 52:4, 88:4, 142:4, 144:4, 145:4, 1:5, 17:5, 18:5, 60:5, 61:5, 62:5, 63:5, 82:5, 83:5, 106:5, 117:5, 133:5, 134:5, 135:5, 68:6, 75:6, 76:6, 106:6

Beatitudes. *See also* **Sermon on the Mount**

   16:P, 18:P, 28:P, 28:1, 49:3, 41:5, 82:5

believe. *See* **faith**

   in order to see

       68:5

Beloved Son. *See also* **Christ**; *See also* **Exemplar**; *See also* **Jehovah**; *See also* **Lamb**; *See also* **Savior**

   47:1, 65:3, 111:3, 55:5, 56:5, 110:5, 115:5

Bible

   39:1, 63:1, 83:1, 54:2, 7:3, 138:3, 203:3, 8:5

blasphemy

   59:1, 82:3

bloodline

   men ordained to priesthood regardless of

       17:1

gold

> 28:P, 38:P, 42:P, 27:1, 50:1, 52:1, 58:1, 59:1, 62:1, 76:1, 96:1, 22:2, 80:2, 94:2, 129:3, 151:3, 9:4, 40:4, 44:4, 82:4, 101:4, 103:4, 106:4, 109:4, 116:4, 118:4, 124:4, 132:4, 139:4, 140:4, 145:4, 146:4, 3:5, 21:5, 23:5, 24:5, 25:5, 26:5, 17:6, 19:6, 22:6, 27:6, 35:6, 36:6, 44:6, 55:6, 64:6, 65:6, 68:6, 69:6, 70:6

good

> definition of
>> 9:1

goods. *See* mammon

Gordon B. Hinckley

> 6:P, 7:1, 28:2, 55:3, 172:3, 211:3, 37:4, 40:4, 41:4, 56:4, 59:4, 60:4, 164:4, 170:4, 87:5, 78:6, 83:6, 93:6

grace. *See also* mercy

> 15:P, 19:P, 22:P, 4:1, 6:1, 10:1, 11:1, 28:1, 42:1, 4:2, 17:2, 18:2, 19:2, 20:2, 22:2, 23:2, 26:2, 29:2, 36:2, 38:2, 43:2, 45:2, 78:2, 16:3, 21:3, 24:3, 52:3, 53:3, 54:3, 55:3, 60:3, 64:3, 86:3, 104:3, 153:3, 198:3, 200:3, 57:4, 66:4, 79:4, 89:4, 92:4, 139:4, 146:4, 174:4, 175:4, 177:4, 181:4, 184:4, 7:5, 20:5, 31:5, 32:5, 45:5, 90:5, 124:5, 64:6, 70:6, 75:6, 80:6, 81:6, 82:6, 83:6, 89:6, 90:6, 100:6, 101:6

Harold B. Lee

> 16:P, 28:P, 28:1, 82:1, 49:3, 130:3, 131:3, 204:3, 82:5, 147:5

heal

> 21:P, 1:1, 2:1, 46:1, 135:3, 142:3, 152:3, 165:3, 171:3, 73:4, 77:4, 142:4, 144:4, 159:4, 160:4, 161:4, 184:4, 15:5, 113:5, 68:6, 86:6

healing

> we prepare for Zion by experiencing
>> 160:4

health

> 23:P, 9:1, 76:1, 90:1, 100:1, 24:2, 29:2, 123:3, 18:4, 161:4, 180:4, 185:4, 15:5, 24:5, 25:5, 37:5, 57:5, 71:5, 72:5, 1:6, 86:6, 103:6, 109:6

heart

> a discussion of
>> pure in
>>> 77–108:5
> is altar of soul
>> 49:5
> must be changed to attain Zion
>> 12:1

Heber C. Kimball

> 114:1, 83:3, 100:3, 101:3, 148:5

heir

> 11:1, 53:1, 101:1, 29:3, 76:3, 195:3, 45:5

157:3, 164:3, 176:3, 179:3, 181:3, 184:3, 190:3, 191:3, 192:3, 198:3, 9:4, 62:4, 66:4,
89:4, 106:4, 146:4, 153:4, 159:4, 164:4, 182:4, 26:5, 46:5, 47:5, 54:5, 64:5, 66:5,
87:5, 88:5, 108:5, 134:5, 22:6, 70:6, 94:6, 106:6, 108:6

King Benjamin

20:P, 19:1, 20:1, 21:1, 22:1, 23:1, 24:1, 25:1, 26:1, 8:2, 66:2, 7:3, 8:3, 9:3, 10:3, 11:3,
20:3, 51:3, 67:3, 152:3, 9:4, 35:4, 39:4, 78:4, 120:4, 121:4, 126:4, 127:4, 170:4, 36:5,
42:5, 59:5, 62:5, 63:5, 64:5, 66:5, 106:5, 108:5, 39:6, 46:6, 48:6, 76:6, 79:6, 106:6

king(s)

15:1, 16:1, 20:1, 21:1, 23:1, 25:1, 49:1, 85:2, 90:2, 92:2, 94:2, 95:2, 5:3, 7:3, 9:3,
10:3, 11:3, 29:3, 45:3, 111:3, 112:3, 113:3, 119:3, 139:3, 152:3, 198:3, 199:3, 20:4,
39:4, 76:4, 100:4, 108:4, 134:4, 8:5, 9:5, 39:5, 51:5, 54:5, 58:5, 60:5, 62:5, 63:5,
89:5, 1:6, 2:6, 16:6, 26:6, 46:6, 58:6

Korihor

50:1, 79:1, 127:4, 175:4, 47:6, 88:6

labor. See also work

35:P, 37:P, 38:P, 42:P, 20:1, 24:1, 27:1, 30:1, 42:1, 84:1, 39:2, 7:3, 19:3, 55:3, 146:3,
171:3, 17:4, 19:4, 39:4, 58:4, 62:4, 70:4, 71:4, 80:4, 82:4, 83:4, 84:4, 85:4, 86:4,
87:4, 88:4, 89:4, 90:4, 91:4, 92:4, 127:4, 135:4, 136:4, 140:4, 141:4, 151:4, 152:4,
156:4, 174:4, 176:4, 183:4, 185:4, 4:5, 26:5, 32:5, 33:5, 50:5, 92:5, 93:5, 95:5, 122:5,
137:5, 48:6, 59:6, 60:6, 65:6, 66:6, 71:6, 72:6, 100:6

lack. See poor

Laman

101:1, 20:5, 27:5

Lamb. See also Christ, Jesus; See also Exemplar; See also Jehovah; See also Savior

18:1, 172:4, 98:6

lawyers

86:1, 90:1, 119:4, 103:5, 37:6

Lehi

17:P, 27:P, 63:1, 64:1, 74:1, 94:1, 52:2, 58:2, 78:2, 195:3, 21:4, 42:4, 59:4, 3:5, 8:5,
9:5, 10:5, 17:5, 19:5, 21:5, 23:5, 26:5, 28:5, 31:5, 34:5, 41:5, 42:5, 51:5, 52:5, 58:5,
67:5, 73:5

lies

30:P, 9:1, 18:1, 22:1, 51:1, 63:1, 72:1, 19:2, 97:2, 9:3, 55:3, 60:3, 95:3, 97:3, 117:3,
139:3, 160:3, 181:3, 13:4, 41:4, 47:4, 65:4, 74:4, 137:4, 142:4, 156:4, 166:4, 7:5, 9:5,
19:5, 26:5, 87:5, 2:6, 60:6, 67:6, 101:6, 112:6

Lorenzo Snow

78:1, 6:4, 15:4, 17:4, 31:4, 47:4, 4:5, 94:5, 95:5, 100:5, 131:5, 136:5, 148:5

love. See also charity; See also heart

2:P, 7:P, 9:P, 10:P, 11:P, 12:P, 17:P, 20:P, 21:P, 22:P, 24:P, 27:P, 28:P, 34:P, 39:P,
43:P, 19:1, 22:1, 23:1, 24:1, 26:1, 29:1, 30:1, 33:1, 34:1, 42:1, 49:1, 64:1, 65:1, 70:1,
71:1, 76:1, 77:1, 79:1, 86:1, 87:1, 89:1, 91:1, 99:1, 3:2, 4:2, 5:2, 18:2, 19:2, 27:2,
38:2, 41:2, 44:2, 50:2, 54:2, 56:2, 57:2, 60:2, 61:2, 62:2, 66:2, 67:2, 69:2, 70:2,

materialism. *See also* **mammon**

    25:P, 41:P, 62:1, 64:1, 68:1, 102:1, 109:4, 93:5, 26:6, 76:6

Matthew Cowley

    3:P, 4:P, 6:1, 46:1, 105:6

Melchizedek

    administered priesthood to Abraham/built temple in Salem

        16:1

Melchizedek Priesthood. *See also* **Aaronic Priesthood**; *See also* **oath and covenant of the priesthood**; *See also* **patriarchal order of the priesthood**; *See also* **priesthood**

    a discussion of

        4–209:3

merchandise. *See* **mammon**; *See* **money**

mercy. *See also* **grace**

    10:P, 17:P, 20:P, 21:P, 22:P, 23:P, 24:P, 23:1, 26:1, 30:1, 66:1, 100:1, 4:2, 6:2, 7:2, 8:2, 9:2, 10:2, 15:2, 16:2, 17:2, 18:2, 20:2, 23:2, 24:2, 26:2, 27:2, 28:2, 29:2, 30:2, 32:2, 34:2, 35:2, 36:2, 45:2, 57:2, 97:2, 54:3, 71:3, 156:3, 159:3, 165:3, 167:3, 98:4, 112:4, 122:4, 129:4, 130:4, 143:4, 148:4, 151:4, 179:4, 15:5, 16:5, 19:5, 44:5, 64:5, 77:5, 106:5, 113:5, 114:5, 124:5, 12:6, 29:6, 41:6, 49:6, 51:6, 82:6, 102:6

miracle

    17:P, 25:1, 30:1, 66:1, 64:2, 155:3, 9:4, 36:4, 51:4, 57:4, 60:4, 67:4, 70:4, 159:4, 160:4, 162:4, 163:4, 173:4, 25:5, 32:5, 39:5, 66:5, 101:5, 109:5, 99:6

miserable

    49:1, 50:1, 51:1, 60:1, 77:1, 78:1, 8:2, 16:2, 89:2, 132:3, 63:4, 13:5, 14:5, 16:5, 56:5, 30:6

money. *See also* **mammon**; *See also* **materialism**; *See also* **riches**

    love of, is root of all evil

        70:1

Moroni

    1:1, 31:1, 61:1, 90:1, 91:1, 92:1, 103:1, 12:3, 65:3, 68:3, 92:3, 166:3, 195:3, 209:3, 210:3, 5:4, 6:4, 107:4, 123:4, 124:4, 149:4, 165:4, 166:4, 174:4, 175:4, 178:4, 181:4, 182:4, 183:4, 31:5, 44:5, 53:5, 55:5, 70:5, 77:5, 109:5, 112:5, 118:5, 119:5, 22:6, 23:6, 43:6, 86:6, 100:6

mortality

    is testing ground for our genuine desires

        47:1

Moses

    4:P, 26:P, 18:1, 19:1, 28:1, 32:1, 34:1, 51:1, 74:1, 87:1, 88:1, 8:2, 22:2, 40:2, 81:2, 84:2, 14:3, 15:3, 16:3, 17:3, 18:3, 20:3, 23:3, 24:3, 40:3, 55:3, 63:3, 65:3, 66:3, 76:3, 77:3, 88:3, 89:3, 99:3, 104:3, 110:3, 175:3, 176:3, 177:3, 184:3, 195:3, 207:3, 208:3, 47:4, 50:4, 100:4, 101:4, 112:4, 118:4, 120:4, 126:4, 129:4, 151:4, 165:4, 166:4, 8:5, 9:5, 18:5, 23:5, 31:5, 32:5, 35:5, 41:5, 42:5, 54:5, 55:5, 67:5, 72:5, 74:5, 79:5, 86:5, 89:5, 112:5, 131:5, 16:6, 17:6, 29:6, 36:6, 38:6, 46:6, 49:6, 50:6, 94:6, 95:6

mother

46:1, 61:1, 62:1, 25:2, 51:2, 85:2, 59:3, 126:3, 158:3, 28:4, 110:4, 172:4, 21:5, 129:5, 27:6, 52:6, 98:6, 106:6, 109:6

murder

50:1, 53:1, 60:1, 62:1, 63:1, 69:1, 80:1, 90:1, 102:1, 96:2, 119:3, 146:3, 160:3, 53:4, 118:4, 137:4, 14:5, 108:5, 36:6, 60:6

murmur

22:2, 26:5

mysteries

26:P, 32:P, 39:P, 40:P, 18:1, 61:1, 44:2, 8:3, 10:3, 24:3, 30:3, 31:3, 43:3, 47:3, 49:3, 57:3, 72:3, 81:3, 87:3, 93:3, 95:3, 96:3, 97:3, 98:3, 176:3, 177:3, 181:3, 183:3, 187:3, 188:3, 189:3, 190:3, 191:3, 192:3, 46:4, 100:4, 108:4, 149:4, 59:5, 60:5, 66:5, 79:5, 85:5, 86:5, 87:5, 88:5, 116:5, 119:5, 16:6, 25:6, 115:6

natural man

25:P, 22:1, 78:1, 20:2, 21:2, 50:2, 178:3, 64:4, 95:4, 169:4, 182:4, 23:5, 25:5, 42:5, 43:5, 44:5, 45:5, 68:5, 76:5, 84:5, 91:5, 9:6, 86:6

Neal A. Maxwell

12:1, 40:1, 110:3, 118:3, 148:3, 15:4, 27:4, 57:4, 79:4, 148:5

needy. *See also* poor

3:1, 20:1, 24:1, 27:1, 56:1, 80:1, 91:1, 48:3, 114:3, 129:3, 7:4, 11:4, 14:4, 23:4, 24:4, 29:4, 33:4, 40:4, 54:4, 72:4, 75:4, 82:4, 90:4, 107:4, 117:4, 121:4, 122:4, 123:4, 124:4, 125:4, 126:4, 129:4, 130:4, 133:4, 139:4, 144:4, 149:4, 153:4, 158:4, 170:4, 179:4, 180:4, 71:5, 5:6, 8:6, 23:6, 36:6, 41:6, 43:6, 44:6, 45:6, 46:6, 50:6, 52:6, 56:6, 63:6, 67:6, 72:6, 76:6, 87:6, 95:6, 104:6, 105:6, 106:6, 107:6, 109:6, 113:6

Nehor

26:1, 84:1, 145:3

neighbor

7:P, 8:P, 9:P, 28:P, 30:P, 19:1, 29:1, 66:1, 18:3, 49:3, 96:3, 182:3, 21:4, 26:4, 33:4, 38:4, 56:4, 58:4, 77:4, 91:4, 100:4, 104:4, 118:4, 122:4, 158:4, 164:4, 165:4, 169:4, 184:4, 93:5, 94:5, 127:5, 16:6, 20:6, 36:6, 41:6, 77:6, 93:6, 94:6, 113:6

new and everlasting covenant. *See also* marriage

a discussion of

how it's likened to marriage

72–99:2

Nimrod

51:1, 52:1, 53:1, 54:1, 55:1, 58:1, 61:1, 101:1

Noah

15:P, 14:1, 15:1, 16:1, 18:1, 36:1, 53:1, 55:1, 86:1, 87:1, 101:1, 102:1, 103:1, 7:3, 27:3, 207:3, 107:4, 32:5, 88:5, 101:5, 124:5, 125:5, 127:5, 22:6

oath and covenant of the priesthood. *See also* priesthood

1:P, 6:1, 32:1, 9:2, 34:2, 36:2, 47:2, 61:2, 98:2, 1:3, 2:3, 3:3, 4:3, 6:3, 21:3, 25:3, 30:3, 33:3, 35:3, 36:3, 39:3, 40:3, 41:3, 43:3, 47:3, 49:3, 53:3, 54:3, 55:3, 58:3, 59:3, 60:3, 61:3, 63:3,

About the Author

Larry Barkdull is a longtime publisher and writer of books, music, art, and magazines. For nine years, he owned Sonos Music Resources and published the Tabernacle Choir Performance Library. He was also the owner and publisher of Keepsake Books. Over the past thirty years, he's published some six hundred products for numerous authors, composers, and artists. He's founded two nonprofit organizations: The Latter-day Foundation for the Arts, Education and Humanity (to promote LDS arts), and Gospel Ideals International (to promote the gospel of Jesus Christ on the Internet).

His books have sold in excess of 300,000 copies, and they have been translated into Japanese, Korean, Italian, and Hebrew. He is the recipient of the American Family Literary Award; the Benjamin Franklin Book Award; and *Foreword Magazine's* GOLD Book of the Year Award for best fiction. His most recent books are *Priesthood Power—Blessing the Sick and the Afflicted*; *Rescuing Wayward Children*; and *The Shepherd Song*.

He and his wife, Elizabeth, have ten children and a growing number of grandchildren. They live in Orem, Utah. Read more of his writings at Meridian Magazine.com.

www.ingramcontent.com/pod-product-compliance
Lightning Source LLC
Chambersburg PA
CBHW080514090426
42734CB00015B/3049